# CAREFREE!
## CHELSEA CHANTS
## AND
## TERRACE CULTURE

MARK WORRALL & WALTER OTTON

**Carefree!**
**Chelsea chants and terrace culture**

Copyright Mark Worrall and Walter Otton 2017
Published by Gate 17
www.gate17.co.uk

THE MORAL RIGHT OF THE AUTHORS HAS BEEN ASSERTED

Apart from any fair dealing for the purposes of research or private study, or criticism or review, as permitted under the Copyright, Designs and Patents Act 1988, this publication may only be reproduced, stored or transmitted, in any means, with the prior permission in writing of GATE 17, or in the case of reprographic reproduction in accordance with the terms of licenses issued by the Copyright Licensing Agency. Enquiries concerning reproduction outside those terms should be sent to the publishers.

enquiries@gate17.co.uk
Cover photograph: The Shed by Hugh Hastings
3 May 1980, Division Two, Chelsea 3 Oldham Athletic 0, Mike Fillery, Clive Walker x2
Cover design: Gate 17

## CONTENTS

GROUND RULES ................................................................... 1
ACKNOWLEDGEMENTS ........................................................ 3
FOREWORD ........................................................................... 9

### PART ONE

CAREFREE! ........................................................................... 15
THE GREENAWAY LEGACY ................................................ 17
CAROUSEL ............................................................................ 23
WE ARE THE MODS .............................................................. 27
BIRTH OF THE SHED ........................................................... 29
ZIGGER ZAGGER .................................................................. 34
BORN IS THE KING ............................................................... 38
SHEDITES .............................................................................. 41
THE MIDDLE OF THE SHED ................................................ 57
THE 'AND LEICESTER' MYSTERY ..................................... 64
THE LIQUIDATOR ................................................................. 70
BOOTBOY ANTHEMS ........................................................... 72
LEEDS AND LEEDS .............................................................. 82
DARK BACK STREETS ......................................................... 89
CAPITAL CAPERS ................................................................. 91
BLUE IS THE COLOUR ......................................................... 98
THERE WAS A MIGHTY BATTLE ...................................... 104
COME ALONG AND SING THIS SONG ............................ 109
CELERY! .............................................................................. 112
ONE MAN WENT TO MOW ................................................ 115
SING WHEN YOU'RE WINNING ........................................ 118
IS THERE A FIRE DRILL? ................................................... 125
CHANGE ............................................................................... 138
ONLY A POUND ................................................................... 143

### PART TWO

WHERE IT ALL BEGAN FOR ME ....................................... 155
TOTTENHAM, SHEFFIELD UNITED AND RUUD BOY 155
ENGLISH CIVIL WAR .......................................................... 168

| | |
|---|---|
| THE WIGAN TRAIN | 180 |
| IVANOVIC | 189 |
| WILLIAN | 196 |
| KANTÉ | 207 |

## PART THREE

| | |
|---|---|
| BEST OF THE REST | 215 |
| FINAL WORDS | 262 |

# GROUND RULES

*Carefree!* is an exploration of the terrace culture and chants associated with Chelsea Football Club. Given the fact that many different groups of supporters have followed the Blues down the years, and continue to do so, it's inevitable that there are many different accounts of the events that have shaped history. For the same reason, there are plenty of chants with slight variations which occasionally provoke 'lively' debate about which is correct.

With the shared belief that Chelsea is a broad church, in *Carefree!* Mark and Walter have used an even mix of interviews, research and personal experience to explain significant culture-forming events and historic rivalries and they have stayed true to the versions of chants and songs familiar to them without being precious about whether they are right or wrong.

At every tier of the game, the match-going experience was for many years tarnished by various forms of xenophobia, racism, homophobia, bigotry and prejudice. The Football Offences Act 1991 and subsequent initiatives of pioneering bodies like *Kick It Out*, football's equality and inclusion organisation, changed perspectives and led to clubs adopting a zero-tolerance policy to all forms of discrimination. Despite this, in the modern era, while far less prevalent, chants and taunts directing discriminatory abuse at clubs / owners / players / supporters can still be heard in stadiums when teams with a deep-seated historic rivalry are in opposition.

In 2010 Chelsea launched *Building Bridges,* an initiative to promote equality within the club, its stadium and its communities. The Club remains clear and consistent in its condemnation of all forms of discriminatory behaviour and language. Wholly supportive of Chelsea's endeavours, Mark and Walter took the decision at the outset that *Carefree!* would not include chants and songs deemed to be discriminatory. Re-oxygenating such material would be detrimental to the initiatives in place to eliminate it.

*Carefree!* contains a number of chants and songs that incorporate bad language. While this has been asterisked, the authors accept that some readers may be offended by this aspect of the book's content and apologise in advance. To make capital out of causing offence was not the purpose behind writing *Carefree!* which has taken many years of research to piece together. Mark and Walter hope that this will shine through, and that your reading experience will be both enjoyable and informative.

# ACKNOWLEDGEMENTS

The authors would like to thank Mick Greenaway RIP; Brian Hapted RIP; Jack Horner RIP; Matthew Harding RIP; Alan 'Garrison' Tomkins; Kerry Dixon; David Johnstone; Nicholas Hapted; Tim Rolls; Rick Glanvill; Neil Smith; Vince Cooper; Martin Goggins; Tom Broderick; Wendy Groussin; Keith Smith; Thomas Smith; Les Allen; Paul Barnard; Christopher Smitheram; Andrew Smith; Denis Thomas; Alan Thompson RIP; Paul Jervis; Rachel Jervis; Zack Jervis; Chris Holland; Alexandra Churchill; Callum West; Steve Winters; Stephen Lorch; Sally Lorch; Simon Lorch; Charles Wass; Dave Carroll; Doug Vigar; Peter Queally; Pete King; David Rodriguez; Andy Hawthorn; Simon Hawthorn; Scott Rennison; Bartholomew Barrett; Shaun Long; James Ellard; Thomas Ellard; Ben Rebuck; Ben Sewell; Jack Cosby; Brad Paget; Russell Baldry; Tim Scaping; Gary Gornall; Garry Sparks; Peter Trenter; Cliff Auger; Liz Nurse; David Chidgey; Daniel Shiel; Antony Barrett; David Barrett; Johnny Gleeson; Michael Campion; Jake Cohen; John Dawes; Kerry Swift; Kraig Dixon; Barry New; Kenneth Rice; Ryan Arif.

A very special thank you to Hugh Hastings who kindly provided the superb photo of The Shed which adorns the cover of *Carefree!* Hugh first worked for Chelsea FC in 1977 when he became the Club's Official Photographer, a post he held for ten years. Hugh was also the Editor of the Chelsea FC programme from 1980 to 1986. He was the same age as many members of the playing squad and enjoyed a hugely memorable time working alongside players, fans and staff, a fact which has made the recent passing of two players from that era, Ian Britton and David Stride, especially sad. One of Hugh's images from this era, a photo of Paul Canoville, the first black player to play for Chelsea, is a part of the National Portrait Gallery's collection.

In May 1984, Hugh appeared as a substitute for the Chelsea first team in a testimonial game against Brentford held for Bees legend Eddie Lyons (14 May, Brentford 3 Chelsea 6). Eddie was sixty-three-years old at that time and played the last fifteen minutes of the match! Hugh replaced Kerry Dixon who scored five for the Blues that night, the other goal came from David Speedie. The game was played on a Monday evening at Griffin Park, and if the thought of Hugh replacing Kerry makes you smile, then the knowledge that Pat Nevin came off at half-time so he could go and see his favourite band the Cocteau Twins will surely make you laugh out loud. Proper Chels!

Today, Hugh continues his work for Chelsea as part of the Club's Cobham training-ground-based Comms team, managing and developing Chelsea's historical archive in addition to assisting as second photographer when needed at major events. He also edits current images and helps manage the Club's day-to-day digital image workflow in support of Chelsea's long-standing official photographer Darren Walsh.

Find out more about Hugh's work at www.hughhastings.co.uk

*Carefree!*
*Chelsea Chants And Terrace Culture*

dedicated to

Mick Greenaway and Brian Hapted
RIP

# FOREWORD

## KERRY DIXON

My earliest recollection of being in the company of Chelsea supporters' dates back to the mid-1970s when I was in my early teens. When I wasn't playing football, I would go and support my local team Luton Town and stand on the terraces at Kenilworth Road. Back then, it's fair to say that when the Hatters played the Blues I didn't want to be in their company, but we had no choice! I loved the thrill of going to the football, but it was quite scary. I would learn later when I played for the club that Chelsea always travelled to away games in huge numbers.

*Carefree!* I remember that chant ringing in my ears as well as getting chased around the Oak Road end on a few occasions. It's funny how things turned out.

What I do recall specifically is the Chelsea crowd being very supportive of their team when they came to Luton even though the football was poor and they weren't doing well. Both teams got relegated together from the old Division One in 1975 and renewed acquaintances in Division Two the following season. There was a riot when Luton won 3-0 (30 August 1975), me and my mates didn't get involved in any of the fighting, but we learned how to run that's for sure!

I started playing regularly on Saturday afternoons soon after, and then when I got my first taste of league football with Reading I got a completely different perspective of the atmosphere generated by football supporters. The home crowd were always behind me, and I was l lucky in that respect pretty much throughout my whole career. Interestingly enough, it was still the away fans, the diehards, who made things that little bit more intimidating and hostile.

Moving to Chelsea, the crowds were bigger and the support I got was outstanding for most of the nine years I was at Stamford Bridge. As a Blues player, I really got a feel for how passionate the away support was in particular. Obviously, I had my experiences as a kid on the terraces, but this was completely different. The game at Highbury when we'd just been promoted back to the First Division (25 August 1984, Arsenal 1 Chelsea 1), Chelsea fans were all round the ground and the support for the team was fantastic. When I scored in front of the Clock End were most of them were gathered and they started chanting *One Kerry Dixon* the noise was incredible!

There was a tricky period at the beginning of 1988 when the team was struggling under John Hollins and Arsenal and West Ham came in for me with bids. The Chelsea crowd went a bit quiet on me and I could hear a few things being said which got to me a little as I'd never mentioned anything about leaving the club. It was the press that speculated on my future – but that's football. I can tell you now, the way it was reported that I'd rejected West Ham – every time I played at Upton Park after that I got volleys of abuse from their supporters.

Leading up to that time, many fans were chanting for Hollins to go and it was difficult. There were players who agreed with the crowd, and of course there were problems. It's not easy when things go against you and the manager is changing the team around. I was on the bench. Hollins had previously signed Gordon Durie and was trying to work out how to play him with me and David Speedie. Throughout though, once again, the Chelsea supporters were always behind me and the rest of the players.

All of us seemed to get our names chanted before we came out, and though there were obvious favourites, it definitely helped to keep us motivated. The players wanted to perform for the fans, and we knew the fans wanted to perform for us – to encourage us. I get the same feeling as a spectator at Stamford Bridge today. It seems quite unique to Chelsea… that the team, and the players, are given every encouragement even when things aren't going well… the 2015/2016 season being a recent example.

It was the usual places that you think of that were hostile to play at. Millwall, until I played for them. They gave me a bit of stick at first, but once I started scoring a few goals they were very supportive. Leeds, Birmingham, Cardiff, Leicester, when they had the cages at Filbert Street, all those places were intimidating.

Playing at Anfield was always an event. Liverpool fans made the greatest noise and everyone knew that. The whole ground singing *You'll Never Walk Alone* I'll never forget that. When I was there commentating at the Champions League semi-final (3 May 2005, Liverpool 1 Chelsea 0), the Luis Garcia 'ghost goal' game… the noise they made that night was amazing. It had to help their players. And saying that though, when Chelsea were at home to Barcelona earlier the same season (8 March 2005), when we won 4-2 at the Bridge (Eidur Gudjohnsen, Frank Lampard, Damien Duff, John Terry) and went through 5-4 on aggregate, the atmosphere was truly outstanding. Maybe the best I've ever experienced there. The noise levels were unreal… the players would have thrived on it. *Boring, boring, Chelsea!* Blues fans always have a good line in humour.

## CAREFREE! CHELSEA CHANTS AND TERRACE CULTURE

I used to like playing at Tottenham for Chelsea because of the rivalry, and the fact Blues fans of course would always turn up in big numbers. I remember a Fifth Round League Cup replay at White Hart Lane (23 January 1991)… we'd drawn 0-0 at the Bridge and went over there and won 3-0 (Andy Townsend, Kerry Dixon, Dennis Wise). They had Gazza and Lineker in their team, but all you could hear all the way through the match were 5,000 Chelsea fans belting out their support for us. They drowned out the Spurs crowd.

I'd have to say that a certain element of raucousness and edginess has been lost to the game since I retired. Back then, certain matches, Spurs as a good example, used to bristle with atmosphere. When a goal was scored, sometimes it would all kick off. You still had to play your game, but the way the crowd were definitely could affect your performance for better or worse… more so than I think it would today.

I remember Gordon Durie, who'd played for us in that 3-0 League Cup win, moved to Tottenham in the summer. The press reported that he wanted to leave London because his wife wanted to be nearer to her family in Scotland… so when he moved across the Capital to the Lane it didn't go down too well with Chelsea supporters.

Unluckily for Gordon, Spurs played us at their place really early on at the start of the new season (24 August 1991) and Blues fans gave him stick every time he touched the ball. Again, we were much better than them that day anyway, winning 3-1 (Kerry Dixon, Kevin Wilson, Andy Townsend) – but it's fair to say our crowd played its part, and if Jukebox had an off day well it might have been the reason. In fairness to Chelsea supporters, who I've always found very appreciative of former players, more so perhaps than fans of other clubs, Gordon's situation was rather unique.

I've got two memories that I hold very dear to my heart when it comes to Chelsea supporters and the way they have been with me. Coincidentally to that last story, both of them relate to clubs I played for after I'd left Stamford Bridge.

3 January 1993: I was playing for Southampton. The Saints were away at Nottingham Forest in a Third Round FA Cup tie. The gate was about 14,000, so it wasn't packed by any means. Anyway, I've gone up early for a corner and there's a mob of twenty or so fellas shouting my name and they did it again every time I touched the ball. They were Chelsea fans, and they soon made their allegiance known. The Blues had been drawn away to Middlesbrough, but the game had been called off so they decided as they

were up north to come and support me. They were singing *One Kerry Dixon* all the way through the game. I thought it was brilliant. Unbelievable really.

9 April 1994: Just over a year later on, I was playing for my home-town club Luton Town in an FA Cup semi-final against Chelsea at Wembley. Luton lost the game 2-0 (Gavin Peacock x2), the final whistle goes and suddenly there's almost 60,000 fans, most of them Chelsea, singing *There's only one Kerry Dixon*. Obviously I just wanted to get off the pitch as it didn't feel right, but Denis Wise who was the Blues captain that day told me to stay out there and enjoy it as I deserved it. I clapped everyone for a while, but did head off pretty quickly. It was the most incredible, humbling situation I've ever experienced in football, I've never forgot it.

The atmosphere at football is different these days. The stadiums are all-seated, the crowds are more cosmopolitan – clubs like Chelsea are reaching out to the world. I think it's amazing that Blues fans from different countries are so well organised, they learn all the songs. Sweden, Norway, the USA and plenty more… some of those fans have been following Chelsea for years; they've also become diehards. I remember going to do a question and answer session in Malaysia and there were 150 Malaysian Chelsea singing *Carefree!* Who'd have believed that back in the '80s!

One thing that has definitely improved when it comes to atmosphere though is that there seems to be a lot more humour and straight back at you banter these days.

The *loads and loads of money* chants when Roman Abramovich took over Chelsea set this tone. I remember when we played Lazio in the Champions League in Rome (4 November 2003, Lazio 0 Chelsea 4, Hernan Crespo, Eidur Gudjohnsen, Damien Duff, Frank Lampard) and their fans were giving us stick about Roman's money and our lot were waving their cash at them. Brilliant! And there's plenty more examples in the pages of this book which certainly kept me entertained and I hope like me you will enjoy the memories associated with them.

Chelsea supporters, you've always been good to me. You're a fantastic crowd. Thank you.

Kerry Dixon
London 2017

# PART ONE

## THE ORIGINALS

# CAREFREE!

**Mark:** When poet and songwriter Sydney Carter died in 2004 at the ripe old age of 88, an obituary in the Daily Telegraph noted that his lyrical composition *Lord of the Dance* set to a melody adapted from the Shaker dance tune *Simple Gifts* was the most celebrated religious song of the 20th Century. Praise indeed.

Carter was a Londoner by birth, and while it's not known if he had any allegiance to any of the Capital's football teams it's highly likely that long before he passed away he would have become aware of a rewrite of *Lord of the Dance* by Chelsea supporters which has become one of the signature chants at Stamford Bridge.

*Carefree, wherever you may be, we are the famous CFC,*
*And we don't give a f\*ck whoever you may be,*
*'cause we are the famous CFC.*

My memory isn't as good as it should be, but I can't recall ever going to a Chelsea game, home or away, where *Carefree!* hasn't been sung at some stage. I remember following the Blues on their travels outside London in the mid '80s, back then, *Carefree!* wasn't just a chant... it was a statement. Walking from station to stadium in some nondescript town, casually-attired in a nice bit of Pringle or Lyle and Scott, shod in Forest Hills, arms outstretched 10-to-2-style, hollering *and we don't give a f\*ck whoever you may be,* and meaning it, was a wonderful, character-forming experience.

Some years ago a tourist tarrying at the *cfcuk* stall after a game asked me 'Who's Geoffrey?' 'Geoffrey who?' I replied. 'Geoffrey, the man Chelsea supporters were singing about in the ground.' I'd looked at him puzzled. 'Geoffrey? I've never heard that. Can you sing it?' 'Sure. It goes like this. *Geoffrey whoever you maybe, we are the famous CFC...*'

It still makes me laugh now thinking about it... as does one amusing explanation about *Geoffrey* that can be found online on an old *CFCnet* forum. A statement is made that *Carefree!* started out life as *Geoffrey*... by way of being a reference to Conservative politician Geoffrey Howe. The post details that in the late '70s, Howe had been responsible for banning Chelsea fans from travelling to away games because of serious hooligan-related issues associated with the London club at the time.

7 May 1977: Eddie McCreadie's Blue and White Army thwarted the ban

and piled into Wolverhampton Wanderers Molineux stadium in their thousands for a top of the old Second Division table clash (1-1, Tommy Langley). Gleefully, they chanted *Geoffrey, wherever you may be* to stick two fingers up at Howe. It's a fantastic story that deserves to be true... except it isn't. It was then Labour Sports Minister Dennis Howell who had instigated the ban in April 1977 following recent public order incidents at Chelsea games.

By way of an amusing aside, worth mentioning at this point is the story Blues supporter, author and former Chairman of the Chelsea Supporters Trust, Tim Rolls tells about a chant related to the ban.

**Tim:** "A song that was unable to be sung by Chelsea supporters for many years was *We're the famous Chelsea FC and we're going to Wembley*, though in the past two decades it has had regular airings. One bowdlerised version was sung in the Nell Gwynne before beating Sheffield United 4-0 on 30 April 1977, (Tommy Langley, Ray Lewington, Ray Wilkins, Steve Finnieston), this was a week before the Wolves away promotion game where Chelsea supporters were famously banned. The pub chant of *We're all pi\*sed up and we're going to Molineux* implied that quite a few of the drinking hordes had illicitly acquired tickets for Wolves. As it turned out, they had, and so had thousands of their compadres."

**Mark:** Back with *Carefree!* Online encyclopaedia *Wikipedia*, while having undoubted merits as a source of genuine information, is also open to abuse as witnessed by an entry clearly made by a supporter of Chesterfield Football Club, the only other English football team with the initials CFC, claiming that Spireites fans originated the chant.

Arsenal supporters, evidently lacking imagination, subsequently swapped *C* for *A* are often heard singing *Carefree!* while Everton fans concocted an altogether more sinister version which goes like this: *Run, run whoever you may be, we are the famous EFC, and we'll f\*ck you all whoever you may be, 'cos we are the famous EFC.*

Then of course there are Everton's antiquity-obsessed, neighbours from across Stanley Park Liverpool whose spiteful use of the melody beget: *F\*ck off Chelsea FC, you ain't got no history, five European Cups, eighteen Leagues, that's what we call history.*

No history eh.

Let's get into that now.

# THE GREENAWAY LEGACY

**Mark:** What fans of Arsenal, Everton… and Chesterfield are unlikely to know is that the conversion of *Lord of the Dance* into *Carefree!* and its popularization on the terraces, like a number of celebrated Chelsea chants you will come across in the pages of this book, was largely related to the efforts of legendary Blues supporter Mick Greenaway who passed away in tragic circumstances in 1999.

As Walts now describes, there's a story within a story here that recalls his first meeting in March 2017 with Blues fanatic Nicholas Hapted. An encounter which turned out to be crucial in respect of understanding Greenaway's phenomenal legacy to Chelsea supporters.

**Walter:** Nick is one of those people where he and I had historically been in the same places (pubs, concourses, stands) at the same time, but never met. It was due to social media where formal introductions were finally made and we eventually connected on *Twitter* – Walts: @WalterOtton and Nick: @MrNH11.

Nick was complimentary about an article or two that I'd written. Subsequently, he sorted me a ticket to a game at Old Trafford one season when I didn't have enough loyalty points to apply. We've met for beers a couple of times, and regularly chat on *Twitter*.

In 2015, Nick's Dad, Brian Hapted, passed away. Nick found letters that Mickey Greenaway had written to Brian – they really were something special. These letters (penned in 1993) sparked the platform for this book. They were the inspiration. If Nick hadn't have found the letters – who knows if these words would ever have been written. Out of respect to Nick and Brian Hapted – and to Mickey – it is only good and proper that we acknowledge them now.

**Nick:** "My Dad was born in 1937 – he was a war child. He attended the friendly match against Dynamo Moscow in 1945 (13 November, Chelsea 3 Dynamo Moscow 3, Reg Williams, Len Goulden, Tommy Lawton), because he would always refer to it and go on about the size of the crowd. (Official attendance 74,496, actual match attendance between 100,000 and 120,000!)

He would have been eight-years-old, so this must have been his first match at Stamford Bridge because the Football League didn't resume after World War II until the 1946-47 season. Dad said that Frankie Blunstone

(1953-1964, 317 appearances, 47 goals) was his favourite player – he used to love him. I was born in 1972.

Dad always went in The Shed, the Bovril Entrance, and liked to stand by the Tea Bar. After I was born and he used to take me, we used to drift about a little bit. I have that same trait, I liked to go in different stands. I can remember one of his friends called Mick Quartemaine. Dad knew he was always in the North Stand sitting in the seats above. It struck me that Dad always knew where his friends and acquaintances were situated in various parts of the Bridge. Mick Quartemaine passed away in 2009. Dad was also good mates with the Webb brothers. As you know, these days you're stuck in your seats – back then you could drift around the ground and meet up.

My Dad and Mickey Greenaway were great mates. The both worked for British Rail – out of Waterloo or Wimbledon Park. They'd go on the piss together. My Mum used to get the right hump! Pubs used to shut at 2.00pm on a Sunday, so if the cricket was on they'd go to the Oval to watch the cricket because the bars there would carry on serving. Mickey loved cricket. He was Middlesex and my Dad was Surrey – they would always go together. Mickey would come back and stay for a night and he'd still be there two or three weeks later! That's what used to happen. He'd overstay his welcome all the time! Not in a rude way – he just didn't know when to leave!

Dad started taking me when I was very young. I remember an away game at Blackpool – this was my earliest memory. I've researched it online and it was either 1975 or 1976. I'm fairly sure it was 1976 because the match was in September, (26 September 1976, 1-0, Steve Finnieston), so the weather would have been a bit warmer.

I went with both my parents. We went up on the train. I remember Blackpool's kit because it was bright orange – it really stood out. I recall being along the side of the pitch. After my Mum passed away, Mick Quartemaine told me a story about that match. We got off at Euston and there were opposing fans waiting to travel back north – could've been United or Liverpool, I don't know, and one of them knocked me over. I've always had it in my head that it was United fans. My Mum turned to my Dad and said: "Ain't you gonna do anything?" She then turned round and cracked the bloke who pushed me over! When she punched him, her diamond fell out her wedding ring. It went bouncing *'ching ching ching'* down the marble floor and my Dad starts running along, chasing this runaway diamond until he managed to collect it!"

## CAREFREE! CHELSEA CHANTS AND TERRACE CULTURE

*Walter's research on fixtures played that day uncovered that Manchester United were away at near neighbours Manchester City while Liverpool played at Newcastle United. The opposing 'red and white' fans that knocked Nick over at Euston and got an almighty whack from his Mum could have been Sunderland who had drawn 1-1 at West Ham or Stoke City who'd lost 2-0 at QPR. Going with Nick's hunch, it's possible they were London based United fans, 'Cockney Reds', who'd travelled back from Maine Road to Euston.*

**Nick:** "Dad got me a season ticket with him from the 1975/76 season in the West Stand above the benches. My early, vivid memories were of Clive Walker, (1976-1984, 224 appearances, 65 goals), because he stood out with his wild hair. The most stand-out memory for me was his goal versus Liverpool in 1978, (FA Cup Third Round 7 January, Chelsea 4 Liverpool 2, Clive Walker x2, Steve Finnieston, Tommy Langley), he was my first favourite player. We lived in Southfields, and when we got off the tube to walk along Wimbledon Park Road I'd be begging my Dad to put me on his shoulders. I can remember the big Church (Saint Michael's) on the walk home – as it towered above the houses it was always a reminder to ask Dad to haul me up on his shoulders for the journey home.

Other things that stick out when I was growing up, was admiring Clive Allen. I remember a night game, he must've been a teenager – I was understanding football a lot more and as a young, opposing striker his movement and ability stuck with me. He was at QPR then Palace between 1978 and 1981 so it was in that time frame. He eventually signed for Chelsea in 1991 – a decade too late!

Another thing that is firmly in my memory, is one match the Old Bill done a show with their police dogs jumping through hoops on the pitch. Weird! I loved it. As a kid it was brilliant entertainment – in that moment it was more exciting for me than the football. One thing that will never leave me, is the buzz walking with my Dad from Fulham Broadway to the stadium. The walk, the turnstiles, the stairs, getting into my seat. If I could see the *LWT* crane with a cameraman positioned on the top, I got a right buzz because being on the TV only happened once or twice a year!

I'd always run up the stairs – we were always five minutes late getting in. It wasn't because Dad took me in the pub – that always happened afterwards. Nine times out of ten we'd go straight to the game and go in the Working Man's Club (CIU) after the match – or sometimes head to Waterloo and go into the CIU there.

My later memories of Mick Greenaway were bumping into him after winning at Elland Road in 1988. Johnny B scored, (24 September 1988, Leeds United 0 Chelsea 2, John Bumstead, Gordon Durie), but Mickey didn't look great. He used to take a few digs, which was sad. As everyone knows, he was the cheerleader for the fans. We saw him up there but he was a bit distant – I was younger so I didn't really take it in, but reflecting on it years later it sticks in my mind. The last time I saw him was on the Fulham Road in the late 90s. Because of my hair, he used to call me Dennis Waterman off of Minder on the TV. He'd say: "Here's little Minder" – I loved it. Then in 1999 Mickey passed away.

My Dad didn't get involved in creating the atmosphere like Mickey did – well, not when I was with him. During home games, I'd be in the West Stand but we could hear Mickey in The Shed. Once we had a televised Cup game at Watford (1 February 1987) and Brian Clough was co-commentating. I remember watching the match on ITV and hearing Mickey and hearing our fans – it was something else. We lost 1-0 (Luther Blissett), but Clough praised our travelling support, paying them a massive compliment, and everyone remembered that.

Kerry Dixon was on the bench that day. Rumours were that he was off – he stayed, of course. My Dad's favourite song was *Chelsea Chelsea Chelsea* over and over. He loved it. That constant chanting led to the Osgood goal in the 1970 Cup Final replay (29 April, Chelsea 2 Leeds United 1, Peter Osgood, David Webb) – that's why he loved it. He loved Charlie Cooke and Peter Osgood – he only called him Ossie – they were his favourite players of that era. He loved Ossie's song *Born is the King*, and I know the opening line can be contentious, but Dad always sang, *The Shed looked up and it saw a great star!*

He used to go away regularly back then, and then come back on the train and have a drink with the players in their carriage. It was so more relaxed in those days. Mickey and my Dad would time it – they'd get the later train to London after an away game up north to coincide with the players on that train, and they'd mingle with them. He said George Graham always had a scotch on him and was always on the piss! He said he didn't like him as a player, though. Dad also loved songs to do with taking piss out of Scousers. He hated Scousers. Out of all the fans he despised them, and Sheffield United for some reason!

The other thing about my Dad, is that he got on with my mates – especially Tony Bentley who I've known since the early nineties. We met through a mutual friend and, of course, our love for Chelsea Football Club. We were both in the same boat in the fact that we'd been born in West

London but had moved across to the East side of the Capital. It was an experience to say the least being Chelsea fans in a staunch West Ham area. Tony and I ended up getting a season ticket together and obviously still go to this very day.

My Dad loved Tony. Tony is a very funny bloke and is the most knowledgably football fan I know – not just everything Chelsea, but football in general. My Dad and Tony used to really bounce off each other. Before 2005 (winning the league) he'd constantly tease Tony saying, "I've seen us win the league – have you?" It was the only thing that used to shut him up, which is saying something! But then a few years later, around 2008, my Dad let it slip that he'd been doing his National Service in that 1955 season when Chelsea first won the Football League. You can only imagine how Tony then made my Dad's life a misery – usually after every game I could see it in my Dad's face that he was waiting for Tony to tee him up, so he could joke with him, "You didn't even see us win the league, you were doing your National Service!" It was a regular comical thing – it is a thing I miss dearly.

Once my Dad became very ill, he ended up bed ridden in the Royal London Hospital. Tony came to the hospital in the last few evenings after grafting all day on a building site. He sat with me by Dad's bedside and when Dad was in pain, he held his hand with me. When I cried, he cried with me. He was the mate I needed the most. I will never forget our friendship – I class Tony as family now along with his own amazing family. I'll never forget it.

Tony reminded me recently that he bumped into Mick in Florida, Fort Lauderdale when Chelsea had a pre-season tour line up there in 1981. Tony says that Mick was wearing a sheepskin jacket in ninety-degree heat! Incredibly, the tour was cancelled because not enough people had booked through the Club. The friendly was due to be played against the Fort Lauderdale strikers and had been advertised in the match day programme. However, a lot of Chelsea – like Tony and Mick – had booked travel so they went out there anyway.

As for me, personally, when it comes to chants, the current one I love is *Fàbregas is Magic* – he is such a quality player. At the time, the *Stevie G / Demba Ba* song had me in stitches – I loved it. Supporters of so many other clubs were singing it when they played Liverpool – shows you just how much they're loathed around the country. Obviously, our media would have you believe otherwise. But I don't think that song should be sung now, it's irrelevant.

I want our support to get behind our team and our players. I prefer that. I loved *Super Frank* and *Oh Jimmy, Jimmy!* When Jimmy pulled one out the bag – he was some finisher! I loved Hasselbaink and I loved that song. It's incredible really – after my Dad passed away and I found those letters to him in his loft from Mickey – they were like gold dust – I never thought they'd be a springboard for this book. All the best with it. Walts – I really appreciate what you and Mark have done."

# CAROUSEL

**Mark:** Born in 1945 and raised in Billing Street, London SW10... shouting distance from Stamford Bridge, Mick Greenaway's influence in developing Chelsea's terrace culture from the mid '60s through the '70s and '80s cannot be understated.

Attending games at Bridge with his father, young Mick was soon smitten by Chelsea. His proudest moment as a boyhood supporter came during the 1954/55 season when he was chosen to be a matchday mascot for the Blues home game with West Bromwich Albion.

On 2 October 1954, assisted over the fence, resplendent in a Chelsea kit he had been given as a present the previous Christmas, Greenaway made his way to the centre circle there to witness Chelsea captain Roy Bentley win the coin toss to determine who would kick off. Bentley won the toss and handed the coin to Mick which he proudly kept as a memento for the rest of his life. On that day, a huge crowd of 67,440 saw Bentley score Chelsea's first goal in a thrilling 3-3 draw (Roy Bentley, Jim Lewis, Eric Parsons), little did master Mick and his fellow supporters know that the Blues would go on to win the First Division title at the end of the season.

Despite the large crowds, Greenaway was perplexed by what he described as the 'polite applause' which Chelsea's goals were met with. By the time he was twenty-years old his thoughts on how to generate atmosphere at the Bridge were published in the Blues matchday programme.

16 December 1964
Chelsea 2 Workington 0
(Peter Osgood x2)

*"I have found more vocal support away from home because there is not the atmosphere at the Bridge for shouting for the Blues. If everyone capable of cheering would shout powerfully at every home game (especially early on in the game), then Chelsea will know they have supporters on the terraces and Chelsea would be inspired by such support."*

This game marked Ossie's debut for Chelsea. The attendance, 7,936, was on the low side for Stamford Bridge, though the unglamorous Third Division opposition and the fact it was a League Cup match (quarter-final second leg), a competition still in its infancy, clearly lessened the appeal of the fixture.

Coincidentally, in the same programme, a letter from M. Winnett and P. Slattery suggested the following adaption to *Hello Dolly* the Jerry Herman-penned title song from the Broadway musical of the same name which had been first sung by Carol Channing when the show opened in 1964.

*Come on, Chelsea. Well come on, Chelsea.*
*It's so nice to have you back on scoring form.*
*You're looking swell, Chelsea. We can tell, Chelsea.*
*You're still scoring, we're still roaring, you're still going strong.*
*Don't make us sad, Chelsea, make us glad, Chelsea, we're still like your Royal Blue and your White.*
*So score some goals, Chelsea, make the net full of holes, Chelsea, Chelsea don't you ever lose a game,* HOORAY.

*Come on, Chelsea*, didn't catch on. At that time, what was having a profound on many Blues supporters and Mick Greenaway in particular was hearing Liverpool supporters chanting in unison their version of soon to become terrace classic *You'll Never Walk Alone*… and the Scousers gained a wider audience in 1965 (1 May) when the Reds beat Leeds United 2-1 in the FA Cup Final at Wembley.

Commentating on that Cup Final for the BBC, Kenneth Wolstenholme remarked that *You'll Never Walk Alone* was Liverpool's signature tune. Nobody argued with Wolstenholme's observation, and over fifty years later the song pretty much remains the same.

What is both remarkable and interesting to note however is that *You'll Never Walk Alone* had an association with football long before Mersey Beat group Gerry and the Pacemakers recorded the version which topped the UK singles charts in November 1963 and was adopted by The Kop as Liverpool's scarf-waving anthem.

*You'll Never Walk Alone* was written by Richard Rodgers and Oscar Hammerstein for the musical *Carousel* which opened on Broadway in 1945 and came to London's West End in 1950.

Prior to his death in 2002, Chelsea supporter 'Little' Jack Horner (kids nursery rhymes have a lot to answer for!) lived in happy retirement on the Italian Riviera for many years. I first made his acquaintance in the Portovecchio Bar when staying in San Remo (my Aunt Luisa lived there) during the Italia '90 World Cup. I holidayed in the town many times thereafter and always sought out his company and never tired of his sepia-tinged memories of watching the Blues.

## CAREFREE! CHELSEA CHANTS AND TERRACE CULTURE

On 25 September 1937, six-year old Jack, who hailed from Filmer Road, London SW6, made the short walk from his home to Stamford Bridge for the first time with his father. Wilf Chitty and James Argue scored Chelsea's goals as the Blues beat Stoke City in front of 39,504 spectators. World War II saw Jack go and live with relatives in Cornwall and by the time he returned to London he was old enough to attend matches on his own. British Railways' issue football rattle in hand, he spent each half at the end of the ground Chelsea were attacking... the vast expanse of the north terrace or what was then known as the Fulham Road End.

Like Mick Greenaway, 'Little' Jack remembered Stamford Bridge being quite reserved back then, and again like Mick, he had nothing to compare it with. Small groups of supporters standing on the terraces would often break into popular songs of the day that had been heard in music halls and theatres and occasionally adapt the refrains so they made reference to Chelsea.

*Carousel* proved hugely popular when it opened at the Theatre Royal, in London's Drury Lane (7 June 1950) and Jack recalled being told that a couple of songs that he'd heard older supporters stood near him singing came from the show... so he went to see it for himself in order to make more sense of them!

*Blow High, Blow Low* was transformed to *Shoot High, Shoot Low* and sung enthusiastically:

*Shoot high, shoot low, away then we will go.*
*We'll go away with the Chelsea away. Away we'll go.*

*You'll Never Walk Alone* was quite sedate in its original phrasing and on the terraces the *Walk On, Walk On* verse was replaced by *Chelsea, Chelsea*.

Without the coordination of massed ranks that would come later, there was little longevity for much of what 'Little' Jack heard being sung at Stamford Bridge in the '50s, *You'll Never Walk Alone*, being a prime case in point. When Liverpool fans, thanks to Gerry and the Pacemakers, later championed the song as a football chant, for many years it became a standard across football terraces. In the modern era, it's hard to imagine The Shed in full flow singing *You'll Never Walk Alone*... and when it happened Jack Horner always used to think wistfully about his trip to the theatre to see *Carousel*.

By the summer of 1960, Jack had all but forgotten about *You'll Never*

*Walk Alone*. At this time, French chanteuse Edith Piaf had a worldwide hit with *Milord (Ombre de la Rue)*. He loved the song, everyone did… particularly the Chelsea faithful who retitled *Milord* as *Come On And Cheer Again*, and sang it enthusiastically for the next decade.

*Come on and cheer again, 'cos Chelsea's here again.*
*They are the greatest football team you've ever seen*
*We are the best in town. We are the best around.*
*We are the greatest football team you've ever seen*
*La, la, la, la, la – la. La, la, la, la, la – la.*

Another favourite of Jack's which continues to be sung today is the Chelsea version of the much-covered Jimmie Davis and Charles Mitchell composition *You Are My Sunshine* which was originally recorded by the Pine Ridge Boys in 1939.

*You are my Chelsea, my only Chelsea.*
*You make me happy when skies are grey.*
*You'll never notice how much I love you, until you've taken my Chelsea away. La la la la la…*

# WE ARE THE MODS

**Mark:** North Stand terrace legend Alan 'Garrison' Tomkins began his Chelsea adventures as a five year old in 1951 (10 November) when his father marched him along Britannia Road to Stamford Bridge for the first time to see the Blues in top-flight action against Manchester United. Chelsea beat eventual champions United 4-2 with Seamus D'Arcy netting twice and Roy Bentley and Bobby Smith also getting on the score sheet in a an exciting and comprehensive victory for Billy Birrell's side.

Just like Mick Greenaway and Jack Horner, Garrison was hooked immediately and started attending Chelsea games regularly. In parallel with football, as he got into his teenage years, like many kids of the day, music and clothes became an equally important part of his life... and these three burgeoning obsessions started to blur into one.

I interviewed Garrison in June 2016 and more missing pieces of the complex jigsaw puzzle that forms the roots of Chelsea's terrace culture fell into place.

**Garrison:** "The identity of Chelsea supporters as a group began early on in 1962 as Mod started. I was still a teenager. Mod had its roots in a nightclub called La Discotheque (Wardour Street, London) which was run by Peter Rachman and popular with the Kray twins and their crowd."

**Mark:** Rachman was a notorious landlord who employed retired heavyweight wrestling champion Bert Assirati to manage the door alongside fabled West End hardman Norbert Rondel. Originally favoured by socialites, La Discotheque's high-brow clientele deserted the venue in the wake of a police raid related to the scandal associated with high ranking politician John Profumo and wannabe model Christine Keeler.

Teenagers started frequenting the club which at the time was playing mainstream pop music, and among them was Garrison who thanks to Radio Luxembourg had already had a passion for R&B and Motown and was buying select 45s from DJs at another fabled Wardour Street night club The Flamingo and playing them at La Discotheque, where he'd convinced the manager he was eighteen-years old.

Despite being almost seventy-years old at the time of the interview, Garrison's eyes twinkled with youthful enthusiasm as he recalled those early days.

**Garrison:** "I'd go back to the North End Road where the lads I went to Chelsea with hung out and tell them to come up to La Discotheque. Modernists caught our eye and we started copying the way they were dressed. It might not sound like much today, but stone-washed jeans and plain white T-Shirts were very different to what everyone else was wearing then… especially at the football, which is what we started doing.

Warren Gold (Lord John) opened up a shop in Camden Town selling the latest Italian designer wear. A polo shirt could cost as much as five quid, and given the weekly wage at the time was seven or eight quid it was a fortune, but we would buy them.

We'd go to Chelsea away games and everyone would laugh because of the way we were dressed… and then the following year we'd go to that game and they'd be wearing the clobber we had on… except we'd moved on with the latest fashion trends.

We always tried to keep one step ahead and be different from the rest. We'd buy cloth from Dormeuil in Golden Square, Soho and take it to a tailor's in nearby Brewer Street. He'd put a unique cut at the foot end of the trousers with a vent in the back so they were lower than the front… they were called Step Bottoms and we'd wear them with Chelsea boots.

At Stamford Bridge, we'd all congregate on the west bank of the ground which at that time was just an open terrace. We stood by the half way line and called ourselves the Half Way Liners. *Half way line, half way line* we'd chant to the melody of kids' nursery rhyme *Three Blind Mice*.

Groups from Pimlico and Battersea started joining us, and each mob would shout where they were from to the same tune so we'd sing *North End Road, North End Road*. The whole Modernist look really was a Chelsea thing to start with, although QPR and Tottenham weren't too far behind. The Spurs lot had the Royal on the High Road near White Hart Lane which was a big Mod venue and there was a similar scene developing in the QPR heartland of Shepherds Bush."

# BIRTH OF THE SHED

**Mark:** Having already noted the way Liverpool fans unified their vocal support of the Reds at Anfield… watching the 1965 FA Cup final on television motivated Mick Greenaway to get a first-hand understanding of the audio-visual and portable dynamics of chanting the Scousers were perfecting.

14 August 1965 and Mick travelled to Old Trafford on a fact-finding mission to watch Liverpool, the FA Cup winners, play First Division champions Manchester United for the FA Charity Shield. Known as the FA Community Shield since 2002, the FA Charity Shield was initially contested at guest venues until 1974 when the fixture was moved permanently to Wembley and the attendant temporary switch to the Millennium Stadium.

*Editor's note: In the memoir letters that Mick Greenaway sent to Brian Hapted he referred to himself as Mick. The conversational sections of* Carefree! *that quote from them are pre-fixed throughout in the following way.*

**Mick:** "I was impressed by the vocal support generated by both sets of fans, especially the travelling Kop some of whom I met that evening when I stayed on socially with the Scousers. The ones I met were really okay. I remember thinking the Chelsea support could be developed along the same lines."

**Mark:** By virtue of finishing third in the First Division, the Blues qualified to play in Europe (Inter Cities Fairs Cup) and Mick Greenaway wasn't alone in using the matchday programme to bring ideas about generating atmosphere at Stamford Bridge to a wider audience. M. Keady from Battersea requested the attention of all *ninety minute shouters*:

1 September 1965
Chelsea 1 Stoke City 2
(John Hollins)

*"Now that Chelsea are to play in European football, they will need our support more than ever before. Many people have written to the club about the lack of vocal support for the team. May I suggest that all Chelsea supporters who are prepared to shout throughout the game congregate between the new West Stand and the North Stand. If all the 'fanatics' are in the same part of the ground, the roar will be much louder than when the shouters were spread all round the ground. At other clubs such as Liverpool, all the noise comes from one end of the ground, so let's try it at the Bridge and give the team some real*

*encouragement for a change."*

A couple of weeks later A.P Randall writing on behalf of S. Donan, M. Moore, M. Clune and M. Benneker, the 'Chelsea contingent with Ealing Celtic FC' had a letter published in the matchday programme entitled *'Is this the Chelsea song?'* It makes for interesting reading in the context of the observations and endeavours of Greenaway and Keady.

25 September 1965
Chelsea 1 Newcastle United 1
(George Graham)

*"During the past season or two I have read with interest the many and varied suggestions put forward for a 'Chelsea song'. This season at Highbury and Fulham, the Chelsea choir showed tremendous potential, and proved they can and WILL (with the coming of the new stand?) match the best.*

*Let us Chelsea followers then provide an original song, simple, easy to learn, one that is well known and if possible one associated with London. I feel that Chelsea followers should not have to 'borrow' themes from Liverpool, Manchester or Tottenham.*

*The LAMBETH WALK with the lyrics as below is a winner all the way – it has proved immensely popular on our own club nights (Ealing Celtic FC) – and soon has <u>everyone</u> joining in.*

*Anytime you're Chelsea way. Any evening, any day.*
*You'll find them all, playing the best football (roar) hoi!*

*Chelsea play it hard but fair. There's no team that compare.*
*You'll find them all, playing the best football (roar) hoi!*

*Stamford Bridge is where they go,*
*Up and down the Old King's Road.*
*We all love Chelsea, they're gonna win the league hoi!*

*Followed by chants of Chelsea, Chelsea etc. I, and my friends, Chelsea supporters all, feel that this will catch on in a big way if publicised through the medium of the Club Programme.*

*So come on all of you that chanted so well at Highbury and Fulham, let's hear you add this one to your ever increasing repertoire, and drop the 'Ee Aye Addios.' After all, Chelsea is a London side not a Lancashire One."*

## CAREFREE! CHELSEA CHANTS AND TERRACE CULTURE

**Mark:** Garrison recalled the North End Road boys and other groups of Chelsea Mods whose preferred vantage point on the half way line on the west terrace having to move when the construction of the original West Stand commenced in 1965.

**Garrison:** "We moved along a bit and then into the North Stand. But because that's where the away supporters went and because there were quite a lot of us, the police moved us on… so we moved to the front of the East Stand. There wasn't much room at all there because of the seating and I remember well-known supporter Cliff Webb suggesting we went to the southern terrace at the Fulham Road end of the ground and stand under the roof which had been built to provide shelter for bookmakers and punters attending the greyhound race meetings."

**Mark:** Greyhound racing was held at Stamford Bridge from 1937 to 1968. The corrugated steel roof covered about a fifth of the terrace and had been constructed in 1930 when the concrete-stepped south terrace had been laid to accommodate a greater number of standing football spectators. It was the only standing area in the ground that afforded shelter from the elements… and the acoustics of the low roof meant that the noise generated by chanting was pushed out towards the pitch and the players rather than dissipating into the sky.

Aided by the willingness of fans such as Garrison and others like him who were able to marshal the different groups of Chelsea supporters, Mick Greenaway along with Cliff Webb continued to champion their cause to the matchday masses via the programme and they weren't alone in their endeavours. Here are the thoughts of Norman Taylor.

22 February 1966
Chelsea 3 Sunderland 2
(George Graham, Barry Bridges, Peter Osgood)

*"This season there has been more vocal support than I have ever known at Chelsea, especially at the Fulham Road End, but when, for example, at the Spurs match, the 'other' Chelsea supporters have started chanting, they have been over-enthusiastic and have chanted 'Chelsea! Chelsea! Chelsea!' all in a mad rush. Alas! this has petered out in fifteen seconds or so; to overcome this, they should have clapped three times in between, which in turn would have made it last longer and sound twice as loud. If any true Chelsea supporters are prepared to chant and sing throughout the game would come and help us at the Fulham Road End, their support would be appreciated."*

Persistence eventually paid off as more groups of supporters began to congregate at the Fulham Road End in larger numbers. Published in a Chelsea programme shortly after the start of the following season, a letter from Cliff Webb announced the birth of something truly special… The Shed! The name is derived from the old south terrace standing area at Leeds United's Elland Road ground which in the 1920s had been covered with a similar curved, wooden barrel-shaped roof and been christened The Scratching Shed.

> 7 September 1966
> Chelsea 2 Leicester City 2
> (Peter Osgood, Charlie Cooke)

> *"From now on we wish the Fulham Road End to be called 'The Shed'. This is the section where the fanatics stand – and while we are on fanatics, why don't more people come in The Shed and join in the singing and chanting, not just at big games like last season's Fairs Cup? If we could have had support all through the League and Cup, we would have won them both. This year we must have this attitude at every game, so please help us make the Shed as fanatical as The Kop."*

In his excellent book about this period of Blues history, *Diamonds, Dynamos and Devils, the transformation of Chelsea FC under Tommy Docherty*, Tim Rolls writes… *Supporter David Collis remembers that Webb's letter followed discussions with other die-hard Chelsea supporters including Mick Greenaway, Danny Harkins and Dave Stevens about the need to create a vibrant end at Stamford Bridge. From that day to this, that end of the ground is called The Shed, despite demolition in 1994 and a rebuild as an all-seater stand, it indeed became the place to stand if you wanted to sing and chant.*

Programme Editor Albert Sewell's response was *'Must say "The Shed" sounds a likely place to keep that "Blue Submarine" you've all been singing about. And by the way, don't forget that visiting supporters have a right to shout and sing for their team too'.*

(More on Chelsea's *Blue Submarine* in the *Shedites* chapter.)

It's worth highlighting that during the 1965/66 season, then Chelsea manager Tommy Docherty and his team 'thanked' travelling Blues supporters for their support at Anfield where a notable 2-1 victory (22 January 1966, Peter Osgood, Bobby Tambling) had been secured in an FA Cup 3rd Round tie.

The programme for Chelsea's home game with Fulham (5 February, 2-1, Bobby Tambling, Peter Osgood) noted: *your support was terrific and we hope that*

## CAREFREE! CHELSEA CHANTS AND TERRACE CULTURE

*not only the four thousand or so that went to Liverpool but everyone supporting us here next Saturday will give the same full-voiced encouragement against Leeds United.*

The words of thanks obviously helped gee the Stamford Bridge crowd up as Chelsea beat Leeds 1-0 (12 February, Bobby Tambling) to ensure further progress in the competition.

# ZIGGER ZAGGER

**Mark:** Mick Greenaway will forever be associated with the classic *Zigger Zagger, Zigger Zagger… Oi, Oi, Oi,* chant, and his memoirs provide a fascinating insight into both its origin and purpose.

**Mick:** "The Zigger Zagger chant was really a fun character chant which dates back to about 1966 (it was 1964) when heard at a Blackburn (Rovers) v Leeds (United) game at Ewood Park, when a Chelsea game in the area was called off. (28 December 1964 Blackburn Rovers 0 Leeds United 2. Chelsea's away fixture at Blackpool was postponed because of snow.) Although not there myself, a number of other Chelsea fans were, and this chant was redeveloped to its present form."

*Zigger Zagger, Zigger Zagger. Oi, Oi, Oi.*
*Zigger Zagger, Zigger Zagger. Oi, Oi, Oi.*
*Zigger… Oi… Zagger… Oi.*
*ZiggerZagger, Zigger Zagger. Oi, Oi, Oi.*

"It was originally introduced as a rallying call for supporters to get together, and get behind the Blues support-wise. Although that still applies now, it should be regarded as a character 'fun' chant more than any other thing, certainly not as a signal for crowd troubles or disorders, which has been wrongly attributed previously by media coverage."

**Mark:** Although *Zigger Zagger* is associated with football supporters and Chelsea in particular, it is predated by the drinking song *Oggie, Oggie, Oggie* much loved by rugby union players which can be traced back to Cornwall's tin-mining industry. Oggie is slang for a Cornish pastie and the womenfolk of men who laboured down the mines would arrive at the pit-shafts at lunchtime hollering *Oggie, Oggie, Oggie* which would be met with the reply *Oi Oi Oi.*

Mick Greenaway's Chelsea's version of *Zigger Zagger* was further developed with the addition of a 10, 9, 8, 7, 6, 5, 4, 3, 2, 1 countdown at the start… and a rewrite of the American Gospel Hymn *When the Saints Go Marching In* at the end. *Oh when the Blues, go steaming in, Oh when the Blues go steaming in. I wanna be in that number, oh when the Blues go steaming in.* The anthem being completed with a repetitive three-clapped chant of *Chelsea!* In the modern era, *Zigger Zagger* has been led to very good effect by both CFC Cathy (McDonnell) and Martin 'Scoggsy' Goggins – more on Scoggy's vocal efforts later.

## CAREFREE! CHELSEA CHANTS AND TERRACE CULTURE

Not everyone was impressed with *Zigger Zagger* though! A letter from 'exiled' Glasgow Rangers fan Ian McKissack which appeared in a special edition of the Chelsea programme sold at a CCTV screening at Stamford Bridge of the Blues Inter Cities Fairs Cup semi-final playoff with Barcelona at the Camp Nou (25 May 1966, Barcelona 5 Chelsea 0) was less than complimentary about Greenaway's chant and support in general.

*"With regards to cheering the team, the juvenile chanting and singing makes me want to turn my head in shame. There is a certain chant which goes like this: 'Zigger, Zagger, Zigger, Zagger, How, How, How!!!' I have to pinch myself that I am at a League match and not in a kindergarten. When I hear that one, I want to run 400 miles back to Ibrox Park and sanity. Another thing, rattles are surely for babies in prams!!! It is time the Chelsea fans started to grow up and learn to cheer properly."*

Good job Mr. McKissack hadn't heard another version of *When The Saints Go Marching In* that had started doing the rounds of the away grounds Chelsea played at.

*Oh West London is wonderful!*
*Oh West London is wonderful!*
*It's full of tits, fanny and Chelsea.*
*Oh West London is wonderful!*

A letter from Peter House published (8 October) in the Chelsea v Burnley (1-3, Tommy Baldwin) programme had also expressed concern about recent developments on the vocal front at Stamford Bridge.

*"In reply to C. Webb, who wishes the Fulham Road End to be named the 'Shed', I would like to rename it 'The Foulmouthed End'. I find myself... and probably many more supporters are, too... sick and tired of hearing these so-called 'fanatics' finding any excuse to call players and officials of opposing clubs any filth which comes into their heads."*

In the same programme, in a letter entitled *Lay Off The Shed*, Mick Greenaway replied 'on behalf of The Shed' to media comments about Chelsea supporters.

*"I personally have made persistent attempts to curb the bad language that has been used at various matches, and there is now a crowd of us who will stamp this out with our own methods. I believe matches are won 90% on the terraces by giving encouragement (no disrespects to Bobby, Ossie, Charlie & Co.). This has been proved successfully up to now... we are top of the League... and will continue (cleanly) from the true chanting, singing, swaying Shedites."*

Less imaginative than *Zigger Zagger* but perhaps more amenable to Mr. McKissack and Mr House, was another favourite of Mick Greenaway's that has also stood the test of time. *Chelsea, Chelsea, Chelsea,* repeatedly sung to the tune of English poet and clergyman John Newton's 18th Century hymn *Amazing Grace* became increasingly popular when American folk singer Judy Collins recorded a version which spent a total of 75 weeks in the UK charts between 1970 and 1972. As a consequence of this, the tune was never off the radio… and the Stamford Bridge tannoy. Singing along was inevitable and the words needed no powers of recall.

**Walter:** When it comes to Chelsea Football Club, the *Chelsea, Chelsea, Chelsea. Chelsea, Chelsea, Chelsea* chant defines our support. I love how it goes in waves – when it dies down there's a hard-core handful who carry it on, and then it gathers more voices again, often coupled with a deeper defiance, it grows and grows once more into a bigger wave, the whole away end banging it out… *Chelsea, Chelsea, Chelsea. Chelsea, Chelsea, Chelsea* repeat to fade.

Over all my years going to the football, the most spine-tingling and defiant I have ever heard it was at Anfield in May 2010 (2 May, Liverpool 0 Chelsea 2, Didier Drogba, Frank Lampard) as The Kop sang *You'll Never Walk Alone* the away end drowned it out. If we could beat Liverpool, we had Wigan Athletic at home next game. We needed six points to win the league. We ended up beating Liverpool 2-0 and thrashed Wigan 8-0 a week later (9 May, Nicolas Anelka x2, Frank Lampard, Salomon Kalou, Didier Drogba x3, Ashley Cole.)

Our Club. Our support. Our vociferousness. Our Chelsea. It's probably our most significant song, and it is sung to the tune of the most significant hymn of all time – *Amazing Grace.*

*Amazing Grace how sweet the sound*
*That saved a wretch like me*
*I was once was lost but now I'm found*
*Was blind but now I see*
*'Twas grace that taught my heart to fear*
*And grace my fears relieved*
*How precious did that grace appear*
*The hour I first believed*
*When we've been there ten thousand years bright shining as the sun*
*We've no less days to sing God's praise*
*Then when we first begun*

## CAREFREE! CHELSEA CHANTS AND TERRACE CULTURE

2 October 1965 A very young-looking Frank Bough fronted BBC TV *Match of the Day* highlights of a Chelsea 2-1 away victory (Barry Bridges, George Graham) at West Bromwich Albion that can be found on *YouTube*.

Among the chants of visiting fans that can be clearly heard are *Zigger Zagger, Why Don't You Give Me A C* in which the letters that spell out Chelsea are called and repeated, *Johnny Boyle, Johnny Boyle* in reverence of the popular Blues midfielder, the humming of Chopin's *Funeral March* when Baggies defender Ray Fairfax goes down injured… and a sparkling rendition of World War I Armistice Night classic *Knees Up Mother Brown* which still warms the cockles of the heart over fifty years later.

*Knees up Mother Brown, knees up Mother Brown.*
*Under the table you must go eee-aye eee-aye eee-aye-oh.*
*If I catch you bending, I'll saw your legs right off,*
*Knees up knees up, don't you get a breeze up, knees up Mother Brown.*
*Oh my what a rotten song, sing, what a rotten song, sing, what a rotten song.*
*Oh my what a rotten song, and what a rotten singer too ooh ooh.*
*Chelsea! (clap clap clap) Chelsea! (clap clap clap) Chelsea!'*

Chelsea manager at the time, Tommy Docherty, would be treated to a slightly different version of *Knees Up Mother Brown* just over a decade later when he was in charge of Manchester United. As news broke that Docherty was embroiled in an extramarital affair with Mary Brown the wife of United physio Laurie Brown, terrace wags changed *Knees Up Mother Brown* to *Who's up Mary Brown?*

# BORN IS THE KING

**Mark:** In tandem with the significant improvement in the way support for Chelsea was being orchestrated, the team upped their game. Maybe it was just a coincidence… maybe not. Tommy Docherty had fashioned a side of exciting young players such as Peter Bonetti, Ron Harris, Eddie McCreadie, Barry Bridges and Bobby Tambling who had featured in the two-legged 1965 League Cup Final triumph over Leicester City. (First Leg, 15 March, Chelsea 3 Leicester 2, Bobby Tambling, Terry Venables, Eddie McCreadie. Second Leg, 5 April, Leicester 0 Chelsea 0.)

Among the players Docherty had blooded at Chelsea was Peter Osgood. Osgood made his Stamford Bridge debut as a seventeen-year old (16 December 1964) scoring both goals in a 2-0 win over Workington AFC in the League Cup. The following season, Ossie established himself in the first team, and Blues fans rapidly took the skilful striker to their heart.

On 8 January 1966, a sizeable crowd of 48,529, some of them seated in the newly opened West Stand, gathered at Stamford Bridge to witness a keenly contested London derby between Chelsea and Tottenham Hotspur.

Irrespective of vantage point, Blues supporters looked on in awe as Osgood scored a late winner in a 2-1 (George Graham, Peter Osgood) victory for the home side. Just five minutes remained when the Wizard of Os nipped in to take the ball away from teammate George Graham… jinking sideways and then striding forward, Ossie unleashed a rising shot that whistled past Spurs keeper Pat Jennings into the back of the net.

Osgood only beat Jennings from near and from far on two more occasions while playing for Chelsea.

31 August 1968 – a penalty in a 2-2 league draw at Stamford Bridge (Alan Birchenall, Peter Osgood.)

22 December 1971 – the opening goal in a dramatic 3-2 (Peter Osgood, Chris Garland, John Hollins) League Cup semi-final first leg tie win at the Bridge.

It didn't matter to Blues supporters however who always remembered that stunning late festive season present against Spurs and along the way rewrote the Christmas Carol, *The First Noël* in his honour. There are several subtle variations of this chant that can be heard from time-to-time and debates are frequent about which is correct. The version below is the one the authors most readily identify with:

*The Shed looked up and they saw a great star,*
*Scoring goals past Pat Jennings from near and from far.*
*And Chelsea won, as we all knew they would.*
*And the star of that great team was Peter Osgood.*
*Osgood, Osgood, Osgood, Osgood, born is the King of Stamford Bridge.*

*The First Noël...* Walter delves deeper and recalls a special moment:

**Walter:** No, we are not singing about the first bloke named Noel in history, or remembering TV 'personality' Mr Edmonds – the word 'Noël' deriving from the Latin word 'Natalis' means 'birthday' and some suggest that by the time it reached our shores, the Cornish used 'Noël' as their word for Christmas. The Christmas Carol, "The First Noël", is of Cornish origin. It was first published in Carols Ancient and Modern (1823) and Gilbert and Sandys Carols (1833), both of which were edited by William Sandys.

*The First Noël, the Angels did say*
*Was to certain poor shepherds in fields as they lay*
*In fields where they lay keeping their sheep*
*On a cold winter's night that was so deep.*
*Noël, Noël, Noël, Noël*
*Born is the King of Israel!'*

The full lyrics are too long to print here. The complete story detailing 'the first Christmas' and the birth of Jesus, is recorded in The Bible in The Gospel of Luke, Chapter 2.

The most magical memory I have of singing this song was in Stockholm in 1998 after lifting the Cup Winners' Cup, (13 May, VFB Stuttgart 0 Chelsea 1, Gianfranco Zola), I was with Den, Tall Paul and Jervo the Pervo. As we finally left our seats after celebrating and the players had long left the pitch, we turned to the exits and Den bumped straight into Peter Osgood!!

In a rush of euphoria, Den threw his arms around Osgood, who hugged him back magnificently. As people crowded around and noticed our former striker, his song was started and everyone sang it to him. Den took his Chelsea baseball cap off and gave it to his idol. Den and Peter went down the steps together, Peter wearing Den's cap.

As we left the ground more and more people heard the song, saw that

Peter Osgood was amongst us and the singing continued with Peter embracing more and more fans. A truly wonderful moment.

**Mark:** As befitting a player who would go on to become a true Chelsea icon, Born is the King is still regularly reprised today. There is no doubt in my mind that this wonderful tribute to Ossie, who scored 150 goals in 380 appearances for the Blues, will be sung decades from now.

Sadly, Peter Osgood died tragically young (1 March 2006) at just fifty-nine-years of age. I was a kid when he made his name with Chelsea, and like many young fans he was my first football hero. Accessible, personable and endearingly humble about his status within the Blues community, I met Ossie many times at social events after his playing career ended and never tired of hearing his stories about the old days and his fellow kings of the King's Road.

It was 11 March 2006 and as fate decreed, the first game Chelsea would play at Stamford Bridge following Osgood's sudden death was against Spurs. Ossie's family and former teammates were at the match, and supporters paid their tributes in song and with a minute's applause. Chelsea won (as we all knew they would) 2-1 with goals coming from Michael Essien and William Gallas.

On 1 October 2006, Peter Osgood's memorial service held at Stamford Bridge conducted by Blues supporter and Matthew Harding Stand season ticket holder Reverend Martin Swan remains to this day one of the most moving events I have ever attended as those present paid tribute to the King as his ashes were laid to rest under the penalty spot in front of The Shed End.

Peter Osgood
20 February 1947 – 1 March 2006
King of Stamford Bridge
Rest in Peace

# SHEDITES

**Mark:** Mick Greenaway's recollections of The Shed's development into a fully-fledged football 'end' are enthralling.

**Mick:** "At first there were only about 150-200 fans vocally cheering the Blues from this area. However, this gradually increased through the season (1966/67) to up to about 1000 for bigger games. Song sheets that were introduced to adapt popular records with Chelsea words in them – for example *(we all live in a) Yellow Submarine* (Beatles single released August 1966) became *We all live in a Blue and White Shed* – were well promoted."

In his interview with Mark, Garrison recalled Cliff Webb having the use of a Gestetner copying machine to produce the song sheets and that it was Webb who was responsible for revising many of the lyrics while Greenaway started off the chants.

*In the land where I was born, lived a manager of a football team.*
*And he told us of the time when the Blue and Whites were the cream.*
*So we walked the Fulham Road, till we found Stamford Bridge, then we started to support the best team of our age.*
*We all live in a Blue and White Shed, a Blue and White Shed, a Blue and White Shed.*

**Mark:** 17 September 1966, and the first versions of the chant featured the chorus *We all live in a Blue Submarine* can be heard being sung by Chelsea supporters during an exceptional 47 minutes' worth of *Match of The Day* highlights of a Blues away game with Aston Villa (Aston Villa 2 Chelsea 6, Bobby Tambling x5, John Boyle) that can be found on *YouTube*. It's recommended viewing, not only because Chelsea thrash Villa but also because the sound is faultless and provides a wonderfully audible testament to Greenaway's description of evolving fan culture.

Vociferous Blues followers travelled in numbers that day and constituted a sizeable portion of the 18,233 spectators at Villa Park. Their chants can be heard clearly, with impressed commentator Kenneth Wolstenholme often making reference to them.

"And so the Chelsea supporters all live in a *Blue Submarine* they tell us in their song," he advises. "Ringo Starr lives in a *Yellow Submarine*, but the Chelsea fans of course live in a *Blue Submarine*… the normal colours of their club." (Chelsea wore plain white shirts without the club crest for this particular game.)

5 November 1966, a couple of months after the Villa game, the Chelsea matchday programme for the home game with Manchester United (1-3 John Hollins) featured a letter from D.J Imray, a Geordie Blues fan living in Battersea entitled *That "Submarine" – New Words.*

"As Chelsea supporters seem to have adopted a slight variation of *Yellow Submarine*, I would be grateful if you would consider publishing the following verse in the programme to help the lads along."

The version printed in the programme has a different chorus to the Greenaway/Webb original, replacing *We all live in a Blue Submarine / Blue and White Shed* is *We all support the Blue and White team. Chelsea! The Blue and White team. Chelsea!*

*Blue Submarine* in any of its guises is definitely a Chelsea chant of the past, however there is a whacky Blues song that borrowed heavily from parent tune *Yellow Submarine* which remains popular in the matchday pubs around Stamford Bridge today.

It was 13 August 1992, at the dawn of what was then known as the Premiership, Chelsea paid a club record fee of £2.1 million to Norwich City for the services of Scotland international striker Robert Fleck. Fleck had a prolific goal-scoring career for the Canaries for whom he always seemed to find the net when they faced the Blues, but his prowess deserted him at Stamford Bridge. Four goals in 48 appearances for Chelsea didn't do Fleck any favours and in September 1995 he was sold back to Norwich for a cut price £650,000.

As has often been the case with Chelsea supporters, rather than berate an underachieving player, Fleck became a cult hero commemorated in song.

*Number 1 is Robert Fleck, Number 2 is Robert Fleck. Number 3 is Robert Fleck, Number 4 is Robert Fleck. Number 5 is Robert Fleck, Number 6 is Robert Fleck. Number 7 is Robert Fleck, Number 8 is Robert Fleck. Number 9 is Robert Fleck, Number 10 is Robert Fleck. Number 11 is Robert Fleck, Number 12 is Robert Fleck. We all live in a Robert Fleck world, a Robert Fleck world, a Robert Fleck world.*

Since 2012, the principal use of the *Yellow Submarine* melody has been to remind Arsenal supporters that their former left-back Ashley Cole won the Champions League playing for Chelsea. *Ashley Cole's won the European Cup, the European Cup, the European Cup. Ashley Cole's won the European Cup, the*

## CAREFREE! CHELSEA CHANTS AND TERRACE CULTURE

*European Cup, the European Cup.* Perfect!

**Walter:** Back in the summer of 1992, Chelsea and Spurs apparently had a gentleman's agreement that the Blues would bid for Fleck, and Teddy Sheringham would leave Forest for White Hart Lane. It does make you think how different things may have panned out if the transfers of the two players had been the other way around. One of the best moments singing the *Ashley Cole* version was on 19 December 2012 when the Chelsea away end was locked in after a League Cup game at Elland Road. Ashley came out to warm down and was duly serenaded vociferously.

**Mark:** Back to the Aston Villa highlights:

The repetitive three-clap and klaxon accompanied chants of *Chelsea!* prompted Wolstenholme to quip, "judging by the noise being made from the terraces, you'd think that everybody here was a Chelsea supporter."

The simple *Chelsea!* chant, modified for use by supporters of many clubs, had its origins in the Dave Dee, Dozy, Beaky, Mick & Tich song *Hold Tight* which had reached number 4 in UK singles chart earlier in the year. During the World Cup tournament, England fans had sung an *England!* version and given that all the games were screened live on television this no doubt explained its rapid rise in use across the nations terraces.

*Molly Malone,* still sung today, albeit infrequently, was aired enthusiastically on numerous occasions at Villa Park.

*In Dublin's fair city, where the girls are so pretty, I first set my eyes on sweet Molly Malone.*
*She wheeled her wheel-barrow, through streets broad and narrow, singing* (clap clap, clap clap clap, clap clap clap) *Chelsea!*

The Blues galloping into a 3-0 lead courtesy of a Bobby Tambling brace and a goal from John Boyle ensured travelling supporters remained in good voice.

*Oh when the Blues, go marching in, oh when the Blues go marching in.*
*I wanna be in that number, oh when the Blues go marching in.*

Given Chelsea's dominance in the game, the chanting remained good-natured. Only an ever so slightly tweaked version of the Geordie folk song *Blaydon Races* provided an inkling of the confrontational aspect of following football that was slowly, surely and sinisterly gaining momentum.

*Oh my lads, you should have seen them running.*
*Asked them, why? And they replied, the Chelsea boys are coming.*
*All the lads and lasses, with smiles upon their faces.*
*Walking down the Fulham Road… to see the Chelsea aces.*

*'Running'* had taken on a new meaning when singing this chant compared to its earlier innocence… more on this later.

Barely six weeks earlier (30 July 1966), Wolstenholme had uttered the immortal line "some people are on the pitch… they think it's all over… it is now!" as Geoff Hurst scored England's fourth goal against West Germany in the World Cup Final at Wembley. Now he was waxing lyrical about Blues supporters.

"Chelsea fans really taking the mickey out of Villa now by singing the tune of *Strolling*," he advises. "And that's really what Chelsea are doing. They're strolling through this match, deservedly 3-0 up."

*Strolling, just strolling in the cool of the evening air.*
*I don't envy the rich, in their automobiles.*
*For a motor car is phoney, I'd rather sh\*g a pony!*
*When I'm strolling, just strolling, in the light of the moon above.*
*Every night I go out strolling, and I know my luck is rolling, when I'm strolling, with the one I love.*
*Chelsea* (clap clap clap) *Chelsea* (clap clap clap)

This ever so slightly adapted *sh\*g a pony* rendition of *Strolling* (original version made popular during World War II by British comedy double act Bud Flanagan and Chesney Allen) was sung by Chelsea supporters for a number of years, but became neglected as more ambitious and provocative chants found favour.

Gone, but not forgotten, *Strolling* was resurrected decades later by David Chidgey, host of the excellent *Chelsea Fancast*, who along with the guests on his weekly show sang it for the benefit of the podcast's burgeoning global audience.

Meanwhile, nostalgically back at Villa Park, Bobby Tambling would soon complete his hattrick and finish the game with five goals in a remarkable 6-2 Chelsea victory.

*You're all going home, you're all going home. Ee Eye Addio, you're all going home* sang the visiting crowd gleefully to the melody of the nursery rhyme *The*

## CAREFREE! CHELSEA CHANTS AND TERRACE CULTURE

*Farmer's In His Den* as Villa fans made for the exits well before the final whistle.

*****

Another chant that made a bow during the 1966/67 season borrowed the melody from *Distant Drums* which Jim Reeves had a posthumous No.1 UK chart hit with in September 1966.

Targeted at opposition fans, *And do they smell, like f*cking hell. Over there, over there* was an entertaining addition to The Shed's growing repertoire of chants. Like the Beatles *Yellow Submarine* which charted at the same time, *Distant Drums* was another track played before games over the Tannoy system at Stamford Bridge which on hearing prompted Chelsea supporters to begin singing their own versions.

Tim Rolls remembers *And do they smell* being the first chant he heard at the Bridge at his first big match. 25 November 1967, Manchester United, 1-1, (Tommy Baldwin.)

**Tim:** "I am pretty sure it had been sung around the country for several months. Until the mid-1960s very little football was shown on TV and, until August 1966, *Match of The Day* was on BBC2 which almost nobody had. National coverage, and the growth of 'ends' at every league club, meant that chants one end sang that was heard on television could be picked up across the country by different crowds the following Saturday. *And Do They Smell* was one of the 'obscene chants' the papers had got into a lather about."

> *I hear the sound, clap-clap-clap clap-clap-clap,*
> *Of distant bums, clap-clap-clap clap-clap-clap,*
> *Over there, over there (fingers pointing at away fans under old North Stand)*
> *And do they smell? clap-clap-clap clap-clap-clap,*
> *Like f*cking hell clap-clap-clap clap-clap-clap*
> *Over there, over there (fingers pointing at away fans under old North Stand)*

**Mark:** The 1966 World Cup tournament had seen England beat Mexico 2-0 at Wembley in Group One (16 July). Despite seeing their team outclassed, Mexico's supporters were in a carnival mood throughout the game repeatedly singing *Cielito Lindo* aka the *Ay, Ay, Ay, Ay* song.

While underdogs Mexico's challenge had ended at the group stages, unfancied Portugal and Russia made it through to the semi-finals largely thanks to the exploits of two legendary players who were cult heroes for all football fans at that time. Striker Eusebio finished the tournament with nine goals for Portugal winning the Golden Boot, while goalkeeper Lev Yashin's agile saves for Russia were largely responsible for propelling his country to the last four.

Chelsea supporters absorbed what they'd heard and seen during the World Cup and came up with a version of the *Ay, Ay, Ay, Ay* chant first heard on The Shed in October 1966 which paid homage to Blues goalkeeper Peter Bonetti and new striker Tommy Baldwin who'd arrived at Stamford Bridge from Arsenal in a part-exchange deal which took George Graham to Highbury on 29 September.

On 1 October, Baldwin scored on his debut for Chelsea in a 4-1 (Bobby Tambling, Tommy Baldwin, Joe Kirkup, Peter Osgood) rout of Manchester City at Maine Road, a game in which Bonetti pulled off a string of outstanding saves.

*Ay, Ay, Ay, Ay. Bonetti is better than Yashin.*
*Baldwin is better than Eusebio, and Tottenham are in for a thrashing.*

At the time, Peter Osgood was, apart maybe from George Best, the best young player in England, and opposition fans began marking him out for special treatment. Chelsea's thrashing of Man City reinforced their top-of-the-table status and an imperious Ossie had skated through the City defence to score a superb solo goal to round of the victory.

As Tim Rolls recounts in *Diamonds, Dynamos and Devils*, Osgood's reaction to scoring was both unique (at that time) and controversial. He immediately gave a 'modified Churchillian' two-fingered salute to the City fans who had, not entirely originally, been jeering and baiting him with *Osgood, No Good* chants to the melody of the *Pompey Chimes*. There was a minor furore in the press, especially as the incident was shown on *Match of The Day* (and can be found on *YouTube*), though commentator Ken Wolstenholme did not mention it.

Osgood later apologised and manager Tommy Docherty commented "The goal was enough. The gesture was unnecessary. It was a damned silly thing to do."

Unfortunately, just four days later in a League Cup tie away at Blackpool (5 October 1966) Ossie was on the receiving end of an horrific leg-breaking tackle perpetrated by Tangerines left-half Emlyn Hughes. The game at Bloomfield Road ended in a 1-1 draw (Peter Houseman). A fortnight later

# CAREFREE! CHELSEA CHANTS AND TERRACE CULTURE

(17 October) Chelsea lost the replay 3-1 (Peter Houseman) at Stamford Bridge. Hughes, who went on to play for Liverpool and England, featured in the match and was barracked every time he touched the ball. The Shed's affection for Osgood was undimmed, however, and on his return the following season he was as popular as ever.

On 26 October, the Tottenham prediction came true when Baldwin fired home a brace in a pleasing 3-0 (Bobby Tambling, Tommy Baldwin x 2) victory over Spurs at the Bridge.

The value of Baldwin's currency with The Shed continued to rise, and a chant to the melody of *McNamara's Band* was soon being sung in his honour. A chart hit for Bing Crosby and the Jesters in 1945, a version of *McNamara's Band* had been sung for some time by Tottenham fans at White Hart Lane where the track was played as the teams came out for the second-half... and so in purloining the melody, Chelsea fans knew they would be irking their rivals.

> *His name is Tommy Baldwin he's the leader of the team.*
> *(What team?)*
> *The finest football team that the world has ever seen.*
> *We're the Fulham Road supporters and we're louder than The Kop.*
> *(What Kop?)*
> *If anyone wants to argue, we'll kill the f\*cking lot.*
> *La la la la.*

Nicknamed 'Sponge' by his teammates for his ability to soak up alcohol at parties, Baldwin would feature prominently in the great Chelsea side of the late '60s and early '70s. A regular at Stamford Bridge today, the sight of Tommy walking down the Fulham Road is all it takes for Blues fans in the vicinity to launch into *His name is Tommy Baldwin*.

*****

Walter's friend Champagne Les Allen was one of the original Shedites. Like all my co-author's friends he has a nickname that merits explanation.

**Walter:** Les was always simply Les. A glint in his eye, a spring in his step, a sparkle in his grin and a couple of pints of Guinness before the game. Then one New Year's Day, we've got Fulham away. I'm walking towards the Eight Bells pub with Big Chris, Tall Paul and Smiffy when the door opens and Les sticks his head out and shouts *"Happy New Year!"* at us, pushes the door open further and lifts a bottle of champagne in the air. It was a memorable moment and since then he's always been known in the contacts in my phone as simply 'Champagne.'

On 22 January 2017, I interviewed Champagne Les in fabled SW6 drinker the Malt House a few hours before Chelsea's home game with Hull City (Chelsea 2 Hull City 0, Diego Costa, Gary Cahill.)

Les Allen was born in February 1949. I watched him sip his Guinness between recollections – brow sometimes furrowed, a head scratch here and there to nail a memory down, mixed in with bucketsful of smiles of remembrance:

**Les:** "I can't recall my first game, I was probably five or six. My Granddad was a Fulham supporter, and my Uncle was Chelsea. One week I'd go to Fulham with Granddad, the next week to Chelsea with my Uncle. All the family went together – Fulham one week, Chelsea the next.

I've got five brothers – two of them are Chelsea, two are Fulham. One brother doesn't like football – so he must've been the milkman's! I'd been to watch Chelsea away when we played London teams, but I'd never been out of London – except in the Cup. You see, my Mum was Fulham. She said to me, *"When you're old enough to go to work and bring money into the house, you can go to away games outside London."* I remember it so well – but she made exceptions three years in a row though! All because Chelsea got to consecutive FA Cup semi-finals. She understood – she got it. She let me go to the Cup semis. They were all played at Villa Park. In 1965, we lost to Liverpool (29 March, Chelsea 0 Liverpool 2). In 1966, we lost to Sheffield Wednesday (23 April, Chelsea 0 Sheffield Wednesday 2). In 1967, we beat Leeds! (29 April, Chelsea 1 Leeds United 0, Tony Hateley.)

My first league game outside of London was against Southampton at the Dell. On the Friday night before the match, I was at Walham Green Youth Club with Colin Butler and John 'Irish'. I never knew John's surname, but he was Irish, so there you go. We'd play billiards, darts and table tennis. Well we decided we were going to go to Southampton so we left the Youth Club and started walking down the A3, trying to hitchhike. We had a flag that we took with is – the girls at the Youth Club had made it for us! It took them hours to sew together. A Union Jack was sewn into the back of a great big Chelsea flag. I can remember the names of the girls – they were Wendy Game and Sue Gould. Sue ended up marrying Colin Butler!

While hitchhiking down the A3, I got knocked over by a push-bike. I don't know how far we got, but I remember seeing a sign for Guildford but

## CAREFREE! CHELSEA CHANTS AND TERRACE CULTURE

I don't know how close we were to Guildford. This bloke had pulled over for a kip, we looked in his motor and he woke up. He yelled, "*What you doing here? You frightened me!*" He was going to Portsmouth, so he gave us a lift. He even let us put our big flag with flag poles in the car. We kipped on some grass opposite the Town Hall. It was Saturday 3 September 1966 – I remember it because it was the only game Alex Stepney played for Chelsea. We won 3-0." (George Graham, Peter Osgood, Bobby Tambling)

**Walter:** With a pause in his story, I asked him where Walham Green Youth Club was based? Les smiled and pointed to the window gesturing to the Church. I could walk across the pub floor, glance out the window and be looking at St. John's on the North End Road. Things like this are mad. Personally, I've walked past that Church hundreds of times – in both directions. I always look up at it.

Nearly fifty-one years after Les, Colin and John went for a walk down the A3 from Walham Green and here he is telling me the story from the pub opposite the church where he went to Youth Club. As I often do when things like this crop up, I go to the wonder of the internet. Walham Green tube station was opened on 1 March 1880. In 1905, the original station was replaced with a new entrance to cope with the crowds flocking to the newly build Stamford Bridge Stadium. On 1 March 1952, the name was changed to Fulham Broadway. Don't you just love stuff like this? I realised I had to spend more time – much more time, listening to Les. I gestured at him to continue.

**Les:** "So that was my first time out of London for a league game. I'd only experienced Cup games outside London – three semi-finals up at Villa Park – losing two but winning one. In the early hours in Southampton we went to Terry Paine's caff. (Paine made over 800 appearances for The Saints.) It wasn't open, but the milk had been delivered, so we helped ourselves to a bottle from the crate thinking they wouldn't miss one bottle. So, we drank it for breakfast. After the match, we got the train home."

Walter and Champagne Les are then joined by Vastly Intelligent Keef and his son Tax Dodging Tommy.

**Walter:** First off, I need to tell you about Vastly Intelligent Keef.
In 1987 my cousin Gioja and Keef got married. My big sister was a bridesmaid. Champagne Les was there, but I didn't know him at the time. I knew that Keef loved Chelsea and betting on the horses and that the newlyweds wouldn't be living anywhere near where I did in Chessington, Surrey.

I was very fond of my cousin Gioja, in fact reflecting on it I was fond of all my cousins and Aunt's and Uncle's from my Mum's side of the family. They all lived in Malvern, Worcestershire. My earliest memory of Keef was playing football with him.

When he started going out with Gioja he was brought over to be introduced to Granny in Malvern. I think it was Easter time, and I was up there with my sisters and parents visiting. Keef and I went outside and played football for ages on the green. I can remember kicking the ball backwards and forwards, I can even remember what we talked about, which is crazy because we might have only been playing for ten or twenty minutes and this would've been about 1985 or 1986 or something.

My first trip to the Bridge didn't happen until 1990 (more on this later), and I wasn't expecting Keef to take me or anything, the thought hadn't crossed my mind, and, why would he? I was his girlfriend's little cousin with holes in his jeans and a bad haircut. Keef wouldn't want to be lumbered with me – he had pints to drink and horses to bet on and travelled into London for games in completely the opposite direction to where I lived.

Fast-forward a few years and I'm eighteen-plus and drinking in pubs and going as often as I can. I can't remember the exact games or concourses, but every time I went away I'd bump into Keef. Of course, we'd chat and have a beer, our connection was still there, even though (two kids later) his marriage to my cousin had come to a sad end. I remember a time up in Middlesbrough when we bumped straight into each other! Keef always invited me down the Wheatsheaf in Parsons Green. (This pub is now a Sainsbury's. Every time I think about it, it's like a punch in the guts!)

So – now and again on home match days I'd pop in – especially if his two kids were with him. I mean, we're family, and that means something. It was through Keef that I met Les. Best pals. Been going for years. The Wheatsheaf was a brilliant pub. One summer, the Cock was yuppied up. Speaking to Den recently, he thinks it was the summer of 2009 or 2010 when this yuppying up occurred.

I wasn't going to the first home match that season, but Den rings me and he's all wound up. He tells me that security wouldn't let anyone in wearing Chelsea colours. What's the matter with these people? Don't they want to earn money? It was so out of touch I could barely believe it. So, the next home match we all gravitated permanently to the Wheatsheaf, rather than it just being the odd beer in there intermittently.

They were happy times – Les, Keef, Tax Dodging Tommy (Keef's son), Taxi Alan, Den, Smiffy, Tall Paul, Big Chris et al. (As the season progressed, the Cock management clearly realised they needed their pub full on match days and changed their policy to welcome back Chelsea supporters – but even now I still get the hump going in there and buying a drink.)

So, it's October 2010 and we're on the motorway going to Blackburn (30 October, Blackburn Rovers 1 Chelsea 2, Nicolas Anelka, Branislav Ivanović), Keef is driving, Les is in the passenger seat with Tommy and I in the back. We're discussing Fulham's proposal to extend Craven Cottage, and whether a stand backing up and over the River Thames was viable. As this discussion went on, Keef was getting more and more irate to the point where he exploded:

"I know what I'm talking about you lot, I'm Vastly Intelligent on these matters!"

To which, of course, we all burst out laughing, and his nickname was born. Which brings us onto Tax Dodging Tommy.

Tom was a student at Canterbury University. When sending in articles for the *cfcuk* fanzine, I needed a nickname for him to keep up with the tradition of people I drink with having a nickname. He wasn't paying tax because he as a student, so that was that. Then, after Uni when he started working, he became Tax Paying Tommy.

I have two favourite memories of Tom.

Firstly, drinking with him before Munich (19 May 2012, Champions League Final, Bayern Munich 1 Chelsea 1, Didier Drogba, AET, Chelsea win 4-3 on penalties, David Luiz, Frank Lampard, Ashley Cole, Didier Drogba) and stopping him from starting on a meathead twice his size who was dressed as Biggles and disrespecting our generous German hosts with taunts regarding WWII.

Secondly, at a game at Hillsborough in December 1997, I was in the upper tier with Tall Paul, Ravishing Rachel and Jervo the Pervo. For his seventh birthday Tom was the mascot and ran out with Dennis Wise – he was such a sweet kid with the fairest hair in the land. Chelsea won 4-1 (20 December, Sheffield Wednesday 1 Chelsea 4, Dan Petrescu, Gianluca Vialli, Frank Leboeuf, Tore Andre Flo), and on the way home we passed the team coach and Tore Andre Flo gave us a wave.

Thinking about it, Tommy the Mascot seems a more suitable nickname. During the summer of 2010, Tommy told me that in the Green Man at Wembley after Chelsea had won the FA Cup (15 May, Chelsea 1 Portsmouth 0, Didier Drogba), Champagne Les had started a song on the spot. The table picked up on it – the table opposite joined in and in minutes the whole place was singing it. This is how Les explained to me:

**Les:** "We were in the Green Man after winning the FA Cup. Everyone was singing the Wayne Bridge song. (6 April 2004, Champions League quarter-final Second Leg, Arsenal 1 Chelsea 2, Frank Lampard, Wayne Bridge.)

*Follow, follow, follow, there was only two minutes to go.*
*It was Wayne Bridge's Goal, That sent us out of control,*
*And sent the Arsenal out of Euro.... two, three, four…*

I was toying with the *follow, follow, follow* line and starting singing *double, double, double* and then it grew from there. (Melody courtesy of Scott Joplin's classic piano rag *The Entertainer* which dates all the way back to 1902.) The *John Terry* line got added as it caught momentum across the pub, but originally it was *Super Chelsea*. See – the way I see it is that John Terry didn't win the double on his own, Chelsea won the double. And, another thing – the bad language was added, there was no cursing in my original, others' put in the swearing. But we were basically singing it back and forth, one table to another, and then it grew and grew and eventually hundreds of fans were belting it out."

*Double! Double! Double!*
*Super Chelsea have won the Double.*
*And the Spurs from the Lane have won nothing again…*
*But Super Chelsea have won the Double.*

**Walter:** *The Entertainer* would also provide the melody for a tribute chant conceived when Frank Lampard broke Bobby Tambling's long-standing goal-scoring record. Super Frank netted a brace at Villa Park (11 May 2013, Aston Villa 1 Chelsea 2), there are a couple of different versions of this song… some fans sing 'got' and others sing 'broke':

*Record, record, record. Frankie Lampard has got the record.*
*It was Villa away on the eleventh of May,*
*Frank Lampard has got the record.*

What a man!

## CAREFREE! CHELSEA CHANTS AND TERRACE CULTURE

For supporters of a certain generation, you don't need me to tell you that football has evolved massively. From the working mans' game to corporate hospitality. One of the things I've noticed is that, for me, the spirit in the pub has replaced the spirit on the terracing. You meet who you want, where you want. You might be gathered for drinks before going to the ground to watch the match, you might be gathered for drinks after returning from the ground. You might be gathered because you and your mates want to watch it in the pub because you're priced out, you're banned or it's a game you can't make for whatever reason, but whatever the scenario – basically there's a whole load of you in the boozer because of the football. And there's no buzz like it – for me, anyway. It's unique. Last minute winners are unique. Organic chants formulating on trains and concourses are unique. And pre-or post-match gatherings are unique too – and they are the constant – the consistent – the addiction.

On this occasion featuring Keef, Tommy and Les – it was a post-match gathering full of celebrations after winning the Double. The jubilation was tangible. A song springs organically, catches on and then goes that final step to become a fan favourite sung every game. Keef recalled another song Les had written after the 1994 Cup Final defeat to Man United (14 May, Manchester United 4 Chelsea 0), in a Wembley boozer.

After the loss, Tall Paul and I went back to West Ewell and sat all vacant in a pub, also called the Green Man, funnily enough. I felt sick and my face paint was no doubt smudged. Turns out though, that where they went drinking post-match (oh how I wish I was with them) to drown their sorrows, those in the boozer came up with a cracker.

**Les:** "Keef and I hit the pub after the '94 Cup Final – we're with Mickey G and although I cannot remember who was involved with the conversation, it did go along the lines of not winning the League and whether that would ever happen, and Cup runs being so important to us fans, we get all the way to the final but end up getting thumped. We didn't win the League and we didn't win the Cup. Then the conversation develops into going to Europe and the next thing a bit of singing and conversation mingle and then within a minute or two everyone is singing:

*Hello! Hello! We are the Chelsea boys!*
*Hello! Hello! We make a lot of noise.*
*We did not win the Football League, we did not win the Cup…*
*But we're all going to Europe!*

Mickey was a bit older than me and my mates, but because we started going every game as young men, we always knew him to talk to. I wasn't tight with him – he had his bond of friends – but he was a nice guy to say the least. We all looked up to him! He was like our Godfather – I mean, he looked after us for tickets if he could. No-one can compete with his *Zigger Zagger*. He was top notch."

Walter was keen to find out how Champagne Les and Keef first met…

**Les:** "Forty-five years ago, I was working in Grantham in Lincolnshire. Someone tells me that a Chelsea fan was running a bus to Leicester away. I rang up, booked a space and jumped on. And that was I how I met Keith. We've been going together ever since."

As he readied himself to reply Keef was smiling, like he'd taken some chemicals, but this was a natural high.

**Keef:** "I was sixteen! Too young to book the coach, so my Dad had to book the coach for me!"

Walter asks if there anything about trips in the past that spring to Keef's mind?
Of course there are hundreds to choose from. Here's the first…

**Keef:** "We went to Hull in 1982 at the time when the FA had banned Chelsea supporters from travelling to away matches. (FA Cup 3rd Round Replay, Hull City 0 Chelsea 2, Alan Mayes, John Bumstead.) We park up and our pal Winnie wants to go for a drink, but I want to go to the ticket office and try and get tickets. Winnie convinces us to go to the pub, so in we go. There's about fifty Chelsea already in there including Mickey Greenaway, and he's got loads of match tickets! We buy some off him. We always said hello to each other after that. It felt good to be on speaking terms with the characters like Mick and Babs – I'd always tell my mates, I felt so proud.

I was born and still lived in Lincoln, but I was a Chelsea supporter. My Dad, John, is a Nottingham Forest fan. In 1966 when I was still a kid he took me to Forest v Chelsea at the City Ground. (12 April, Notts Forest 1 Chelsea 2, Bobby Tambling x2), I've still got the match programme. Forest came out the tunnel, and Chelsea ran out all in blue. I fell in love! Just like that! Dad never took me to Chelsea, but from that point onwards I followed their results. I'd sit on kitchen floor and listen to the radio or I'd be up and about kicking a ball around the room and using my imagination. 7 October 1967 Chelsea lost 7-0 at Leeds and I felt like my whole school taunted me. But this made me more determined! I remember Boots the pharmacy had *CHELSEA* sprayed on it.

I'll tell you how I met Steve 'Winnie' Winters. You see, I had long hair and he had a skinhead. After a local disco, I got kicked in – to be honest I took a bit of a bashing. It was 1973. Soon after, I was in The Shed and we were playing Birmingham City (5 September, Chelsea 3 Birmingham City 1, Ian Hutchinson, John Hollins, Steve Kember) – and I see Winnie is in there, in The Shed! I got to know him and his mates. Even though I was a student with shoulder length hair, they accepted me.

I loved rock festivals and I loved Chelsea. They didn't mix. I went to the first ever Reading festival and I also remember a festival in Bardney in Lincolnshire. In those hippy days, you had communal sleeping areas. There was a terrible gale and we were all in a marquee. I'd rung my Dad to come and pick me up, but then, in the meantime, I'd somehow found a lift home. He was six hours at the festival trying to find me before he gave up!

Then, Winnie and I found ourselves working in the same factory. I was in the office, he was on the shop floor! We were an odd couple, but opposites attract. We played together for the works football team. I was striker and he was a left back. I was best man at his wedding! We still go all over together. We were two people who couldn't be mates and we became mates. We hit it off at Chelsea.

I'll tell you something – because I lived in Lincoln, I hadn't gone on a football special from London to an away game. I really wanted to get a special. So to fix this, one time I drove from Lincoln to London with Les and Winnie, but my car broke down. I was devastated! I decided to leave the car and get a train to London so we didn't miss the special! I found out the next day that at 10.30am the police rang my Dad. I'd abandoned the car across the entrance to the bus station so no buses could get in. I was eighteen-years old. Back then I read the *Guardian* so I was 'Vastly Intelligent' even back then! (Walter's note: "Apart from abandoning your car across the entrance to a bus station!") On the special, everyone would swap newspapers. There'd be the *Daily Sketch* or the *Sun* or the *Daily Mirror* – if I swapped newspapers then they'd end up giving the *Guardian* straight back to me!"

**Walter:** A waitress turns up with the food order. Champagne Les shuffles some papers and pushes them over to me. He's handwritten a few songs from back in the day, songs like *Blue Submarine* and *Bonetti is better than Yashin* which are mentioned earlier in this chapter... and a few more which are coming up in subsequent chapters.

The lads tuck into their Sunday roasts, I sink back in my chair and study Les' notes – I feel this mad sensation prickling all over me, like I'm sitting here in the present in a pub I've drank in numerous times with friends and family I've seen a thousand times, but at the same time it's like I'm not really here, like I'm behind the bar or up high on another level – people watching and looking down at myself – I have this sensation of Chelsea history rushing up at me for such a time as this, and it might sound daft but I feel incredibly privileged to be the one typing all of this up.

# THE MIDDLE OF THE SHED

**Mark:** By the late 1960s, the Horner family had moved to Thessally Road, Battersea, and Little Jack used to walk to Stamford Bridge with a sizeable contingent of Blues supporters who lived just south of the River Thames.

Jack remembered the friendly rivalry with fans from neighbouring Stockwell… and the chant the two mobs traded which harnessed the melody of *Camptown Races,* an American minstrel song composed in the 19th Century that found a global audience via cartoon character Foghorn Leghorn!

The Stockwell would sing; *We all come from Stockwell, doo-da, doo-da. We all come from Stockwell, doo-da, doo-da-day.* And the Battersea would reply *We all come from Battersea, woof-woof, woof-woof. We all come from Battersea, woof-woof, woof-woof-woof.*

Although the *Stockwell / Battersea* chant has sadly been consigned to history, as noted later in *Carefree!* the *Camptown Races* melody would be used again to a wider and longer-lasting effect on the European stage.

Trading chants was fun and got the atmosphere going, particularly if the crowd following the opposition was scarce. The weather would determine where Little Jack and his friends stood on The Shed whose curiously juxtaposed roof didn't afford cover to everyone on the terrace. On dry days, they would stand on the west side… when it rained they would pack into the middle or make for the whitewashed wall which jutted down the broad concrete steps and split the wrought iron stanchions.

Atmosphere-wise, the middle was the place to be… and those gathered there would try and out sing supporters either side of them.

*We're the middle, we're the middle, we're the middle of The Shed.* Those stood by the whitewashed wall would reply, *We're the white wall, we're the white wall, we're the white wall of The Shed* to which those stood towards the West Stand would add *We're the west side, we're the west side, we're the west side of The Shed.*

The chant would continue until the terrace unified in singing *We're The Shed End, we're The Shed End, we're The Shed End, Stamford Bridge!*

Notwithstanding the redevelopment of the Bridge in the mid-1990s which saw the old Shed demolished and re-modelled as an all-seated stand which also houses away fans in its east side, *We're the middle of The Shed* has retained its popularity.

Despite vocal support improving thanks to the efforts of those prepared to sing in The Shed, letters continued to feature in the matchday programme's *In Off The Post* section criticising the general atmosphere at Stamford Bridge.

7 January 1967
Chelsea 4 Southampton 1
(John Boyle, Tommy Baldwin x2, Bobby Tambling.)

*"There can be no other club in the country that has only 400 or so REAL SUPPORTERS. No wonder the home record is poor. The team needs support, and if the skill and effort of Chelsea are to receive the great reward they so richly deserve, let's have the support. From everywhere!"*
Duncan S. Dymond

16 September 1967
Chelsea 2 Stoke City 2
(Bobby Tambling, Peter Osgood.)

*"Stamford Bridge is like a mausoleum. How can we expect players to reach a peak in this deathly atmosphere?"*
Francis McGettigan

\*\*\*\*\*

Despite the grumblings of Messrs Dymond and McGettigan, there are plenty of supporters who will happily testify that Stamford Bridge was very much alive at that time… among them Champagne Les who fondly recalled to Walter several Shed classics from the mid '60s which were belted out on the terrace with gusto.

The first made use of *Bless 'Em All*, a war song written by Fred Godfrey in 1917 and set to a melody composed by Robert Kewley which banjo-twanger George Formby was among many to record.

*Bless 'em all! Bless 'em all!*
*The long and the short and the tall.*
*Docherty's diamonds in bright royal blue.*
*There's Ossie, Bonetti and Charlie Cooke too,*

*And we're saying goodbye to them all, as we make Spurs look small,*
*We're going to get goals and two points to go with them, so cheer up you lads*
*Bless 'em all!*

Spurs was substituted with the name of any one of a number of rival clubs depending on the circumstances.

A favourite for FA Cup games was *Come on score, score, score. When you get one you'll get more. We'll sing your assembly when we get to Wembley, so come on you Chelsea and score.*

In the modern era, *Bless 'Em All* is still represented on the Chelsea song sheet with the version which denounce rival teams.

*F\*ck 'em all, f\*ck 'em all, United, West Ham, Liverpool. Cos we are the Chelsea and we are the best. We are the Chelsea, so f\*ck all the rest.*

Wouldn't it be funny to have a George Formby impersonator playing the banjo and singing those words?

*Daisy Bell (Bicycle Built for Two)*, written by Harry Dacre in 1892 is said to have been inspired by Daisy Greville a mistress of King Edward VII. It's well-known chorus *Daisy Daisy, give me your answer do. I'm half-crazy oh for the love of you* was a standard singalong in London's pubs for decades before The Shed minstrels transformed it into the equally wonderful:

*Chelsea, Chelsea give us a goal or two.*
*We're all for you so we shout, 'Up the Blues!'*
*They may be stylish and dashing, but we'll give them a thrashing,*
*And we'll look sweet, when Spurs are beat, and our points go up two by two!*

A letter from R.J. Otter published (12 September 1964) in the Chelsea v Fulham (1-0, Barry Bridges) programme (the first time supporters letters featured) championed the song and advised:

"*Surely Chelsea needs a victory song now. It's not good enough to echo Spurs'* Marching on, *or* Chel-sea, Chel-sea. West Ham have Bubbles *and Liverpool's* Saints Go Marching In. *Can't we have something simple like this to the tune of* Daisy Daisy *which everyone knows.*"

As with *Bless 'Em All*, Spurs could be interchanged with the name of a rival team. It seems funny seeing a song referring to win being worth two points. It was visionary football legend Jimmy Hill who first proposed the three-point win in 1981 and the way the game is being changed to suit the whims of the television moguls it's quite possible this might change again or be amended in the not too distant future.

Listening to Les reminiscing about *Daisy Daisy* gave Walter a flashback to his primary school playground days and an altogether different version which merits inclusion on the basis that he couldn't believe the teachers didn't put a stop to it. Maybe they were too busy laughing!

*Daisy, Daisy give me your tits to chew.*
*I'm half-crazy my balls are turning blue!*
*I can't afford a johnny, a plastic bag will do.*
*You do look sweet, under the sheet, with me on top of you.*

Last but not least a Chelsea version of the traditional American spiritual *He's Got the Whole World in His Hands* which had been a top twenty hit for Laurie London accompanied by the Geoff Love Orchestra back in 1957.

*We've got the best team in the land! We've got the best team in the land! We've got the best team in the land! We've got the best team in the land!*
*We've got Peter Osgood in our team!*
*We've got Charlie Cooke in our team!*
*We've got Peter Bonetti in our team!*
*We've got the best team in the land!*

*****

For Champagne Les, the mid 60s was definitely the period when the terrace culture that had slowly been evolving at football grounds up and down the land began to take on a harder, edgier incarnation.

**Les:** "It must have been about 1965 when I noticed an increase in away ends at Chelsea and at Fulham. I'd watch the first half with my Uncle (at Stamford Bridge) or my Granddad (at Craven Cottage) and then we'd move around the ground at half-time and stood where we wanted for the second half.

Sometimes there'd be a bit of noise – *Come on Chelsea! Come on Chelsea!* or *Come on Fulham! Come on Fulham!* but no specific other songs spring to mind. There was no segregation, and you'd all have a chat, you know? I remember going to Upton Park and talking with opposing fans, it's what you did, especially with the World Cup on the horizon. Pop music gave birth to chants and songs on the terraces – *Yellow Submarine (as mentioned earlier)* the obvious example.

After the 1966 World Cup there much more excitement about football. England was alive and kicking because of football and if you had an England player belonging in the team you followed, then you were buzzing – look at West Ham and the players they had. It really resounded. In my mind, it was after the World Cup when songs, crowd segregation and mobs all mixed together, taking off. The culture quickly changed. There were instances in 1965, some violence between opposing supporters, but it was after the World Cup when it became more regular and organised."

**Walter:** Coincidence or not, the first Chelsea game after the 1966 World Cup Final was away at West Ham! The players of both teams applauded Bobby Moore, Martin Peters and Geoff Hurst onto the pitch. (20 August, West Ham 1 Chelsea 2, Charlie Cooke, John Hollins.) There is a fantastic clip on *YouTube* featuring omnipresent commentator Kenneth Wolstenholme's unique introduction to the game, and this dove-tails perfectly with Champagne Les' memories:

*"And what a sizzling start to a new soccer season for this West Ham United versus Chelsea match. A big crowd, a shirt-sleeved crowd. In fact, in many places, a shirt-less crowd! Now I think we must at this point say welcome to our new viewers…. The new fans who have been won over to soccer by the World Cup. We hope that you'll go along to watch your local team as well as watching Match of the Day. And in reply to your many requests, yes I will explain the more technical points of the game as we go along."*

**Les:** "I'll tell you something, thinking about it now, if I'm really honest, it must have been 1965 when it was my first recollection of violence. I was sixteen or seventeen years of age. A lot of lads my age were angry boys – they wanted to argue and fight. Some young lads with energy took it out on the football pitch playing, like me – jumping for headers, tackling all over the pitch, exerting your energy playing the game. When it came to going to Chelsea, others wanted to fight. I liked to talk, and listen! Rather than talk, they'd fight! Us and them. They split the ends up. I remember chatting with West Ham fans at Upton Park: 'How are you?', 'Yeah I'm good, you?', 'Yeah, getting on okay mate. What about Hurst then?', and you'd have a chat! 'What about Hudson then?' and then you'd discuss the match. And then the authorities split the fans up who essentially became two mobs.

Then I recall the 5-5 home draw with West Ham in 1966 (17 December, Tommy Baldwin, Tony Hateley, Charlie Cooke, Bobby Tambling x2.) We'd beaten them 2-1 in the first game of the season. Well, West Ham all got there first and went in The Shed. There was no limit to the crowds –

40,000, 50,000, 60,000 – until the Police said no more. Anyway – we all go in and West Ham had taken the Shed and it all went off. That's my earliest memory relating to trouble. We did the same thing at Arsenal in the North Bank – probably the same season 1966/67 (4 February 1967, Arsenal 2 Chelsea 1, Bobby Tambling). I distinctly remember that we stopped wearing our colours and scarves.

I've been caught in it, couldn't avoid it, but I've never looked at being involved in it. I got a slap in the Shed from West Ham – everyone hitting each other. I couldn't get away! Leeds and Millwall were bad. I believe there's good and bad in everyone, but maybe I was naïve to think that I was immune to trouble because I wasn't a brawler. Once at Leeds I went in The Peacock because I fancied a drink and I thought it would be all right – and it wasn't. How naïve was I! I ordered the beers in a South London accent! I have never initiated anything. If I was hit on the back of the head, I'd turn around and hit back. Now I'm older, I just avoid it. I've never gone seeking a fight, I was purely a football fan following my team. All my friends were the same. But we wouldn't leave a mate – if a mate was getting it, we'd go in and help.

When we were growing up – this is what we did and what we were taught. We went to church, we went to youth club and we went to the football. They all mingled and mixed together. Whether you believed in God or not, you all went because that's what we did. The Church Lads Brigade played football and all sports – they had a band. If you wanted to play the drums or the bugle, learn an instrument – you could! The community was together and everyone was a football fan. The same group went that went to church, went to football! Around me the majority supported Chelsea, and then Fulham. Back then there were no Man United or Liverpool supporters – all that came in later. In my day, you didn't support a team outside of where you lived – you went to the same schools, it was a community.

I played football for my school teams. I went to St Johns C of E Primary School in Dawes Road. It was a tiny little school with two hundred kids in seven classes. My Secondary school was Henry Compton in Kingwood Road, off the Fulham Palace Road. I played goalkeeper in Primary and had a few games on the wing. I was a striker in Secondary, but I didn't play much. There were 2000 boys in the school so to get in the first eleven was an achievement! I did make the squad a few times, and I played for the House Team. There were four Houses, I was in Burne Jones. The other houses were Coleridge, Sullivan and Cairns. You'd play against each other and get house points. I loved football.

## CAREFREE! CHELSEA CHANTS AND TERRACE CULTURE

So, you had the Church Lads Brigade and other mates that were in the Scouts, and we'd all go to St Johns Walham Green Youth Club. We'd always kick a ball around, especially on a Sunday after church. We started our own team and joined the Fulham Sportsman League. We had to pay for the pitch and the referee. We didn't know what to call our team, so went walked down the North End Road and looked at all the shop names – there was Woolworths and all that – in the end we settled on calling our team Gala United after Gala Hairdressers! We didn't have a manager until the Dad of a friend came and took charge of us. We'd train on a Wednesday night."

**Mark:** December 1966 saw the conviction of Harry Roberts and two other men for the murder in Shepherds Bush, London, of three police officers in what was known as the Massacre of Braybrook Street. All three were sentenced to life imprisonment with the judge recommending that they each served at least thirty years.

The widespread public sympathy for the families and colleagues of the murder victims was not wholly shared on London's football terraces where police were starting to be seen in increasing numbers as the 'ends' became more lawless and hostile to supporters of other clubs and the authorities.

At the first sign of trouble, a thin blue line of police officers would appear accompanied by supporters humming fabled comedy film duo Laurel and Hardy's theme tune *The Dance of the Cuckoos*. Police making moves to eject or arrest perceived miscreants were taunted with a spiteful and antagonistic version of the nursery rhyme *London Bridge is Falling Down*.

*Harry Roberts is our friend, is our friend, is our friend. Harry Roberts is our friend. He kills coppers.*
*Let him out to kill some more, kill some more, kill some more. Let him out to kill some more. Harry Roberts.*

Roberts cultural impact clearly did him no favours. He was eventually released from prison in November 2014 having spent forty-eight years behind bars.

When sung at Chelsea, away supporters joining in with the *Harry Roberts* chant would occasionally continue the melody but change the words to mock the home fans.

*Stamford Bridge is falling down, falling down, falling down.*
*Stamford Bridge is falling down. Poor old Chelsea.*

# THE '*AND LEICESTER*' MYSTERY

**Mark:** Along with *Carefree!* the chant *We all* (some sing *will* instead of *all*) *follow the Chelsea, over land and sea and Leicester!* set to fabled British composer Edward Elgar's *Pomp and Circumstance March No. 1* melody is still sung at every Blues game and, like *Carefree!* and *Zigger Zagger*, urban myths abound regarding its origin and the reference to Leicester in particular.

At the turn of the 20th Century, King Edward VII advised Elgar that *Pomp and Circumstance March No. 1* would make a great song, and so the composer transposed the melody into a work entitled *Coronation Ode* to which poet A.C. Benson added words that included the refrain *Land of Hope and Glory, Mother of the free. How shall we extoll thee, who are born of thee?*

First performed by Clara Butt in June 1902, *Land of Hope and Glory* would go on to become an anthem of stirring patriotic significance.

Sixty-plus-years after it was first aired, *Land of Hope and Glory* was reworked by the bards of the terraces, who despite the burgeoning hostilities between all clubs, were unified by their apparent hatred of one team... Nottingham Forest.

Every club had their own version, Blues supporters started out with *We hate Nottingham Forest, we hate Arsenal too. We hate West Ham United, but Chelsea we love you.* There would be notable variations. The addition of *they're sh\*t* after *we hate Arsenal too* proved particularly popular.

The origins of *We hate Nottingham Forest* date back much further than the late '70s when Forest, managed by the late great Brian Clough, enjoyed a brief period of phenomenal success. Having been promoted to the top-flight in 1977 along with Chelsea and champions Wolverhampton Wanderers, the following season Forest won the First Division title and beat Liverpool in the League Cup Final. Clough's side then inflicted more misery on the Anfield club, knocking the reigning European Cup holders out of the competition on their way to winning the trophy in 1979.

Liverpool fans had every reason to hate Clough's team, and sang the *We hate Nottingham Forest* chant with gusto, but they were not the first bunch of supporters to do so, nor were Chelsea's fans... or indeed any of the clubs whose followers would typically be construed as the usual suspects in such matters.

## CAREFREE! CHELSEA CHANTS AND TERRACE CULTURE

As 'Little' Jack Horner recalled, the honour for this lyrical peach was down to troubled followers of Blackpool. The 1966/67 season saw The Seasiders finish bottom of the English top-flight. Manchester United won the title ahead of runners up Nottingham Forest and third place Tottenham Hotspur.

Over the space of a fraught month, October 1966, basement side Blackpool played all three teams. It wasn't pretty on or off the pitch, and following a 2-0 loss to Forest at the City Ground, a chant was spawned by their angry fans. *We hate Nottingham Forest, we hate Tottenham too. We hate Man United, but Blackpool we love you.*

Unlike the names of other teams, Nottingham Forest fitted perfectly with the melody, and as other sides including Chelsea faced Blackpool their supporters picked up on the chant and adapted it to suit their own rivalries.

Although Chelsea fans opted to 'hate' Arsenal instead of Tottenham (the FA Cup final loss to Spurs would come at the end of the season), and West Ham United instead of Man U, they might also have considered Blackpool for inclusion.

The Blues 2-1 defeat to Spurs at Wembley (20 May 1967, Bobby Tambling) is viewed by many as the catalyst that sparked the long-standing animosity towards the north London club. It's a widely held belief that the result might have gone in Chelsea's favour had Peter Osgood been fit to play in the game but he was still recovering from the previously described leg break injury sustained at Blackpool earlier in the season.

The must-read book, *Chelsea FC The Official Autobiography*, written by Blues historian Rick Glanvill, makes reference to the addition of *and Leicester* to the *We hate Nottingham Forest* chant via information provided by Garrison who is noted as saying it had its roots in hostilities between fans of Chelsea and Leicester City which originated as a consequence of the clubs meeting in the 1965 League Cup Final.

Separately from Rick's book, Garrison detailed for *Carefree!* his first experience of seeing 'trouble' at a game.

It was 4 September 1963, and a crowd of 32,776 gathered at Stamford Bridge for a Wednesday evening fixture with Burnley. Chelsea won 2-0 thanks to a Terry Venables penalty and a last minute goal from Frank Blunstone. Memories of the game are a blur for Garrison, but he remembers it being the first time he'd seen a serious fight on the terraces.

**Garrison:** "We were still standing on the half way line back then on the old west terrace. There was a great big mob of Burnley supporters stood next to us. They were all proper blokes and we were just teenagers and kids. They started taking the piss out of the Chelsea players and one of our lot had enough and clocked one of them and we all piled in. We got a right kicking to be fair as it was men against boys really.

A few days later (7 September) we played Liverpool (1-3 Jimmy Mulholland) at home. We all had scooters and before the game we parked them up in a line outside the Rising Sun (currently known as the Butchers Hook situated on Fulham Road at the junction with Holmead Road) opposite Stamford Bridge and went in the pub for a drink. We came out to go to the match and the first thing we see is all our scooters falling over one by one like dominoes. There were some Liverpool supporters stood across the road and we figured it was them... so we went over and hammered them. It developed from there. The fashion thing as I mentioned led to piss-taking and more and more fights. At away games this led to the notion of taking ends, although obviously back then it was very loose with nothing organised as such especially as all the different groups of Chelsea supporters were doing their own thing."

**Mark:** According to Garrison, the seeds of supporter coordination, particularly at away games, were sown eighteen months later... the League Cup Final with Leicester City.

Chelsea won the first leg at Stamford Bridge (15 March 1965) 3-2 courtesy of goals from Bobby Tambling, Terry Venables and Eddie McCreadie. The second leg at Filbert Street (5 April) ended 0-0 meaning it was Chelsea skipper Venables who lifted the trophy. Garrison had travelled to Leicester to cheer on the Blues but ran into problems outside the ground.

**Garrison:** "There was an ambush after the game followed by a battle in the park by Filbert Street. It was here I met the Scotsman who would become a lifelong friend and partner in the skirmishes we got involved in at football. After Leicester, it was noticeable that people came to the front to lead The Shed. People like Danny 'Eccles' Harkins and later Babs."

**Mark:** Garrison and his associates subsequently used every opportunity they could find to have a go at Leicester including somewhat bizarrely a reserve (Football Combination) game. Rick Glanvill's *Chelsea Autobiography* book refers to a Combination match between the Foxes and the Blues played on a Friday night at Filbert Street in the mid '60s, and while there is no record of such a game being played on a Friday, Garrison's hazy recollection had already been backed up in fine detail by Jack Horner who had previously recalled to me the exact circumstances and the precise date.

On 16 March 1968, Chelsea played Leicester in a First Division game at Stamford Bridge. As on a number of previous occasions, a group of Foxes fans had arrived early and made themselves at 'home' on The Shed. Jack remembered seeing Eccles, Garrison, the Scotsman and other well-known faces of the day 'dealing' with the situation shortly before kick-off.

Chelsea won the match 4-1 thanks to an early Tommy Baldwin header and a Peter Osgood penalty which bisected a brace from Bobby Tambling. It was a good performance, but the talk in the pubs after the game was about the liberties taken by Leicester fans who would be bragging about having 'taken' The Shed.

They say that familiarity breeds contempt, and to add further insults to this 'injury', earlier in the season, Chelsea and Leicester had played each other over two legs in the Football Combination Cup. The first leg at Stamford Bridge (21 October 1967) ended in a 2-2 draw with George Luke and Joe Fascione scoring for Chelsea. The second leg at Filbert Street (28 October) saw Luke score again... but the game ended in a disastrous, fan-anger-inducing 10-1 defeat for the Blues.

Enough was enough. It was time for retribution. Jack Horner heard about a hastily convened plan that would reaffirm Chelsea's hardening reputation on the terraces. It's an astonishing tale and one that was taken with a large pinch of salt for many years until things became a lot clearer.

On 18 March 1968, two days after Chelsea's first team beat Leicester at Stamford Bridge, their reserves travelled to Filbert Street for a rearranged Football Combination game. It takes a unique type of motivation to book an afternoon off work to go and make a point, especially at a reserve game, but that's what Garrison and his associates did... and, having done so, they had a sing-song. *We hate Nottingham Forest, we hate Arsenal too* ... at which point someone shouted *and Leicester.* For the record, the match itself ended in a 1-1 (Roy Summers) draw.

*Editor's note: Crowd disturbances at Chelsea reserve games were nothing new. The programme for a home match with Southampton (2 September 1967, Chelsea 2 Southampton 6, Peter Osgood x2) makes reference to a 'hooligan element' fighting in the stand at a pre-season reserve friendly at Tooting!*

Now onto 20 March 1968 and the games were coming thick and fast for Chelsea, whose first team were back in action at Stamford Bridge forty-eight hours later. Leeds United were the visitors (0-0) and with stories circulating of what had occurred at Filbert Street a couple of days previously, when the *We hate Nottingham Forest* chant started... *and Leicester* was gleefully added once again.

Forest's fortunes would fade in 1972 with relegation from the top-flight, and *We hate Nottingham Forest* was benched for a while by Blues supporters in favour of another *Land of Hope and Glory* inspired chant.

*We all follow the Chelsea over land and sea.*
*We all follow the Chelsea, onto victory... altogether now!*

Having long since been put in their place, Leicester were no longer a part of any Chelsea variation of the *Land of Hope and Glory* chant... but that would amusingly change several years later when relegation for the Blues would bring Nottingham Forest back on the radar.

Onto 17 January 1976, and a coachload of Chelsea supporters, among them Jack Horner, travelling to a Second Division game away at Forest (1-3 Bill Garner, Ray Wilkins, Ian Hutchinson) kept themselves entertained throughout the journey singing a repertoire of chants which included the relevant once more *We hate Nottingham Forest*.

It was the first trip to the City Ground for four years, and as the coach sped up the M1 through the Midlands towards Nottingham with the fans in good voice, one of their number looked out of the window and saw a road sign which read *The North and Leicester*. The sign jogged his memory... *and Leicester* was back in the chant.

Yet again, contrasting fortunes would soon keep Nottingham Forest and Chelsea apart. Although both clubs were promoted in 1977, while Forest went on to domestic and European glory, Chelsea soon fell through the trap door and would spend five seasons in the second tier of English football... where they would eventually lock horns again with Leicester City.

Coaches, road signs, and following *the Chelsea over land and sea... and Leicester* became a staple part of the lives of the sizeable contingent of fans who followed the team to away games. When the Blues returned to the top-flight in 1984, the chant gained a new audience including Arsenal supporters who were somewhat overawed by the sheer numbers of Chelsea followers at Highbury for that fabled first game of the season... the match Kerry Dixon refers to at the start of this book.

Having already purloined *Carefree!* for their own purposes, it came as little surprise when Gunners fans added *and Leicester* to following *Arsenal over land and sea*. Given the history of *and Leicester* which is clearly and ridiculously of no relevance whatsoever to Arsenal, when the Gunners crowd are heard singing it... there are plenty of older Chelsea fans who smile, wink or nod at each other and proffer a masturbation-orientated hand signal or three at their rivals.

Had he been alive Elgar, who passed away in 1934, long before *Land of Hope and Glory* was rewritten for football purposes, would have been hugely impressed by the song's reconstruction by supporters' as he was a massive fan of the game.

An avid follower of Wolverhampton Wanderers, it's a fascinating fact that Elgar was so inspired by Wolves striker Billy Malpass that in 1898 he penned a musical ditty in his honour entitled *He Banged The Leather For Goal* which is recognised by keen students of the genre as being the first-ever football chant!

# THE LIQUIDATOR

**Mark:** November 1969 Jamaican record producer Harry Zephaniah Johnson's session band Harry J. All Stars reached No. 9 in the UK singles chart with the reggae instrumental track *The Liquidator*.

Garrison remembered a white label recording of the track having been played for some time months previously in the Rising Sun. Popular in the clubs, and played pre-match along with other hits of the day at Stamford Bridge, *The Liquidator* struck a chord in particular with Chelsea's stylish skinhead followers who skanked on The Shed terrace to its rocksteady beat while humming along to Winston Wright's infernally catchy Hammond organ melody.

Wright's swirling play and the structure of the tune leant itself perfectly to adding clap, clap, clap, clap, *Chelsea!* The result was so sublime it sounded like it was meant to be part of the track, and before long *The Liquidator* was absorbed deep into the consciousness of Blues supporters where it has remained ever since.

Forever associated with the sight of Chelsea's players running out onto the pitch Stamford Bridge, several other clubs, most notably Black Country rivals West Bromwich Albion and Wolverhampton Wanderers, also used the track in the same way which led to a debate about who originated the trend.

Garrison recalled Chelsea playing Wolves (13 September 2-2 John Dempsey, Peter Osgood) and West Brom (18 October 2-0 Peter Osgood, Charlie Cooke) at Stamford Bridge in the autumn of 1969, and it's his belief that their travelling fans… to say nothing of players and managers, saw the reaction that *Liquidator* got from the home crowd and decided to try it for themselves.

The sleeve notes for the album *Liquidator - The Best of the Harry J All Stars* settled the argument once and for all.

*"Way back in 1969, supporters of the Chelsea football team revered players such as Bonetti, Osgood and Hollins. The boys performed under the watchful eye of manager Dave Sexton to the tune of Harry J All Stars chartbuster,* The Liquidator. *Whether the tune helped the squad in their successful 1970 FA Cup campaign and subsequent Cup Winners Cup victory we shall never know. One thing is certain – the theme to those victories was undoubtedly* The Liquidator, *with its Hammond organ crescendos that*

## CAREFREE! CHELSEA CHANTS AND TERRACE CULTURE

*lead to the chant of CHEL-SEA!"*

It's worth noting that at the time *The Liquidator* gained popularity pre-match at the Bridge it was tradition to chant or sing songs related to each player directly before kick-off. Tim Rolls directed me to *YouTube* and some priceless *Match of the Day* footage dating back to 15 March 1969 (Chelsea 3 Manchester United 2, David Webb, Ian Hutchinson, Bobby Tambling), where *Born Is The King* and chants for Webb and Tambling can clearly be heard as the teams line up.

I certainly recall this still being popular through to the 1980s, with John Neal's team in particular benefitting from this type of support. One-by-one his players would hear their name sung, principally by The Shed, and individually they would immediately acknowledge the crowd with that twee little handclap above the head thing that footballers do. This in turn would draw applause from The Shed who would then move on to the next player.

As Tim rightly advises, these days this custom has ebbed away with only two or three players getting their pre-match salutation. It's a pity because it has to be a confidence booster, and in the old days it certainly increased the bond between the crowd and the player. It's possible things fizzled out in the hub-bub that was created by the American-style announcement pre-match of each player by Neil *'two goal Branislav Ivanović'* Barnett.

Barnett comes in for a lot of criticism at times when he is going through his MC routine on the pitch, but to be honest that's like pulling wings off a butterfly. The fella has dedicated his life to championing our Club, is proper Chels, and as such deserves respect… and besides, his occasional put downs of rival clubs never fail to amuse… particularly when their fans corralled in the away section of The Shed give him stick back.

# BOOTBOY ANTHEMS

**Mark:** Opposition fans arriving early and entering The Shed while its regular occupants were still in the pub became a curious force of habit in the late '60s. Leicester 'taking' The Shed when there was nobody else in it in 1968 was a prime example. Typically, as the Chelsea contingent arrived in numbers, the away fans would either melt away or be pincered out by a combination of vigorous policing (segregation hadn't been conceived by the Constabularies at this time) and kicks and punches from Shedites keen to reclaim their territory.

The example that others tried to follow had been set by travelling Manchester United fans in the pre-Cockney Reds era. 5 November 1966, United followers used sheer numerical superiority to pack out the covered part of The Shed and kept themselves entertained by tying blue and white scarves bullied from Chelsea kids to stanchions and setting them alight. It didn't get much better on the pitch as the Red Devils, who would win the First Division title that year, beat the Blues 3-1 (John Hollins).

The attendance that day was 55,958, and the action of United's fans in The Shed rankled with Garrison and his friends in particular… but beyond standing their ground at home and looking for revenge at away games they had no alternative plan as such with which they could make a statement.

Football-related vandalism was also on the rise and several months later Chelsea used the matchday programme v Manchester City (11 February 1967) to issue a warning statement following criminal damage to three trains carrying Blues followers to Huddersfield for 3rd Round FA Cup tie (28 January 1967, 1-2, Peter Houseman, Bobby Tambling).

*"British Railways Eastern Region have listed a total of 235 items affected… they include broken windows, fire extinguishers stolen or discharged, lamps and lampshades missing or broken, seats slashed, compartment ashtrays stolen, toilet fittings missing or broken, and blinds torn off."*

The statement concludes:

*"It all adds up to a picture of the growing hooligan menace at its worst, and we deeply regret that louts linking themselves with Chelsea should have misconducted themselves in this way. Once again the serious misconduct of a comparative few smears the good name of the many. To the hooligans we say: Stay away from football until you have learned to behave. At the same time, we ask true supporters to do all they can to ensure that the*

# CAREFREE! CHELSEA CHANTS AND TERRACE CULTURE

*good name of Chelsea is not further degraded by the actions of irresponsible youths."*

There is no evidence to suggest this statement, and the many that would follow in subsequent years had any impact whatsoever as football-related lawlessness, anarchy, chaos and mayhem proliferated for decades irrespective of various new legislations and attendant penalties imposed on convicted miscreants.

The next season, 2 September 1967, there was serious disorder at Stamford Bridge when Southampton tried their luck in The Shed and gave as good as they got. Hard to conceive in the later, glamourised era of football hooliganism. To make matters worse, despite a brace from Peter Osgood, the Saints trounced Chelsea 6-2. Visiting fans who had travelled up from the south coast by coach had a well ventilated journey home as bricking windows had become a popular sideshow to the main event at football grounds everywhere.

Ironically, the matchday programme for the Southampton game contained the following statement entitled Notes From The Supporters' Club.

*"It has been brought to the attention of the Supporters' Club Committee that some travellers (as distinct from supporters) who went to West Bromwich on the opening day of the season carried sticks, poles and walking sticks. Hob-nailed boots were also in evidence, and it would appear that this is the modern 'combat uniform' adopted by some when going to football matches."*

The statement concludes:

*We will not tolerate and form of hooliganism, and anyone seen to cause trouble, regardless of its nature, will be banned from all future travel.*

The 14 April 1969 was a pivotal date for Garrison. Chelsea played Arsenal in a Monday evening First Division fixture at Stamford Bridge.

On the pitch, the Blues had the upper hand winning the game 2-1. Long throw specialist Ian Hutchinson had both hands in both Blues goals. First teeing up David Webb who gave Chelsea the lead in the 33rd minute with an overhead kick and then finding Webb again with a throw in the second half. The defender crashed a shot against the bar but Tommy Baldwin was on hand to poke the rebound home. On the terraces, it was a different story, one which Garrison remembers vividly:

**Garrison:** "Arsenal supporters had half The Shed and there was a gap in the middle of the terrace and then there was the Chelsea. Eccles had the Stockwell and Southfields mobs with him and I was with the North End Road, Kilburn and Pimlico boys. When the fighting started we all battled, but others ran. It was that organisation thing again… it was better away from home.

That night, one of my mates Lenny pointed at the North Stand and said, "I've had enough of this, I'm going down the other end". He didn't give a f*ck that the away fans were down there. Me, the Scotsman and another mate called Jim said we'd go with him… and that was the beginning of the North Stand firm."

*Editor's note: Recommended reading:* We're the North Stand, *Garrison's best-selling fact/fiction novel which provides granular detail of how the North Stand firm began.*

\*\*\*\*\*

**Mark:** In parallel with the hardening organisation of football terrace mobs and the violence and vandalism associated with them, fashion was evolving. By 1967, Swinging sixties London had seen some Mods begin to embrace psychedelic rock and the hippie subculture that went with it. Their strutting peacock look gave way to laid back denim and tie-dye… but this look and attitude wasn't for everyone.

On south London's estates in particular, street-orientated Mods, often referred to as hard mods, were at odds with the economics and perceived intellectual pretentions of those involved in the new scene. Melding the traditional elements of mod fashion with the trilby hat and too-short-trousers Rude Boy style of the kids of West Indian immigrants and adding boots and braces for good effect, the hard mods rallied against the hippy ideals of peace and love. Hippies had long hair. The hard mods favoured a shorn look, and in adopting this style became known as skinheads. Skinheads oozed aggression and complemented perfectly the violent way terrace culture was evolving… and the chants heard at football soon mirrored this.

*You'll get a boot wrapped round your head.*
*You'll get a boot wrapped round your head.*

Changing the words to Manfred Mann's 1968 chart-topper *Mighty Quinn,* the sharp-dressed, number two grade, clip-guard-cropped skinheads

## CAREFREE! CHELSEA CHANTS AND TERRACE CULTURE

congregating at Stamford Bridge had a warning statement to make.

*You go in on your feet, you come out on your head.*
*You ain't seen nothing like The Mighty Shed.*

Swathed in button-down, gingham-check shirts from Ben Sherman, Brutus and Jaytex worn with white Sta-Prest trousers or Levi 501s complete with must-have ¼ inch turn-ups, ¾ length sheepskin coats, Crombie-style overcoats or Harrington jackets, Chelsea's 'skins' raised the style bar that had already been set high by their Mod predecessors.

*Mighty Quinn* also beget another tribute to crowd favourite Charlie Cooke which was composed by Champagne Les.

*Come on and see! Come on and look!*
*You've not seen no-one like Charlie Cooke!*
*When Charlie Cooke gets the ball, he makes defenders look so small.*

A TV advert rework of *Teddy Bears Picnic* which eventually evolved into *going down to The Shed* instead of *to the woods*... (and this time with a fictional bear called Jeremy whose smiling face could be found on packets of a kids breakfast cereal called Sugar Puffs)... provided Chelsea's skinheads with a surreal opportunity for opposing fans to listen, look, learn... and of course copy.

*If you go down to the Bridge today, be sure of a big surprise.*
*If you go up to The Shed today, you'll hardly believe your eyes.*
*'Cos Jeremy, the Sugar Puffs Bear, has bought some boots and cropped his hair.*
*And Jeremy is now the King of the skinheads.*

Still sung occasionally by Chelsea's old-school in bars prior to Euro away games, *Jeremy* puzzles the younger crowd who associate Sugar Puffs with the Honey Monster who replaced the bear in the mid '70s. Sugar Puffs themselves were later rebranded Honey Monster Puffs in a bid to address concerns about the amount of sugar in the cereal thereby making the *Jeremy* reference in the chant all the more obscure to novice ears hearing the chant today.

As the skinheads held sway, the bootboy chants started coming thick and fast with the pop charts again providing plenty of inspiration.

April 1969 saw the release of *Bad Moon Rising* by Creedence Clearwater Revival and The Shed wasted no time in rewriting the chorus to *Don't go out tonight, there's sure to be a fight, Chelsea boys are back in town.*

Mick Greenaway, resplendent in a yellow Harrington jacket (the suit would come later) braying *Zigger Zagger*, was the uniting target for Chelsea supporters particularly at away games and they would then follow cues to sing the songs that reflected the changing order of the day. Greenaway had also become a target for opposing mobs who would chant *Greenaway where are you?* though it is both significant and vitally important to understand that Mick was a cheerleader-come-figurehead for The Shed and not a fighter.

March 1970 – tough guy American actor Lee Marvin, who had a singing voice that sounded like gravel and concrete turning in a cement mixer, had a surprise No. 1 hit in the UK with *Wand'rin Star*. Taken from the soundtrack to the film *Paint Your Wagon* which surprisingly flopped at the box office, *Wand'rin Star* proved so popular it managed to keep the classic Beatles track *Let It Be* at No. 2.

The Shed's version of *Wand'rin Star* advised fans of rival clubs that they would regularly find themselves chased (and worse) across the concrete terraces by lairy-socked feet shod in highly polished Dr Martens boots or oxblood and black brogues if they dared try and 'take' their domain.

*I was born under a Chelsea Shed.*
*I was born under a Chelsea Shed.*
*Knives are made for stabbing, guns are made to shoot, if you come under the Chelsea Shed, we'll all stick in the boot.*
*I was born under the Chelsea Shed.*

Beaten by fragrant Irish chanteuse Dana's *All Kinds of Everything*, demure Welsh folk singer Mary Hopkin had the disappointment of coming second in the 1970 Eurovision song contest with *Knock Knock Who's There?* To add to Hopkin's misery, her 1968 UK chart-topper *Those Were the Days* had recently been given an altogether more sinister makeover by Chelsea's lyrical bootboys.

*Those were the days my friend, we took the Stretford End, we took The Kop, we took the f\*cking lot.*
*We'd fight and never lose, then we'd sing Up the Blues, those were the days, oh yes those were the days.*

Quirkily, *Those Were the Days* had been one of four records released simultaneously on 26 August 1968 to launch the Apple record label, the other three were *Thingumybob* by the Black Dyke Mills Band, *Sour Milk Tea*

## CAREFREE! CHELSEA CHANTS AND TERRACE CULTURE

by Jackie Lomax and *Hey Jude* by the Beatles.

At over seven minutes in length (7:11), at the time of its initial release, *Hey Jude* became the longest single ever to top the charts (record currently held by Oasis, *All Around the World* 9:38). It's chorus provided the basis for the epic *La, la la, la la la la, la la la la, Chelsea* chant which still remains capable of making the hairs on the back of true Blue necks stand on end when supporters unify to belt it out.

*Those Were the Days* which replaced *Hey Jude* as the UK No. 1 single in October 1968 would also provide the melody to another bootboy classic that provided a stark warning to opposing fans. *We'll see you all outside, we'll see you all outside. We'll see you all, we'll see you all outside.*

Terser chants such as *Time for You to Run* and *A, G... A, G, R... A, G, R, O, AGRO, (Hold Tight* version) left little to the imagination.

For younger kids back then, the first few times they heard *You're gonna get your f\*cking head kicked in* there was no doubting the intent and purpose of the chant. It made them fearful of the consequences of being in the wrong place at the wrong time. Worse still then for the younger away supporters corralled on the old North Stand terrace (Matthew Harding Stand) hearing those songs and spending the game contemplating their fate.

World War I music hall song *It's a long way to Tipperary* penned by Jack Judge in 1912 provided the inspiration for *It's a long way to Fulham Broadway, it's a long way to run. It's a long way to Fulham Broadway and We'll be there before you.*

*It's a long way to Fulham Broadway* was a lyrical aperitif for away fans. The main course that followed the final whistle at Stamford Bridge often involved running the gauntlet to the station with scarves hidden accompanied by chants of *You'll never reach the station.*

*You're going home in a f\*cking ambulance* shredded nerves, as did the altogether more trouser-browning *We don't carry shotguns, we don't carry lead. We only carry hatchets to bury in your head. We don't carry razors, we don't carry tools, we only wear our bovver boots to kick you in the balls.*

Always in the thick of the action on the North Stand was Alan Garrison Tomkins. The name Garrison wasn't bestowed on Alan by his parents, it's a nickname... a reference to *Garrison's Gorillas* a TV series set in World War II about a fictional character called Craig Garrison (portrayed by Ron

Harper) who was a First Lieutenant in the US Army.

In the show, First Lt. Garrison led a group of commandos on near-suicidal military missions against the Germans, scenarios that drew parallels with improbable skirmishes that the North Stand firm were increasingly getting involved in.

**Garrison:** "We were only interested in fighting like-minded people. We'd go in the café underneath the North Stand and stand by the window and look for the other team's firm and then just before the start of the game we'd go steaming into them.

It was just the four of us at the start. Me, the Scotsman, Lenny and Jim… two at the front, two at the back! Other Chelsea could join us, and we organised them the same way in groups of four… but it was on the understanding that no matter what happened they didn't run.

More often than not, we got a result… but sometimes we got a kicking as well. Before the North Stand, we were just making up the numbers, but now we did our own thing. Danny Harkins couldn't control us, but I think he appreciated what we did.

At an away game, if The Shed went in to try and take an end, we'd hold back and see if they could get a result. If they couldn't then we'd come in like the 7th Cavalry and turn the day. There was a mutual respect. Afterwards there'd always be running street battles down some High Street or another. Harkins would play games. If The Shed were getting run he'd back up for a bit and then turn and shout "charge" and run back at the opposition. The North Stand was always there to help out.

As Chelsea's North Stand regularly asserted their authority and brought the terrace under heavy manners, The Shed would bark out words of encouragement. *North Stand, North Stand, do your job. North Stand do your job* was first heard at Stamford Bridge during a game with Liverpool (12 April 1971) which the Blues won 1-0 thanks to a Derek Smethurst goal.

Just before kick-off we were in the café as usual and watching the Scousers. One of them had this great big machete! The police by now were wising up about what was going on and told us to stay in the café and then nicked the bloke with the machete. As they led him away, we piled out of the café and steamed into Liverpool's firm. It must have looked impressive from The Shed, because that's when they first sang *North Stand, do your job*. I looked at the Scotsman and said we've arrived!"

## CAREFREE! CHELSEA CHANTS AND TERRACE CULTURE

**Mark:** The Shed and The North Stand often traded *We're The Shed End* and *We're The North Stand* chants, but *North Stand, do your job* added a new dimension which merited a creative reply. Garrison remembers the Scotsman taking the popular chants *We are Blue, we are white, we are f\*cking dynamite* and *Chelsea here, Chelsea there, Chelsea every f\*cking where* and changing the words.

Using the same melody borrowed from Edmund L. Gruber's United States Army 5th Artillery Regimental song *The Caissons Go Rolling Along* (later transformed into a march and subsequently renamed *The Army Goes Rolling Along* when becoming the official song of the U.S. Army), the Scotsman came up with *We are mad in the head, we're the North Stand not The Shed*.

Given the fact that the tune has been used in over forty films and TV series, it's easy to understand how it crossed the Atlantic and was adapted by British football supporters.

A more incendiary version of the chant was sung a few years later following an act of flagrant vandalism on a football special returning from one of those notorious Chelsea away games with Luton Town that Kerry Dixon refers to in the foreword to this book.

It was 11 January 1975, Luton Town 1 Chelsea 1 (Steve Kember). Following a day of unbridled hooliganism in and around Kenilworth Road which led to over one hundred arrests, the leading coach on the Luton to London train service was set on fire and destroyed. The headline-grabbing incident was swiftly sanctified in song. *Chelsea sing, Chelsea fight, Chelsea set the train alight.*

The best version however emanated a decade later following one of the most remarkable games Chelsea have ever played.

On 30 January 1985 – a bitter night when 6,000 Chelsea supporters travelled north to Yorkshire to watch the Blues play Sheffield Wednesday in a Milk Cup Fifth Round replay at Hillsborough. A classic game which if everyone who says they attended actually had, the gate would have been 50,000 not 36,505.

3-0 down by half time, it looked like Chelsea fans were in for a shocking evening. Could popular manager John Neal turn things around? Injured Colin Lee was replaced by Paul Canoville at the break and the winger immediately set about transforming the game in Chelsea's favour. Well almost immediately. Eleven seconds after the restart Canoville pulled a goal back. Kerry Dixon further reduced the arrears in the 64th minute, and when Mickey Thomas scored a fabulous equaliser in the 76th minute, Blues fans sensing a famous victory was now possible bellowed encouragement for the team. *We are the famous, the famous Chelsea* reverberated around the ground.

With just four minutes remaining, Canoville netted a Dixon cross. 3-4 to Chelsea. *Let's go f*cking mental, let's go f*cking mental.* Chelsea supporters were in Blue heaven… and then calamity struck. In the final minute, Blues defender Doug 'the thug' Rougvie, exposed for pace by Mel Sterland, brought the Wednesday man down in the box. Penalty! Sterland took the kick and beat Eddie Niedzwiecki. 4-4. Extra time. 4-4 Full time. Glorious unpredictability and all that!

A week later on 6 February 1985, Chelsea won the second replay 2-1 at Stamford Bridge (David Speedie, Mickey Thomas). The chant of the night bubbling up from The Shed and the West Stand 'benches' where we made our home for the evening commemorated Rougvie's error.

The Shed sang *Benches, benches give us a song. Benches, benches give us a song,* and the benches responded with *3-0 down, 4-3 up, Big Doug Rougvie f*cked it up, la la la la, la la la, la la.*

Genius!

***Editor's note:*** *The Benches were a section of benched concrete 'seating' in front of the old West Stand. At the time of the Wednesday replay it was possible to transfer from The Shed to The Benches for 50p. The area proved popular for thrill-seekers as it was possible to get 'close' to the away supporters in the North Stand.*

*****

Perhaps the strangest ditty to evolve from the period of unbridled hooliganism was a lengthy take on a Manchester United song that celebrated the Red Devils 1968 European Cup win over Benfica. An Irish folk song *The Old Orange Flute*, brought to wider attention by The Dubliners, provided the melody and Chelsea's version, very seldom heard today, went something like this.

*We went down to Wembley one fine day in May, a crowd of supporters so happy and gay.*
*And when it was over and when it was done, Benfica were beaten by four goals to*

*one.*

*The first was scored by wee Georgie Best, the second was scored when Bobby out jumped the rest.*

*The Stretford End chanted but I never did, and the third was scored by young Brian Kidd.*

*The Stretford End cried out, they cried out for more, and Bobby obliged them by making it four.*

*A team to remember, a team to recall, was the great Man United, the best of them all.*

*They came down to Chelsea in '75, they took up The North Stand, The Shed and the side, but Chelsea were many, too many to ruck, and the great Man United got battered to f\*ck.*

*We went to Old Trafford in '78, the whole of Manchester was lying in wait, but Chelsea went mental cos we had our pride, and the whole of Manchester United died.*

*Toora lu, toora lay, and the whole of Manchester United died.*

An epic song if ever there was one, except curiously Chelsea didn't play Man U at all in 1975, nor did they play at Old Trafford in 1978. The logical conclusion to be drawn regarding '75 and '78 is that they were included to complete the rhyme within the verses!

Genius again!

# LEEDS AND LEEDS

**Mark:** Retaining the military theme, Eric Coates' iconic soundtrack to World War II film *The Dam Busters* was set to words that reflected hostile feelings towards another football club, Leeds United.

Unlike Nottingham Forest who were perhaps a victim of circumstance and lyrical suitability rather than genuine hardcore hatred, the developing enmity between Chelsea's London-based mobs and their counterparts from Yorkshire meant that *We all hate, Leeds and Leeds and Leeds, Leeds and Leeds and Leeds and Leeds and Leeds and Leeds and Leeds. We all f\*cking hate Leeds!* resonated far more deeply with those who sang it.

206 miles separate Stamford Bridge from Leeds' Elland Road home, and while the north v south, flat caps from the Dales v flash bast\*rds from the King's Road, ingredient to the rivalry added spice to the Blues v Whites fixture – the full flavour of hostility was infused initially by the players.

During a Second Division fixture (15 September 1962) at Elland Road which the home side won 2-0, Leeds right-half Eric Smith suffered a career-ending double leg fracture when challenging Chelsea midfielder Graham Moore for the ball. The Blues won promotion at the end of that season, the Whites had to wait another year. Both teams, packed with precocious talent, acquitted themselves well in the top-flight and the rivalry developed as 1965 saw Leeds finish runners up to champions Manchester United with Chelsea third.

An FA Cup semi-final meeting at Villa Park (29 April 1967) resulted in a 1-0 victory for the Blues (Tony Hateley), but the game was marred by controversy when referee Ken Burns disallowed a late Peter Lorimer equaliser for the Whites. Burns bizarre judgement that the Chelsea wall had not retreated ten yards when Johnny Giles teed up Lorimer infuriated Don Revie's Leeds team and their fans.

Alan Garrison Tomkins recalled being with The Shed mob and being prevented by police from going in the Leeds end:

**Garrison:** "We went back round there after the match, but they all came out at once and obviously because of what happened in the game they were mad and we got run… but we played them again in a league game at the Bridge a week later (6 May 2-2 Tommy Baldwin, Eddie McCreadie) and got into them."

## CAREFREE! CHELSEA CHANTS AND TERRACE CULTURE

**Mark:** Revie's side got their revenge on the pitch the following season (4 October 1967) thrashing Chelsea 7-0 at Elland Road, but it was the FA Cup once more that would provide Blues supporters with an opportunity to gloat over their northern rivals and those who wanted to fight had a field day.

The physicality of the 1970 Wembley final (11 April) which ended in a 2-2 draw, and the replay at Old Trafford (29 April) famously won 2-1 by Chelsea is the stuff of legend and proved to be the point of no return when it came to the supporters of both clubs.

At Wembley, the players toiled on a shockingly muddy pitch. Leeds had the better of the game and took the lead through Jack Charlton. Peter Houseman equalised for Chelsea before half time, but when Mick Jones put the Yorkshire side 2-1 up with six minutes left it looked like the Blues were headed for another cup final defeat. Garrison remembers the Scotsman saying, "Right lets go up their end and have the bast*rds". As they walked round the stadium, Ian Hutchinson headed in a John Hollins cross to level the match. Extra time, meant extra fighting. There were no more goals however, and the game ended in an unprecedented draw, the first ever in a Wembley final. Both squads somewhat bizarrely embarked on a shared lap of honour and with this the anger on and off the pitch dissipated.

With Wembley deemed unplayable, three weeks later the replay took place at Old Trafford. From the starting whistle, referee Eric Jennings struggled to maintain order as Chelsea skipper Ron Harris kicked flying winger Eddie Gray, Jack Charlton kicked Peter Osgood, Eddie McCreadie Kung-Fu kicked Leeds captain Billy Bremner, Mick Jones bullied Peter Bonetti and Ian Hutchinson boxed with Norman Hunter. Remarkably, Jennings only issued one booking (to Hutchinson) and many years later modern referee David Elleray replayed the game and declared that six red cards and twenty yellows shared between the teams would have been a more accurate reflection of the battle for supremacy on the pitch.

That Chelsea won the game scoring goals from headers says much about the difficulty of playing football. Osgood's horizontal dive to meet Charlie Cooke's floating cross was a rare glimmer of beauty on a night of savagery while David Webb's extra-time winner, initiated by a supremely athletic, long-range Hutchinson throw-in exemplified the need to do something different to secure victory.

*We've won the Cup... we've won the Cup!*
*Ee, aye addio, we've won the Cup!*

Inevitably there was trouble after the game, and Garrison remembers there was also mayhem up at Elland Road the next time Chelsea played Leeds after the cup win.

On 5 September 1970, the Blues lost 1-0, but the visiting North Stand got a "result" despite being pelted with coins and bottles as they ascended the steps of the Gelderd End. "It was hard work," says Garrison. "Leeds had a good firm. A very good firm."

In the midst of such anger there was humour, though Leeds first choice goalkeeper at that time Gary Sprake would have struggled to see the funny side of it. Sprake's fumbling of the ball when Peter Houseman's tame shot brought Chelsea's equaliser at Wembley saw the repetitive chant based on the melody from The Troggs 1967 chart hit *Give It To Me* (All Your Love) being sung every time the two sides met for years after.

*Give us a goal, give us a goal, Gary Sprake, Gary Sprake.*

Sprake had already famously thrown the ball into his own net at Anfield in the first half of a league game against Liverpool in December '67 – an act of kindness that had prompted the PA announcer to play Des O'Connor's chart hit *Careless Hands* during the half-time break.

\*\*\*\*\*

The hostilities with Leeds continued unchecked for years, though as hooliganism became increasingly widespread... when the two sides met 'trouble' was taken for granted.

Leeds fans smashing up the North Stand scoreboard following their side's 5-0 (Mickey Thomas, Kerry Dixon x3, Paul Canoville) defeat at Stamford Bridge (28 April 1984), a result which sealed Chelsea's promotion to Division One didn't do much to foster good relations.

Following the incident, Chelsea chairman Ken Bates set fire to the oil on troubled waters bellowing, *"I shall not rest until Leeds United are kicked out of the Football League. Their fans are the scum of the Earth, absolute animals and a disgrace. I will do everything in my power to make this happen".*

It's strange how life turns out. In January 2005, Bates became the principal owner of financially stricken Leeds United who despite having won the Premier League in 1992 were now a struggling Championship side. Bates subsequently installed former Chelsea skipper Dennis Wise as manager with another ex-Blue Gus Poyet as his assistant... and the 'cockney' nightmare wouldn't end there for Leeds fans as their club entered administration and were relegated to League One.

The waning fortunes of the Yorkshire club has restricted face-to-face opportunities for the old enmity with Chelsea to be rekindled to one meeting in the twelve years that followed leading up to the publication date of this book.

19 December 2012 Capital One League Cup, Fifth Round, Elland Road (1-5, Juan Mata, Branislav Ivanović, Victor Moses, Eden Hazard, Fernando Torres).

Wise and Poyet had long since departed, and Leeds were back in the Championship, but with Bates now owning the club outright... that irritating link with Chelsea remained.

Police were so concerned about the possibility of trouble at the match that they forced Leeds to slash Chelsea's ticket allocation from 5,000 to 3,000. A train chartered by the London club to take Blues supporters from London to Leeds terminated at Wakefield, ten miles from Elland Road... fans were put on coaches, bused to the stadium car park and escorted into the ground. The scenario meant supporters traded chants, not blows... but it wasn't pretty or in good humour.

Borrowing the melody from the Doris Day hit single *Que Sera, Sera (whatever will be, will be)* which had long since been reworked by domestic cup final bound football fans as *Que Sera, Sera (whatever will be, will be) we're going to Wembley*, Leeds supporters sang their ages old favourite *Wash your mouth out son, go get your father's gun, and shoot the Chelsea scum...* which obviously went down well with visiting fans.

The response, although topical, was equally unpleasant. Changing the words of 1927 Bahamas folk song *Sloop John B*, a global chart hit for the Beach Boys in 1966, to *He's one of your own, he's one of your own. Jimmy Savile, he's one of your own*, Blues fans mocked their rivals. At the time of the game, Savile, a native and resident of Leeds who'd died the previous year, had recently been the subject of an ITV documentary which examined claims of serial sexual abuse by the former DJ and TV presenter.

Incidentally, playing for Chelsea against Leeds was the excellent César Azpilicueta. Christened 'Dave' (a nod to TV sitcom *Only Fools and Horses* character Trigger who can't remember Rodney's name and always calls him

Dave) by teammates who apparently struggled pronouncing his surname, it didn't take long for a song to be composed which took note of this curious fact and *Sloop John B* provided the melody for the fabulous chant, *We'll just call you Dave, we'll just call you Dave. Azpilicueta, we'll just call you Dave.*

Back to the game:

Leeds leading at half time through a 37th minute Luciano Becchio goal gave the home crowd hope of a famous victory, but cheers turned to tears in the second half as Chelsea ran in five goals and Blues fans had a field day.

There have been numerous terrace versions of disco classic *Go West*, originally a hit for the Village People in 1979 and subsequently the Pet Shop Boys in 1993. Surprisingly, those regular plagiarists who follow Arsenal deserve some credit for the transition from dance-floor to football stadium. *1-0 to the Arsenal* was first heard at the 'exciting' 1994 European Cup Winners Cup Final when the Gunners beat Parma 1-0… an all too familiar score-line for their games at that time.

The world of course has moved thankfully on from this boring dirge with many different versions bubbling up in the years that followed. The beauty of *Go West* is that it lends itself to instant creativity during a match. A situation presents itself, and moments later it is reflected in song. Two memorable instances as far as Chelsea supporters are concerned happened in the second half against Leeds.

*1-0 and you f\*cked it up* bubbled up from the Blues crowd moments after Ivanović put Chelsea 3-1 up in the 64th minute and grew in volume and intensity when Moses made it 4-1 two minutes later. It's creatively ironic replacement came six minutes from time when Torres, whose Blues career was blighted by an inability to find the net on sufficient occasions to justify the £50 million Chelsea had paid Liverpool for his services, did just that. *5-1 even Torres scored* crowed jubilant Blues fans. You can check out the Gate 17 Chelsea *YouTube* channel for a short film of the evening's musical proceedings.

In a discussion to the pass the time, the inevitable lock-in provided the opportunity to remember several other *Go West*-themed chants including a couple honouring former Chelsea players. *Marcel, Marcel Desailly. Marcel, Marcel Desailly* and the curious *Ooh arrr Jesper Gronkjaer, ooh arrr Jesper Gronkjaer*. Weirdly, during Jesper's time with the Blues, I recall thinking the Ooh arrr bit must have had some sort of country bumpkin connotation.

Foolish with hindsight given he was from Denmark... arrr simply rhymed with jaer.

**Walter:** I was in the West Stand with Big Chris when Chelsea were playing Charlton, (it was probably 21 April 2001, lost 1-0), and Jesper came on as a sub. Chris turned to me and asked what rhymed with Grønkjær – I replied, "I don't know – ooh arr?" He laughed and said, "ooh arrr, Jesper Grønkjær" – we both sang it, miraculously it spread and the West Stand joined in, and the chant was born.

**Mark:** Why Desailly and Grønkjær? Well the post-match chat had moved onto Roman Abramovich buying Chelsea in 2003, and the fact that his decision was based on the Blues qualifying for the Champions League via a 2-1 home victory over Liverpool (11 May) when both players scored.

A year later José Mourinho came to town, told the media he was 'a special one'... and as he set about proving it was soon being saluted with another *Go West* remix, *Stand up for the Special One* which beget yet another in *Stand up for the Champions!* when the title was duly won in his first season as Blues boss.

Perhaps the most inventive use of *Go West* was yet to come, though. 18 March 2014 Chelsea beat Galatasaray 2-0 (Oscar, Branislav Ivanović) in a Champions League game at Stamford Bridge. Visiting fans of the Istanbul club made a decent racket throughout despite the poor showing of their team who featured in their ranks none other than Chelsea legend Didier Drogba. For their troubles, they were treated to the creative genius of *You're shish and you know you are...* a chant which had lovers of Turkish cuisine, and kebabs in particular, chuckling for weeks to come.

*Tore, Tore, Andre Flo* was subsequently thrown into the *Go West* players mix which immediately brought memories flooding back of the towering Norwegian's finest day in a Chelsea shirt.

On 6 December 1997, an early Christmas present for Blues fans came in the form of a 6-1 thrashing of Tottenham Hotspur at White Hart Lane. Flo bagged a hattrick with Chelsea's other goals coming from Roberto Di Matteo, Dan Petrescu and Mark Nicholls.

The victory was commemorated in a chant based on The Sutherland Bros. Band song *Sailing* which Rod Stewart had a No. 1 chart hit with in 1975 and which is still sung today.

*We won 6-1, we won 6-1, we won 6-1 at the Lane.*
*We won 6-1, we won 6-1, we won 6-1 at the Lane.*

Later versions of the chant included optional second and third verses *It's so quiet at the Lane* and *You're all w\*nkers at the Lane.*

Reminiscences could have carried on forever, but Elland Road was getting hypothermic by now, and thankfully Chelsea supporters were finally allowed out of the ground, put on buses back to Wakefield where a train was waiting to return them, tired but happy, back to London.

Despite Bates selling Leeds later that year, the Yorkshire club continues to struggle meaning the chances of another meeting with Chelsea is likely to be restricted to possible future cup meetings. Irrespective of the date or occasion, supporters of both sides will no doubt air hand-me-down chants… and those long-in-the-tooth will remember the old days.

# DARK BACK STREETS

**Mark:** That military tunes and songs were increasingly being used for hostile, football hooligan chants could be just a coincidence, but there is no doubt that their stirring tempos were well suited to terrace skirmishes and the United States Marine Corps became the next battle-hardened source for yet another lyrical testament to the fearsome reputation of the North Stand mob. The opening lines of the *Marines Hymn* refer to the First Barbary War and the Mexican-American War, 19th Century conflicts the US was engaged in.

*From the halls of Montezuma, to the shores of Tripoli.*
*We fight our country's battles, in the air, on land and sea.*
*First to fight for right and freedom, and to keep our honour clean, we are proud to claim the title of United States Marine.*

The song featured in the blockbuster World War ll film *Halls of Montezuma* which although released in 1951 was still being regularly screened on British television in the early '70s. It's a long way from Montezuma to Liverpool, but that didn't deter imaginative Chelsea supporters from creating their own version of the hymn that refers to clashes in the northwest of England.

*In the dark back streets of Liverpool, where the Mile End's never been, lies the chewed-up body of a Scouse git, where the North Stand kicked him in.*
*To hell with Liverpool, to hell with Man. City.*
*We'll fight, fight, fight for Chelsea 'til we win the Football League.*

**Garrison:** "Liverpool was always bad. The police were evil... they hated us as much as their fans did. They'd be waiting for us on horseback at Lime Street Station and whack us with long sticks to break us up. The smaller groups would then get ambushed on the way to the ground."

**Mark:** There is no doubt that the mutual loathing that has long existed between many Chelsea and Liverpool supporters had its roots in regional identity. In 1965, Mick Greenaway had had his friendly experience with the Scousers, but for the younger generation growing up in the next ten years or so that followed the perceptions were becoming divisive.

It was a shame for me really because as a kid born into a non-football household at an age when girls weren't remotely interesting, I was into music more than anything else. To me, the Rolling Stones and The Beatles were the genuine face of the London / Liverpool rivalry thing, but as time went on, like the Mods and Rockers confrontations of the day, it became crystal clear that there was more to it than just your accent and manners which were there to betray you. Londoners and Liverpudlians didn't just come from different cities… they came from different planets in different solar systems in different universes.

*You'll Never Walk Alone* (still sung by ends up and down the land not just The Kop at Anfield as is the case in England now) was transformed into *You'll Never Get A Job… Sign on, sign on, with a pen in your hand, and you'll never get a job, you'll never get a job.* And the stereotyping of Scousers gained impetus.

Popular BBC sitcom *The Liver Birds* first aired in 1969. I was too young initially to appreciate the Scouse wit and undeniable female charms of Polly James and Nerys Hughes, the two female stars of the show, but that changed over the next ten years or so!

The Liver Birds theme tune, written and performed by The Scaffold, was infuriatingly catchy and advised that if you were standing on the corner feeling miserable the Liver Birds would come and grab you and cheer you up. Decent enough, but not half as evocative as the version sung on the terraces by Chelsea supporters when Liverpool were the opposition.

*If you're standing on the corner with a red scarf round your neck,*
*Chelsea boys will come and get you and we'll break your f\*cking neck!*

Envy propagated antipathy. The 1970s marked the time in which Liverpool starting writing the main trophy-winning chapter in their history book and dominating the English and European game. Scouse glory coincided with a sharp decline in Chelsea's fortunes.

For a decade or so from the mid '70s, while titles and cups came to Anfield, Stamford Bridge was mainly hosting Second Division fixtures. What goes around comes around though. Come the 21st Century, the pendulum of success would swing from Merseyside to London as Chelsea set about mastering Liverpool in all competitions with title wins and victories over the Reds in FA and League Cup finals. *Have you ever seen Chelsea win the League?* The Scousers had crowed for years. They could hardly expect any sympathy when callous fate turned against them.

# CAPITAL CAPERS

**Mark:** Closer to home, Chelsea's rivalry with Tottenham Hotspur was often overshadowed by events in and around Stamford Bridge and White Hart Lane when the two clubs played each other.

Blues fans adaptation of Fred Leigh and Charles Collins popular music hall song *My Old Man (said follow the van) ... and don't dilly dally on the way*, written just after World War I had ended, illustrated perfectly the more violent aspects of terrace culture that was evolving.

*My old man said be a Tottenham fan, I said f\*ck off bollocks you're a c\*nt.*
*We'll take the Tottenham in half a minute, we'll take the Park Lane and all who's in it.*
*With hatchets and hammers, carving knives and spanners, we'll teach them Tottenham bast\*rds how to fight.*
*Oh they won't take The Shed when the North Stand's in it, cos Chelsea rule okay.*

Just about every club in British football has their own version of the chant tailored to specific rivalries, with some referring to the use of Stanley knives rather than carving knives. Given its wide usage, ends up and down the country has laid claim to being the first to rework *My Old Man* and, once again, there is a suspect Wikipedia entry this time naming Aston Villa as the originators.

The version belted out by the Holte End at Villa Park makes reference to Spinksy, (Nigel Spinks) Birchy (Paul Birch) and Alan McInally who played their trade for the Midlands club in the '80s. *My Old Man* may not have been initiated by Chelsea fans, but there are plenty who recall singing it in the late '60s and early '70s when Messrs Spinks, Birch and McInally were still in short trousers.

A fabled episode of terrace 'bovver' culture that has all but been buried by the passage of time involved taking seemingly innocuous-looking walking sticks to games.

Alan Garrison Tomkins recalls an FA Cup semi-final at Villa Park with Sheffield Wednesday (23 April 1966) which Chelsea lost 2-0.

**Garrison:** "That season, I'd seen a few people had started taking walking sticks to games for self-defence. They'd paint blue stripes on them. At Villa Park though, I remember Mick Greenaway shouting "walking sticks, where are you?" and 3000 sticks went in the air. It was a magic moment. They were needed too as it kicked off outside and Wednesday's mob had steel combs with sharpened edges.

The next year, we got to the final against Tottenham (20 May 1967, Spurs 2 Chelsea 1, Bobby Tambling) and the walking sticks were out in force. There was fighting all the way around the ground. I think it was the first time there was serious trouble at Wembley.

Later that year (18 November, 2-0), we played a league game at White Hart Lane. Obviously, there was trouble… but the police had finally wised up to the walking sticks which were already banned at Stamford Bridge by now and started nicking people who had them… and then the sticks got banned everywhere, and that was that… it was funny to see though."

**Mark:** The event was significant enough to merit a chant which was creatively set to the melody of the song *Heigh-Ho* which featured in the 1937 Walt Disney film *Snow White and the Seven Dwarfs*.

*Heigh-Ho, Heigh-Ho, it's off to Spurs we go.*
*With a bottle and a brick and a walking stick, Heigh-Ho, Heigh-Ho.*

An alternative version surfaced after the walking sticks were banned which was popular for several seasons.

*Heigh-Ho, Heigh-Ho, it's off to Spurs we go.*
*With a bucket and spade and a hand grenade, Heigh-Ho, Heigh-Ho.*

**Walter:** Decades later, I was travelling by train to an away game at Aston Villa, (27 August 2000, Aston Villa 1 Chelsea 1, Marcel Desailly), with Big Chris, Smiffy, Cazbar Caz and his Dad Phil and a new version conceived to welcome summer signing Eidur Gudjohnsen to the club was born.

*Ei-durrrr! Ei-durrrr! Eidur, Eidur, Eidur, Eidur, Eidur.*
*Gudjohnsen, Gudjohnsen…*
*Eidur, Eidur, Eidur, Eidur.*

It successfully went from the train to the pub (The Witton Arms) but it never went to the ground, so that was that. Out of all the chants over the years that have never made the jump, this is the one that really grates with me because it didn't take off.

## CAREFREE! CHELSEA CHANTS AND TERRACE CULTURE

**Mark:** *Montego Bay* was a chart hit for Bobby Bloom in September 1970 and a month later for British reggae outfit Freddie Notes and The Rudies. The song, co-written by American's Bloom and Jeff Barry, is abstractly about the city in Jamaica which neither man had any grand affinity with and its lyrics bore no resemblance to the whimsical anti-Spurs anthem that The Shed concocted.

*500 Tottenham lying dead, just cos they tried to take the Chelsea Shed.*
*Come in the morning, or come at night, don't come at all if you cannot fight. Sing out!*
*Oh, oh oh oh oh oh oh, the Chelsea Shed.*
*Oh, oh oh oh oh oh oh, the Chelsea Shed.*

Chuck Berry's 1972 hit *My Ding-A-Ling* provided the inspiration for the psychopathically entertaining chant:

*When I was a little bitty boy, my Grandfather bought me a cute little toy.*
*A Tottenham fan on a piece of string, he said I should kick his f*cking head in.*

Less violent in emphasis but equally entertaining was another dig at Spurs, a version of *The Prisoner's Song* by Vernon Dalhart which was topped the US singles charts in 1925! Again, just about every football club had their own localized chant… Chelsea's went like this.

*If I had the wings of a sparrow, if I had the arse of a crow.*
*I'd fly over Tottenham tomorrow, and sh*t on those bast*rds below.*
*Sh*t on, sh*t on, sh*t on those bast*rds below, below.*
*Sh*t on, sh*t on, sh*t on those bast*rds below.*

The only chant with a violent anti-Spurs edge to it which was a product of the bygone bootboy era and is still sung today borrows the melody from *Marching Through Georgia* a marching song written in 1865 by Henry Clay Work at the end of the American Civil War! Again, every club has their own version directed at specific rivals… this is Chelsea's.

*Hello hello we are the Chelsea boys.*
*Hello hello we are the Chelsea boys, and if you are a Tottenham fan surrender or you'll die, we all follow the Chelsea.*

*****

West Ham United's signature chant *I'm Forever Blowing Bubbles* has been sung by Hammers' fans since the late 1920s when manager at the time

Charlie Paynter introduced it to the club. Chelsea's aggro-laden version reflected back at Irons' followers also embraced Arsenal and Tottenham in the chorus and the chant is yet another which supporters of many clubs have tailored to their own requirements.

*I'm forever throwing bottles, pretty bottles in the air.*
*They fly so high, they reach the sky and like West Ham they fade and die.*
*Tottenham always running, Arsenal running too.*
*We're the Chelsea bootboys and we're running after you.*

*Chim Chim Cher-ee* found fame originally when sung by Dick Van Dyke and Julie Andrews in the 1964 musical motion picture *Mary Poppins*, beget a terrace format directed at West Ham fans whom many will recall being referred to as 'chimney sweeps' which is still sung today.

*Chim Chim-in-ey Chim Chim-in-ney Chim Chim Cheroo, we hate those bast\*rds in claret and blue.*

West Ham's North Bank in the late '60s was governed by gangs from Barking, Whitechapel and Ilford. Like The Shed, the North Bank only really got organized after hordes from Manchester United muscled in (6 May 1967, West Ham 1 Manchester United 6).

A *Time Out* article written by Chris Lightbown in 1972 entitled *Football Gangs* refers to the Barking and Whitechapel mobs in particular making a concerted effort after the United incident to 'keep the North Bank free'. Lightbown also mentions a 'shock taking by Chelsea' (23 March 1968 0-1 Peter Osgood).

**Garrison:** "After that game, West Ham started to have the hoodoo over us but it didn't stop us trying. 22 August 1970 (2-2 Keith Weller), we went in the North Bank and we got a result mainly because the Mile End were down the other end having a go at the Chelsea. We went back a year later (11 September 1971 2-1 John Hollins) and they were waiting for us. There was only about fifty of us and we got a right hiding. We went back in '72 (27 January 1973 3-1 Bill Garner) and got another hiding. I think they respected us though because we went in."

**Mark:** A few years later (October 1979), a kids group from Manchester called The Ramblers appeared on *Top Of The Pops* and sang their novelty chart hit *I'm Only A Poor Little Sparrow*. Football ends got hold of it and one of the first 'new' versions to be heard on the terraces was a taunt directed at West Ham.

## CAREFREE! CHELSEA CHANTS AND TERRACE CULTURE

*He's only a poor little Hammer, his face is all tattered and torn.*
*He made me feel sick, so I hit him with a brick, and now he don't sing any more.*

Further manipulations followed aimed at Arsenal and Tottenham supporters.

*****

In the modern era of Premier League London derbies, Chelsea v Arsenal comes some way down the feistiness list, certainly below playing Spurs and West Ham. It wasn't always that way though, and the Gunners success on the pitch in winning the Inter Cities Fairs Cup in 1970 and the League and FA Cup Double in 1971 fuelled serious rivalry on the terraces between the hard core mobs of all three clubs, and Arsenal's firm were as capable as the rest.

Two great Chelsea chants which invoke memories of past clashes with Arsenal made imaginative use of a couple of American novelty pop records!

*Tennessee Wig-Walk,* which was a chart hit in 1953 for Bonnie Lou had already generated *I'm a bow-legged chicken, I'm a knock-kneed hen, ain't lost a fight since I don't know when. Walk with a wiggle and a waggle and a waggle and a squawk doing the Chelsea boot walk* also provided the melody to the following gem:

*Bertie Mee said to Bill Shankly, have you heard of the North Bank Highbury?*
*Shanks said, 'no, I don't think so, but I've heard of the Chelsea aggro!'*

The chant, another with many localized versions, is still sung each time the Blues face the Gunners... a curious testament to a discussion that never took place between two legendary managers, Mee of Arsenal and Shankly of Liverpool (where the *bow legged chicken* was first heard) who have long since entered the pearly gates to football heaven.

The Royal Guardsmen may sound British, but they hailed from Florida and were responsible for the 1966 hit, *Snoopy vs. The Red Baron* which was inspired by the comic strip Peanuts and featured the world's favourite beagle Snoopy in the guise of a World War I airman fighting German air ace Manfred von Richthofen aka The Red Baron. A Ska makeover of the track, released in 1973 by the Hotshots which was actually recorded by reggae band The Cimarons also charted and is well worth a listen as it is more in keeping with the terrace skinhead culture of the day.

The Chelsea version which immortalized Danny 'Eccles' Harkins in song has become somewhat of a scarcely heard lost treasure, which is a shame given its originality.

*10, 20, 30, 40, 50 or more, the Chelsea North Stand were running up the score.*
*80 Arsenal died in that spree, when Chelsea ran riot at Highbury.*
*And out from the corner a hero arose, a funny looking geezer with a big red nose.*
*His name is Harkins, they say he's insane, and the North Bank Highbury was taken again.*

Strangely, Harkins was anything but *a funny looking geezer with a big red nose*. The handsome, chiselled, sideburn-sporting skinhead ace face General of The Shed always dressed to impress in a green Harrington and white Sta Prest. A match for sure in the dapper stakes with counterparts Frankie Parish and Sammy Skies of Spurs' Park Lane End, Johnny Hoy and Jenkins who led Arsenal's North Bank and Johnny Williams and Rollo of West Ham fame.

The intensity of London rivalries with Spurs, Arsenal and West Ham manifested themselves perfectly in a chant which 'samples' Anthony Newley's chart hit *Strawberry Fair* that did the rounds of the grounds in the early '70s that is sadly seldom if ever heard today.

*One day I went to Upton Park.*
*Singing, singing, Chelsea are the champions.*
*Singing, singing, Chelsea are the kings.*
*I saw Ron Greenwood standing there. All alone! All alone!*
*I said to him what's up my friend?*
*He said the Mile End's run again.*
*Singing, singing, Chelsea are the Champions.*
*Singing, singing, Chelsea are the Kings.*

Alternatives for Arsenal and Tottenham had the ground, manager and end respectively adjusted to Highbury, Bertie Mee and the North Bank and Tottenham High Road, Bill Nicholson and the Park Lane.

Further adaptations interchanged the names of the football managers with top boys of the day. Sammy Skies (Spurs), Johnny Hoy (Arsenal) and Bill Gardner (West Ham)… and all three clubs had their own versions of the chant.

One-time glam rock superstar Gary Glitter's 1973 chart hit *Hello, Hello, I'm Back Again* may have been kept off the top slot by Dawn featuring Tony Orlando who convinced the record-buying public to *Tie a Yellow Ribbon*

## CAREFREE! CHELSEA CHANTS AND TERRACE CULTURE

*Round the Old Oak Tree*, but the infectious clap-along *Hello, Hello* chorus lent itself perfectly to the football terraces.

At the first sign of trouble kicking off at a Blues game, the chant *Hello, Hello, Chelsea aggro* could be heard – typically sung by the *North Stand, North Stand do your job* scarfer brigade in The Shed – rather than those actually engaged in hand-to-hand combat.

Pretty much every club (even Watford!) used *Hello Hello (insert name of team) aggro*, and the song also gained widespread usage to both salute (in the modern Chelsea era *Hello, Hello, Hernan Crespo* and *Hello, Hello, Samuel Eto'o* proved popular) players and very rarely to mock those who have left under a perceived cloud. When they faced the Blues in the colours of their new team the crowd sang *Hello, Hello, Chelsea reject, Chelsea reject* – the unfortunate Gordon Durie merits another mention in this respect.

Another version, *Hello, Hello, Chelsea are back* brings fond memories of returning to the top-flight in 1977, 1984 and 1989... with that fabled morning at Highbury (24 August 1984) when somewhere in the region of 20,000 fully paid up members of *Johnny Neal's Blue and White Army* packed into Arsenal's old ground to cheer on the Blues probably the pick of the bunch.

Travelling Blues supporters ironically singing *Hello, Hello, Chelsea are back* when Guus Hiddink's temporary charges moved six points clear of relegation with a 3-0 away win at Crystal Palace (3 January 2016, Oscar, Willian, Diego Costa) during the traumatic 2015/16 season which saw José Mourinho sacked is one of the few memories of a deeply troubled campaign to raise a smile.

Other Gary Glitter tunes that provided inspiration to the terrace songsmiths included *Rock and Roll Part I* which reached No. 2 in July 1972 (a track was kept at bay from the top slot by Donny Osmond's *Puppy Love*). Twenty-five years later, the cadence of *Rock and Roll* was a perfect match for new Chelsea goalkeeper Ed de Goey.

These days, *Ed de Goey, Ed de Goey, Ed de Goey, Ed de Goey* gets an airing when Blues fans happen to spot any player, official, steward, supporter or member of the public they come across who bears resemblance to the distinctive-looking, thin-haired, moustachioed Dutch stopper who was a cult hero during his six-year stint at the Bridge.

# BLUE IS THE COLOUR

**Mark:** Chelsea's victory over Leeds United in the FA Cup final brought European football back on the menu the following season in the guise of the Cup Winners Cup and Mick Greenaway and his companions travelled to all the Blues away leg fixtures in the competition including the final in Athens.

Remarkably, Chelsea only faced four opponents en-route to the final against Real Madrid (19 May 1971, 1-1, Peter Osgood. Replay 21 May 2-1 John Dempsey, Peter Osgood). Away matches with Aris Thessaloniki (16 September 1970 1-1 Ian Hutchinson), CSKA Sofia (21 October 0-1 Tommy Baldwin) and Club Brugge (10 March 1971 2-0) saw intrepid Blues fans broaden their horizons – less so perhaps at the semi-final stage when Manchester City (28 April 0-1 Ron Healey own goal) were the opponents.

As Mick Greenaway describes in his memoirs… at that time, it wasn't unusual for players and supporters to share a drink – and his recollections of the trip to Bulgaria to watch Chelsea play CSKA Sofia bear amusing testament to this.

**Mick:** "We made our way to the hotel which we knew the Chelsea players were staying… this was of course after the game and a 1-0 win meant we were celebrating. When we arrived some of the players asked us to start a singsong which we did. One of the comical sights was seeing our present manager (referring to legendary stalwart of the Blues side of the late '60s and early '70s David Webb who managed Chelsea between February and May 1993 – the period when Greenaway was writing his memoirs) getting up on a chair and singing an adopted French tune *Alouette* with saucy English words added to it. The players, fans, stewardesses and friends all joined in to the chorus which was very entertaining to all present."

**Mark:** The Chelsea squad, with Webby as the caller, would go on to record *Alouette* for the *Blue is the Colour* album released on the Penny Farthing label in 1972.

*Alouette* soon became a terrace favourite and featured in a *cfcuk* article I wrote about a Champions League trip to Bulgaria, there's a coincidence, to watch Chelsea play Levski Sofia (27 September 2006). The Blues won the game 3-1 courtesy of a Didier Drogba hattrick, and the customary lock-in at the final whistle provided the opportunity to indulge in lengthier chants of which *Alouette* is a prime example. Normally there is too much going on during a game for a chant of some complexity to survive being broken by one incident or another and so *Alouette* is normally reserved for pubs … and post-match lock-ins.

Detained after the game in the Vassil Levski National Stadium for our own 'comfort and safety' (though the comfort aspect left a lot to be desired) it was Martin 'Scoggsy' Goggins, a man no stranger to starting the *Zigger Zagger* chant when the mood takes him, who took up the mantle of caller for *Alouette*.

*Alouette, Chelsea Alouette, Alouette, Chelsea Alouette. Oh she had a wonkey eye,* hollered Scoggsy.

*Oh she had a wonkey eye,* we responded, waving at the bemused riot police a couple of whom were tapping their batons on their shields helping to keep us all in time.

*A wonkey eye (A wonkey eye) And golden hair.*
*Alouette, Chelsea Alouette, Alouette, Chelsea Alouette.*

The original French version tells of a lark (alouette) being plucked (je te plumerai), but the Chelsea version, a 'borrow' from the lewd *Rugby Songs* series of paperbacks published in the '60s is far more engaging… and so it continued.

*Oh she had a broken nose. (Oh she had a broken nose)*
*A broken nose. (A broken nose)*
*A wonkey eye. (A wonkey eye) and golden hair.*
*Alouette, Chelsea Alouette, Alouette, Chelsea Alouette.*

Scoggsy continued to call out the unfortunate woman's list of problems which included a club foot, a hairy arse, VD, a 48 and a double chin and, as he did so, the chant gathered momentum, reverberating around the emptying stadium, defying anyone who had even just a basic command of the English language not to join in.

The final chorus of *Alouette, Chelsea Alouette, Alouette, Chelsea Alouette* concluded with a boisterous *Chelsea!* (clap clap clap), *Chelsea!* (clap clap clap), *Chelsea!*

Following on from *Alouette* came another lengthy and popular call and response chant *Chelsea Ranger*. With its US military-style rhythm, *Chelsea Ranger* provides the caller with a brilliant opportunity to unify supporter voices.

*I wanna be a Chelsea Ranger.*
*I wanna live a life of danger.*
*I wanna beat Spurs every week.*
*Chase 'em up and down the streets.*
*Here's to the girl who I love best.*
*Every night I suck her breasts.*
*Sh*g her standing.*
*Sh*g her lying.*
*If she had wings, I'd sh*g her flying.*
*Now she's dead.*
*Not forgotten.*
*Dig her up, sh*g her rotten.*

The chant is supplemented with a version of *My Mammy* which Al Jolson had first brought to worldwide attention via 1927 film *The Jazz Singer*.

*Ohh Chelsea, Chelsea.*
*I'd walk a million miles, for one of your goals for Chelsea!*

*Chelsea Ranger* concludes with the popular refrain *We love you Chelsea we do. We love you Chelsea we do. We love you Chelsea we do. Oh Chelsea we love you.*

By the time we were allowed out of the stadium, the Chelsea team were already en-route to Sofia airport. No partying with the players for our loyal crew. The type of bond Mick Greenaway and his friends enjoyed with the legendary kings of the King's Road Blues side is unheard of in the modern era – and football is all the poorer for it.

*****

One player new to Chelsea in the early '70s who played a large part in the journey to European glory was Keith Weller (creator of Baldwin's goal against CSKA Sofia) who signed on the dotted line at Stamford Bridge the week after the FA Cup Final triumph over Leeds United.

Weller, a pricey £100,000 acquisition from Millwall, proved his worth during the 1970/71 season making 54 appearances and finishing the campaign as Chelsea's leading scorer with 14 goals.

Regularly deployed on the right side of midfield, Weller had become a cult hero with Blues fans as early as the third game of the season (22 August

1970) when a two goal send-half salvo against West Ham United rescued a game which appeared to be lost to Chelsea who had trailed 2-0 at the break. On the hour, Alan Hudson floated a beautiful cross over which Peter Osgood headed down for Weller to rifle home. Fifteen minutes later, the trio combined again in similar fashion to salvage an unlikely point for Chelsea.

Blues' Harry Houdini routines have become the stuff of legend and 70/71 was full of them. Away at Blackpool (24 October 1970) in what was Peter Osgood's first game back at Bloomfield Road since he broke his leg there almost four years to the day previously, Chelsea were trailing 3-0 at half-time and looked dead and buried.

In the 67th minute, manager Dave Sexton brought on Charlie Cooke in place of Tommy Baldwin, and three minutes later Cooke created a chance for Weller who blasted the ball home from edge of the box. Shortly after, David Webb, playing up front since Cooke's arrival, scored from an Osgood bicycle kick pass and then Weller levelled the game in the 80th minute firing home a loose ball following more good work from Ossie. A minute from time, Dave Hatton scored a remarkable own goal, directing a wicked Weller cross past his bemused keeper Harry Thomson to hand Chelsea a 4-3 victory.

Weller's brace took his haul to six in the past five games and nine for the season to date. "He's rapidly becoming the complete player," gushed Osgood of his teammate… and Chelsea supporters were equally impressed, composing a wonderful ode to their new hero which creatively harnesses the melody of traditional Irish folk song *Tourelay* with boy scouts campfire favourite *Ging Gang Goolie*!

*The Arsenal have Radford, the Palace have Queen, West Ham have Geoff Hurst, and Tottenham Gilzean.*
*But Chelsea have Osgood and he is the King, and also Keith Weller who plays on the wing.*
*Keithy, Keithy Weller, Keithy Weller on the wing.*
*Keithy, Keithy Weller, Keithy Weller on the wing.*

Despite his achievements and value to the team, in September 1971 Weller was incomprehensibly sold by Chelsea to Leicester City where he cemented his reputation as outstanding player winning four England caps before ending his career playing and then coaching in the North American Soccer League. Having settled in the United States, sadly, on 12 November 2004, Keith Weller succumbed to a rare form of cancer and passed away at the tragically young age of 58.

\*\*\*\*\*

Chelsea's original wizard of dribble, Charlie Cooke, is another player whose legendary status with Blues fans is commemorated in song. The Scaffold had scored a No. 1 hit with *Lily the Pink* in November 1968 and shortly after The Shed amended the lyrics in praise of Cooke and also often maligned and very much misunderstood winger Peter Houseman.

> *We'll drink, a drink, a drink, to Charlie the King, the King, the King, the saviour of the Chelsea team.*
> *For he invented professional football and now we're gonna win the League.*
> *Peter Houseman, played terrible football, and The Shed all called him names.*
> *So they gave him, a kick in the bollocks, and now he plays in every game.*

**Walter:** Over forty years later Big Chris put the tune to good use again singing, *We'll raise a drink a drink a drink, to Guus Hiddink Hiddink Hiddink!* It never caught on.

\*\*\*\*\*

**Mark:** Copyright legislation restricts the use of the lyrics to the title track of *Blue is the Colour*, which isn't a problem since every Chelsea supporter knows the words. The song, written by Daniel Boone and Rod McQueen who prior to its release had recently collaborated on Boone's worldwide hit *Beautiful Sunday*, was recorded by the Chelsea squad to coincide with the club's appearance in the 1972 League Cup Final.

A Peter Osgood goal wasn't enough for Chelsea who despite being red-hot favourites lost at Wembley 2-1 to Stoke City (4 March 1972), *Blue is the Colour* however fared much better finding favour with the record buying public and reaching No. 5 in the UK charts. The song has deservedly stood the test of time and, like *The Liquidator*, is still played before every Chelsea home game and occasionally after notable victories. It's fair to say though that the relatively recent trend of having Chelsea season ticket holder Stuart Pendred singing an operatic version of *Blue is the Colour* before key Champions League games at the Bridge has irked old school purists who prefer the original version and the memories it evokes.

Chelsea fans gathered at Wembley for that League Cup Final with Stoke stridently sang the *Blue Flag* version of the Manchester United *Red Flag* chant, which has its origins in the left-wing political anthem penned by Jim

Connell in 1889 and curiously set to the tune of the German Christmas carol *O Tannenbaum (O Christmas Tree)*.

*Forever and ever (wherever we go), we'll follow our team.*
*For we are the Chelsea, and we are supreme.*
*We'll never be mastered, by no northern bast\*rds,*
*We'll keep the Blue Flag flying high.*
*Flying high, up in the sky, we'll keep the blue flag flying high.*
*From Stamford Bridge to Wembley, we'll keep the Blue Flag flying high.*

Having been popular since the cup runs of the mid '60s, little did those who sang *Blue Flag* at the home of English football in March 1972 know that Chelsea's fortunes were about to plummet and that there would be no return to Wembley for to watch the Blues for many years to come.

# THERE WAS A MIGHTY BATTLE

"We can win the Second Division championship, we can come straight back," Eddie McCreadie, recently appointed Chelsea manager, had said defiantly at the Blues Player of the Year (Charlie Cooke) dinner which had gone ahead as planned on the evening of the final game of the 1974/75 season.

**Mark:** On 24 April 1975, Chelsea drew 1-1 with Everton at Stamford Bridge, a result which confirmed a relegation which seemed inevitable following the preceding Saturday's horrific 2-0 defeat to fellow basement battlers Tottenham Hotspur at riot-torn, pitch-invaded White Hart Lane. New skipper, eighteen-year old Ray Wilkins' 65th minute goal against the Toffees gave supporters a glimmer of hope, but they were dashed five minutes later when Bob Latchford equalised.

Had Chelsea Chairman at the time Brian Mears got his priorities wrong investing £2 million in the midst of a hideous recession to build the East Stand? Probably. Rival supporters had a field day laughing at Mears' folly and claiming the stand had been built facing the wrong way because the quality of Chelsea's football was so poor.

Mears, like most football chairman, was viewed as out of touch with economic reality by Blues fans, but many took consolation from the fact that McCreadie was a bonafide club legend. "We think big, and we will bounce back," said the Scot who'd made 410 appearances for Chelsea. The supporters loved McCreadie for his enthusiasm and for the way he blended youth with experience.

The Blues slide from cup kings to relegation fodder hadn't deterred their followers from turning up in numbers, particularly at away games. A crowd of 51,064 had been at White Hart Lane for McCreadie's first game in charge of Chelsea (almost double Spurs' average attendance for the season) and a further 10,000 were locked outside. Exactly how many of the combined total were visiting fans is pure guesswork, but it would be fair to say Eddie McCreadie's all new Blue and White Army were at least 15,000 strong.

*Editor's note: Eddie Mac Eddie Mac life and times at Chelsea under Eddie McCreadie written by Eddie McCreadie's Blue and White Army is a worthy addition to your library if you haven't got a copy yet.*

Canadian singer Terry Jacks, whose version of *Le Moribond* by Jaques

## CAREFREE! CHELSEA CHANTS AND TERRACE CULTURE

Brel entitled *Seasons in the Sun* had been a worldwide hit the preceding year, provided Chelsea and Spurs fans with melodious ammunition to bait each other throughout the day.

*We had joy we had fun we had Tottenham (Chelsea) on the run, but the joy didn't last cos the bast\*rds ran too fast.*

The chant proved popular with fans of many clubs for the next two decades before fading into obscurity. A brief renaissance came when Irish boy-band Westlife had a Christmas No.1 with *Seasons* in 1999.

*****

Having insisted that *Kung Fu Fighting* by Carl Douglas be released as an A side rather than a B side, it was clear Pye Records supremo Robin Blanchflower (no relation to former Spurs player Danny who would soon manage Chelsea) had an ear for a novelty hit record.

*Kung Fu Fighting* topped the UK singles charts in September 1974 riding the crest of popularity created for the Chinese martial art by the TV series *Kung Fu* which followed the adventures of Kwai Chang Kaine (David Carradine).

Blanchflower had another musical protégé in Johnny Wakelin whose curious penchant for writing songs in praise of boxing champion Muhammad Ali would also bring him chart success. Wakelin, a cabaret artist who hailed from Brighton, scored a top 10 hit in January 1975 with *Black Superman (Muhammad Ali)*, but is best remembered for another Ali tribute, *In Zaire* which peaked at No. 4 in the UK charts in August 1976.

By 1976, lawlessness on the terraces was getting out of control and *Kung Fu Fighting* and *In Zaire* took on new meanings for Chelsea supporters.

14 February, Second Division Chelsea played Third Division Crystal Palace in a Fifth Round FA Cup tie at Stamford Bridge. A phenomenal crowd of 54,407, almost 40,000 higher than the gate for the Blues previous home game against West Brom (31 January, 1-2, Ian Britton), witnessed a 3-2 victory for the Eagles. Nick Chatterton and Peter Taylor had given Palace a 2-0 lead at half-time. After the break, Ray Wilkins and Steve Wicks levelled the tie, but Taylor scored the winner for the visitors who were managed at the time by flamboyant, fedora-wearing Malcolm Allison.

Forty-five minutes before kick-off, Allison had strolled out onto the pitch and walked over to The Shed raising three fingers to signal how many goals Palace were going to score and then he made his way to the North Stand and did the same. Chelsea supporters who were everywhere in the ground voiced their disapproval chanting *Allison is a w\*nker, Allison is a wa\*ker*.

As Palace took the initiative on the pitch in the first half, so did Chelsea's firm in the North Stand. Pockets of space opened up right across the packed open terrace as scarfers celebrating Chatterton's goal were suddenly panicked by the ruckers. Chants of *Hello, hello, Chelsea aggro, Chelsea aggro*, and *You're gonna get your f\*cking heads kicked in* can be clearly heard on BBC TV *Match of the Day* highlights which, following Taylor's subsequent goal cut immediately away to the action on the terraces where flare-trousered Kung Fu kicks were being traded along with punches.

Following the long hot summer of '76, supporter buzz at the Bridge was all about Chelsea facing newly promoted Millwall. There was going to be trouble… big trouble. At that time, and at face value, this seemed remarkable considering the last time the teams had played each other in a first class fixture was 10 October 1960 when the Blues thrashed the Lions 7-1 (Johnny Brooks, Bobby Evans, Peter Sillett x2, Peter Brabrook, Jimmy Greaves x2) in a First Round League Cup tie at The Den.

The key reason why it was going to 'go off' when the two sides met could merit an entire chapter on its own in any book about rivalries between firms, but that's not what *Carefree!* is about. Nevertheless, there's a short version of the story worth telling, and Alan Garrison Tomkins rubbed his hands purposefully before cracking his knuckles, lighting a cigarette and regaling me with the details.

**Garrison:** "It goes back to 1973 (3 February), when Millwall played Everton in an FA Cup tie at Goodison Park. The Lions who were in the Second Division beat their top-flight hosts 2-0. Millwall took a mob up there and tried to take the Gwladys Street End, but they got hammered… the result on the pitch probably didn't help their boys much either.

At that time, me and my North Stand mates used to drink in a pub called the Pineapple near the Elephant… Millwall's manor! A few months after the incident at Goodison, Bomber who was one of the leaders of their firm was in the Pineapple and he came over. He knew we were Chelsea, and he also knew we were due to play Everton at Stamford Bridge soon (10 November) and asked if he could bring a mob down to join up with us to have a go at their mob and help them get revenge.

Sure enough, come that Saturday, we're in the Rising Sun and about fifty Millwall turn up. A mob of Everton came in The Shed and we hammered them. After the game (3-1, Tommy Baldwin, Peter Osgood x2), we waited by the Britannia Gate for them to come out and done them there and then chased them all the way to the King's Road.

After that for a while if the fixtures worked out so Chelsea weren't playing we'd go down The Den and vice versa. We got to know them well. Bomber, Tiny, Ginger and the others… and for the next year or so we'd run with each other.

That however would come to a spectacular end in 1976 when Chelsea played Charlton in a Monday night game at The Valley (19 April 1-1 Les Berry own goal). We arranged for Millwall to come with us because we'd heard West Ham's firm were going with Charlton and we'd also heard that some Arsenal and Tottenham were going with them as well. We said to the Millwall come with us (the North Stand) because we'll be outnumbered as The Shed will be down the other end. We went into the Charlton end and cleared it. Then Bomber's led Millwall in… meanwhile on the other side of the ground Babs and his Shed mob has seen them and is thinking they are West Ham. As we were all jumping around and celebrating, Babs must have thought we were fighting so he led a charge across the pitch. We were going 'oh no', as Chelsea had so many numbers they mullered Millwall.

The Shed boys eventually went back… but fifty of us North Stand stayed. At the end of the game, the double gates have opened and there's a f*cking army waiting for us. Charlton, West Ham, Arsenal, Tottenham… and Millwall who were well pissed off. All the mobs that hate each other had joined up. I said to the Scotsman we need a diversion and he went into the nearby social club grabbed loads of optics, smashed them on the floor and set fire to them. As everyone went to put the fire out, we've steamed into them and there was a running battle all the way to the station. What happened at The Valley that night set the scene for what was soon to follow."

**Mark:** On 4 September 1976, Millwall played Chelsea at The Den in the fifth league game of the season. Unruly Blues fans had already caused chaos on the opening day of the campaign (21 August) with a mini riot at Brisbane Road following a 1-0 win (Steve Finnieston) over Orient.

Among the Chelsea chants started that afternoon at Orient, was a reworked version of Johnny Wakelin's *In Zaire* which was taken up with zest by The Shed at the midweek home game with Notts County (25

August 1-1 Ian Britton) that followed.

*There was a mighty battle there in Mill, in Millwall.*
*100,000 North Stand there, in Mill, in Millwall.*
*All the West Ham gathered round. In Mill, in Millwall.*
*Chelsea battered them into the ground. In Mill, in Millwall.*

As Garrison explains, the bravado of the chant, and what actually transpired at The Den are somewhat different.

**Garrison:** "We took an absolute hammering. It didn't start well and just got worse. Before the game we were walking along Cold Blow Lane and Eccles was with us. This horse and cart has come by with a tarpaulin over the cart and it's stopped and the guy 'driving' turns and pulls back the tarp and under it there's half a dozen Millwall including Ginger with an ice pick! A f*cking ice pick! They wanted Eccles. I think they would have killed him. I told him to run. He had to. It was like the Wild West.

We went in and got hammered. Babs led a small mob of The Shed in with him and took the heat off us but they got it too. Another group who'd missed the horse and cart scene were already in the ground and getting hammered. There were three Chelsea mobs that day, but Millwall got the result. It was hard work, and it was about self-preservation as much as anything. I was black and blue and bleeding. Me and seven other North Stand stayed in there with four Shed. Millwall done us, but we were still there at the end of the game. Bomber came over and said well done, not even West Ham would have stayed in there. He asked us to have a drink with them so we went in their pub. We were mad in the head alright.

To make matters worse, Chelsea lost the game 3-0. Given what happened at The Den, the *battle in Millwall* chant was shelved... although there would be an ironic version that the North Stand sang from time to time."

*There was a mighty battle there in Mill, in Millwall.*
*100,000 North Stand there, in Mill, in Millwall.*
*All The Shed boys stayed at home. In Mill, in Millwall.*

# COME ALONG AND SING THIS SONG

**Mark:** Despite the humbling loss at Millwall, Eddie McCreadie soon galvanised his young team and Chelsea would finish the 1976/77 season promoted back to the First Division as runners up to Wolverhampton Wanderers.

Supporters, optimistic that McCreadie would be able to continue his good work at Stamford Bridge back in the top-flight had their hopes dashed shortly after when the Scot, unhappy with the terms of a new contract offered to him by the Chelsea board, resigned his position and left.

Ken Shellito, who'd spent his entire playing career with Chelsea and subsequently joined the club's coaching staff took over as manager, but the Blues struggled... and the fans sang dolefully about McCreadie with a wistful lament asking him to return.

Amending the lyrics of the Keith West hit *Excerpt from A Teenage Opera* which had charted in 1967 and told the tale of an ageing door-to-door grocer called Jack, The Shed faithful who'd once sang *Eddie Mac, Eddie Mac, is it true we're going back to... Division One?* could now often be heard chanting *Eddie Mac Eddie Mac when are you coming back.*

The melody had already been used to good effect on many football terraces a decade earlier to abuse then Everton goalkeeper Gordon West and Manchester United superstar George Best. *Gordon West, Gordon West, the biggest c\*nt since Georgie Best. Get on your bike and f\*ck off home.*

Under Shellito, in 1978 Chelsea limped to a sixteenth-place finish in the First Division, but the following season the Blues floundered. Bottom of the League approaching Christmas, Shellito was sacked and replaced by Danny Blanchflower who could not prevent another relegation and would soon lose his job to Geoff Hurst.

Coinciding with the confirmation of Chelsea's return to Division Two, in March 1979 popular Euro disco band Boney M released a single entitled *Hooray! Hooray! It's A Holi-Holiday* which borrowed the melody from the nursery rhyme *Polly Wolly Doodle.*

Peaking at No. 3 in the UK charts, *Hooray! Hooray! It's A Holi-Holiday* was transformed by ever-hopeful Blues supporters into what has become a staple part of the Chelsea song-sheet, *Come Along.*

## MARK WORRALL & WALTER OTTON

*Come along, come along, come along and sing this song.*
*Boys in Blue, Division Two. We won't be here for long.*

Had Chelsea bounced straight back to the First Division in 1980, *Come Along* might have faded into obscurity, but it wasn't to be, the Boys in Blue would be playing in the football wilderness for some time to come.

Chelsea did come close to a swift return though. A 1-0 home victory over Notts County (19 April 1980) courtesy of a rare Gary Chivers goal had lifted the Blues into second place, but a 1-1 draw away at Swansea City the following Saturday saw Hurst's side slip out of the promotion places.

An early Tommy Langley goal at Vetch Field had given vociferous visiting fans hope, but Jeremy Charles levelled the game for the Swans and the result left Chelsea going into the final game of the season in fourth place and relying on Leicester City, Sunderland and Birmingham City, the teams above them in the automatic promotion places slipping up.

On 3 May 1980, 28,253 spectators gathered at Stamford Bridge to watch the Blues see off Oldham Athletic 3-0. Mike Fillery opened the scoring and Clive Walker added a brace, but an afternoon when many fans at the Bridge had brought portable radios with them to listen to how Chelsea's promotion rivals were faring would end in disappointment as they all won.

There had been hope and loud cheers when Notts County had taken a brief lead against Birmingham, but as we know all too well... football can be a cruel mistress.

As the afternoon progressed, and the miserable inevitability of another season in the second tier took hold, Chelsea supporters refocused their attention on the dramatic events that had been unfolding for several days a mile or so away from Stamford Bridge.

It was 30 April 1980 when six armed members of the Democratic Revolutionary Front for the Liberation of Arabistan stormed the Iranian Embassy in South Kensington taking twenty-six people hostage and a siege ensued. The SAS were deployed to deal with the tense, drawn-out situation which was being relayed constantly on live TV news bulletins.

Chelsea followers, having achieved notoriety for taking ends at football grounds around the country, began chanting *We're gonna take the Iranian Embassy*.

## CAREFREE! CHELSEA CHANTS AND TERRACE CULTURE

Actions speak louder than words and, after the game, a sizable mob of Blues fans made their way to Kensington where they were eventually dispersed by the police. The siege continued until 5 May when it was the SAS and not the combined forces of Chelsea's North Stand and The Shed who stormed the Embassy, abseiling from the roof of the building and forcing entry through the windows to bring the incident to a heroic end.

# CELERY!

**Mark:** The early 1980s saw Chelsea embark on a series of pre-season tours to Sweden, and Mick Greenaway was one of the prime movers in an ever-growing band of Blues supporters whose summer holidays embraced these trips. These Scandinavian jaunts not only spawned *Carefree!* but a couple of other Shed classics *Celery!* and *One Man Went to Mow*.

Among the music cassette tapes Greenaway had taken with him to keep the troops entertained in the summer of 1981 was the somewhat unseasonal *Christmas Jamboree Bag* which had been recorded by Chas & Dave, a couple of affable Tottenham Hotspur fans whose piano, bass and drums-based 'Rockney-style' music had found favour with the record-buying public of the era.

*Christmas Jamboree Bag* included such gems as *Rabbit* and *The Sideboard Song*, but the track that Mick enjoyed most was a spoof version of Jive Bunny's *Stars on 45* medley entitled *Stars over 45*, which included a fifteen-second burst of an old London music hall standard *Ask Old Brown*. Mick had grown up with this ditty, recalling the family singsongs where as many of the words as possible had been changed so they sounded like swearing.

*Arse ol' Brown to tea. Arse ol' Brown to tea.*
*If 'e don't come, I'll tickle 'is bum with a lump-a celery!*

The transposition to the *Celery!* song Chelsea supporters know and love took place there and then.

*If she don't come, I'll tickle her bum with a lump of celery.*
*Celery, celery!*

For most people, thoughts of the long-stemmed vegetable *Apium graveolens dulce,* to give celery it its correct Latin name, conjured up images of dips and crudité platters, of warming winter broths and healthy summer salads... Chelsea supporters would add a different dimension to that perception that would last for the next twenty-five years.

Bemused greengrocers passed by Blues fans heading to games would see sales of celery rise as the vegetable became an essential matchday accessory, smuggled into stadia and hurled in the air to accompany the singing of Greenaway's song.

## CAREFREE! CHELSEA CHANTS AND TERRACE CULTURE

The truth about the origins of the *Celery* chant buries another myth that can be found lurking on websites that the fad had its roots, literally, at Priestfield home to Gillingham FC where the vegetable was found growing on the pitch one summer. Gills fans subsequently picked up on the Chelsea chant and cradled it to their bosom, however in 1996 following a promotion season in which they had persistently thrown celery at larger-than-life goalkeeper Jim *'he's fat, he's round, he's worth a million pounds'* Stannard, the Kent club banned supporters from bringing it into the stadium.

By this time, meteoric showers of celery stalks had become synonymous with Chelsea supporters... of course, as happened at Gillingham, the authorities were watching and waiting for the opportunity to spoil the fun.

On 14 April 2002, Chelsea supporter Charlie Driver was arrested along with four fellow fans at Villa Park where the Blues played west London rivals Fulham in an FA Cup semi-final (1-0, John Terry).

Celery was everywhere, and unfortunately for the famous five the stalks they launched invoked the wrath of the police who apprehended the men and charged them with the heinous crime of 'throwing celery without lawful authority', a misdemeanour that was later alleged in Birmingham Magistrates Court by prosecutor Frederick Pilkington to have contravened the Football Act 1991.

For the defence, Bret Loveday countered that throwing celery was a tradition at Chelsea. "These young men, for their trouble, had been involved in a traditional ritual. They clearly regret their actions."

Those of you who know Charlie can imagine him trying to keep a straight face as the case was heard. In the end, the five Blues each pleaded guilty to throwing a missile and agreed to be bound over for a year in the sum of £300.

Outside court, a relieved Charlie told the press, "I'm really pleased I haven't been given a banning order, so I can carry on following my team. I won't be throwing or eating any more celery again."

For a while, Celery-gate saw enthusiasm for the tradition wane, however as Chelsea's fortunes rose and rose... regular cup final appearances and the associated party atmosphere brought celery back into vogue again.

Unfortunately, vegetable-influenced over-exuberance at the 2007 Carling

Cup Final, (25 February, 2-1, Didier Drogba x2), match with Arsenal played at the Millennium Stadium would result in the FA launching an investigation into celery throwing incidents during the game which infamously saw then Gunner Cesc Fàbregas pelted with celery every time he went to take a corner.

The killjoy Chelsea officials decided enough was enough and posted a statement on the club website which read: *'The throwing of anything at a football match, including celery, is a criminal offence for which you can be arrested and end up with a criminal record. In future, if anyone is found attempting to bring celery into Stamford Bridge they could be refused entry and anyone caught throwing celery will face a ban.'*

While the club's decision has meant celery is seldom seen at the Bridge, the song is still sung regularly. Away games and European trips of course present opportunities to resurrect the tradition properly though this is seldom planned and happens on an ad hoc basis as and when Blues supporters happen to pass a shop where celery is being sold.

# ONE MAN WENT TO MOW

**Mark:** Another cassette Mick had with him on the Sweden '81 trip was 50 All-Time Children's Favourites by popular British musician and TV personality Wally Whyton.

On 12 August 1981, for sheer novelty value, Greenaway played the tape at a friendly game Chelsea played against IF Flens, (0-2, Colin Lee, Mike Fillery), and among the sing-along tunes was the classic counting nursery rhyme *One Man Went To Mow* which was reprised numerous times during the course of the match.

*One man went to mow, went to mow a meadow.*
*One man and his dog... Spot! Went to mow a meadow.*

As the repetition continued, Mick and his friends added an arm movement prodding out their right elbows at an angle at the *Spot!* stage of the chant. This had such an infectious quality that its use spread to a wider group of Chelsea supporters when the Blues returned to England and played Exeter City in a final pre-season friendly (21 August) at St. James Park.

A sizeable proportion of the 3,139 crowd were there to cheer Chelsea on to a 1-0 (Micky Droy) victory. *One Man Went To Mow*, complete with elbow jig, was the chant of the day and would go on to firmly establish itself as a terrace favourite in the season that followed when the crouching down / springing up element as the rhyme ascended to ten was added.

Over time, the elbow jig ceased, and crouching down and springing up has proved tricky in all seated stadiums, but *One Man Went To Mow* remains hugely popular, an essential, irreplaceable and unforgettable part of Chelsea folklore just like Mick Greenaway.

Unfortunately, Mick would eventually be tarred by the same 'hooligan' brush that the authorities and media began to conveniently daub Blues supporters with during the '80s.

Defamatory and baseless newspaper articles, including a dreadful piece in the thankfully now defunct *News of the World*, which linked Greenaway to the notorious Chelsea Headhunters firm and alleged he had right wing connections, had serious implications for Greenaway who was also falsely reported to have orchestrated the Goldstone Ground riot at an away game with Brighton and Hove Albion (3 September 1983, Brighton 1 Chelsea 2, Kerry Dixon x2).

Caught up in the maelstrom of negative publicity that surrounded the Headhunters, Mick lost his job and was banned from Stamford Bridge by the club he loved. Beset by loneliness, poverty, and ill health, Mick Greenaway passed away on 22 August 1999... a tragic end to a huge life force. Gone but certainly not forgotten.

Mick Greenaway
Spiritual Leader of The Shed
RIP

Had Mick been more fortunate and lived to keep the Blue Flag Flying High, his viewpoint on modern terrace culture would be as valid and insightful now as it was when he gave The Shed its vocal identity in the '60s.

Holding court in the bar named in his honour at Stamford Bridge, Greenaway would have listened with a critical ear to the witty variations of his old compositions being sung by a new generation of Blues supporters.

Roman Abramovich's acquisition of Chelsea in June 2003 soon catapulted the Blues into silverware orbit providing plenty of subject matter for aspiring chant-smiths.

On 17 August 2003, Claudio Ranieri took a Chelsea team to Anfield that had been given a turbocharged £75 million makeover in the summer transfer window. Ranieri's men won 2-1 thanks to goals from new boy Juan Sebastián Verón and old boy Jimmy Floyd Hasselbaink. Other new signings making their Blues Premier League debuts were Glen Johnson, Damien Duff, Geremi, Wayne Bridge and Joe Cole who replaced Duff from the bench. Ironically, match winner Hasselbaink only started because another new signing, Adrian Mutu, had not received international clearance in time to play.

As Chelsea supporters gathered in the Anfield Road End waved their wallets and taunted The Kop with chants of *Loads and Loads of Money*, one wag decided to give Mick Greenaway's *Carefree!* a remix.

*Debt free wherever we may be, we're gonna buy everyone we see... and we don't give a f*ck about the transfer fee, 'cause we are the wealthy CFC.*

## CAREFREE! CHELSEA CHANTS AND TERRACE CULTURE

A few months later, Geremi would score his first goal for Chelsea in a 3-0 home win over Portsmouth. The Cameroon international's thunderous volley was met with a hastily reworked version of Celery!

*Geremi, Geremi.*
*If Damien Duff don't tickle her muff we'll send in Geremi!*

# SING WHEN YOU'RE WINNING

**Mark:** Since reaching the quarter-finals of the 1938 World Cup competition held in France where they were thrashed 8-0 by Sweden, Cuba's fortunes as a football nation have waned. Associated with fine cigars and a missile crisis that brought nearby USA and the old Soviet Union to the brink of nuclear war, it's hard to believe that this small Caribbean island could in some way be responsible for one of the most recognisable chants heard at stadiums the length and breadth of the country… but it is.

The repetitive and wonderfully ironic refrain, *Sing when you're winning, you only sing when you're winning,* and the myriad variations on this theme, are sung along to the melody of *Guantanamera* which was a transatlantic hit for American folk trio The Sandpipers in 1966. Originating as a patriotic poem about a peasant girl from Guantanamo written by Cuban writer and independence hero José Marti and later set to music by composer Julian Orbon and subsequently given a folkier feel by the likes of José Fernandez and Hector Angulo, *Guantanamera* was adapted by American musician and peace activist Pete Seeger who featured it on his 1963 album *We Shall Overcome.*

It was The Sandpipers version however that became lodged between the ears of generations of British football supporters who have had fun with it ever since by spontaneously reworking the words to suit the occasion.

*Sing when you're winning* is typically directed at visiting fans who break into song after their team has taken the lead and as such isn't unique to Chelsea, nor are a number of other iterations which have been a source of amusement in the past.

Away at Barnsley on 10 December 1983, Chelsea drew 0-0 on a bitterly cold winter's day at Oakwell. Blues supporters who'd travelled in numbers to Yorkshire made their own entertainment during a dour game by singing a number of regional-themed chants directed at the locals the (coal) pick of which *Sing when you're mining, you only sing when you're mining.*

On 14 May 1984, regional employment was a source of inspiration for the Chelsea songsmiths once again, this time at Grimsby where Kerry Dixon scored the winner and Pat Nevin had a penalty saved as the Blues completed their Second Division title-winning season with a 1-0 win.

Travelling Chelsea supporters were packed like sardines in the Mariners cosy Blundell Park ground. The official attendance was given as 13,000... but it seemed much higher. The sardines analogy was appropriate enough. *Sing when you're fishing, you only sing when you're fishing* sang Chelsea fans teasing the home crowd. The Cleethorpes Beach Patrol were less than impressed.

Famously, on 23 October 1997, Chelsea lost a European Cup Winners Cup 2nd Round First Leg tie 3-2 (Gianluca Vialli x2) away to Norwegian side Tromso. The game was played in blizzard conditions so bad that Scott of the Antarctic would probably have stayed in his tent. *Sing when it's snowing, you only sing when it's snowing* sang Blues fans as they engaged in snowball fights and associated malarkey.

On 19 December 2007, Chelsea coasted to a 2-0 (Frank Lampard, Andriy Schevchenko) victory over Liverpool in a Fifth Round Carling Cup tie at Stamford Bridge. The Reds starting line-up featured blonde-haired, pony-tailed Ukraine international glamour boy Andriy Voronin who was teased with the fabulous chant, *Fat Paris Hilton, you're just a fat Paris Hilton* every time he touched the ball.

18 September 2011 – former Manchester United winger Nani scored a peach of a goal for the Red Devils and was a constant thorn in the side of the Chelsea defence in a 3-1 (Fernando Torres) Premier League defeat at Old Trafford. The Portugal international was recognised for his endeavours by travelling Blues fans with the chant *Sh\*t Michael Jackson, you're just a sh\*t Michael Jackson...* a reference to the twinkle-toed Red Devil's uncanny resemblance to the one-time King of Pop.

Such was United's dominance on that day that many of the home supporters in a crowd of over 75,000 left early to beat the rush to the motorway network. *We'll race you back to London* jeered Chelsea's followers. Not a play on *Guantanamera* it's fair to say, but a dig at the Man U brigade who live in the south and get taunted when visiting the Bridge with the chant *Live round the corner, you only live round the corner* the melody to which is of course that familiar old tune.

Sung in response to Fulham supporters taunts directed at Chelsea of *Small club in Fulham, you're just a small club in Fulham – Small club in Putney, you're just a small club in Putney* always raises a chuckle. Sadly, with the departure of the Cottagers to the Championship, this wonderful musical geography lesson for tourists won't be available again anytime soon.

*Speak f\*cking English, why don't you speak f\*cking English* directed at chanting opposition supporters pretty much from any region outside the southeast of England (and stadium announcers at away games in Europe), merits inclusion on the basis that one of its most vocal proponents is the astonishingly loud Chelsea Kal – who hails from Hungary.

*Speak f\*cking English* was perhaps most famously directed at the supporters of Newcastle United in a bid to drown out their wonderfully evocative *Fat Eddie Murphy, you're just a fat Eddie Murphy* chant which former Chelsea striker Jimmy Floyd Hasselbaink had to endure during his playing days for the club.

*Here for the Chelsea, you're only here for the Chelsea*, has stood the test of time and is normally saved for cup ties both home and away – typically against lower league opposition whose supporter numbers swell as part-timers come out of the woodwork for the grand occasion.

*One* is the prefix to a long list of chants. *One team in London* beget at appropriate times *One team in Europe* – but the most stirring *One's* are those directed at players and managers especially on those occasions when they had some added significance.

A incredible occasion it was on 9 April 1994. Chelsea beat Luton Town 2-0 (Gavin Peacock x2) at Wembley in an FA Cup semi-final. Lining up for the Hatters, his hometown club, was 193-goal Chelsea legend Kerry Dixon who was reaching the end of his playing career.

It's fair to say that *One Kerry Dixon, there's only one Kerry Dixon* had been sung at almost all of Dixon's 420 appearances for Chelsea from 27 August 1983 when he scored twice on his debut against Derby County (5-0, Nigel Spackman, Clive Walker, Chris Hutchings, Kerry Dixon x2) to 2 May 1992 when he played his last game for the Blues, an away loss to Everton (2-1, Eddie Newton), but the rendition at Wembley was remarkable as both sets of supporters joined together in unison to salute King Kerry. Those who were there will testify to never witnessing anything quite like it since. It was a truly special moment, and it's brilliant to know that after all these years it still resonates with the great man himself.

**Walter:** I was with Tall Paul, and for me that was, at the time, the best day at the football for me. Drinking in Baker Street, jibbing the tube, Wembley packed with Chelsea. As soon as I saw Kerry was gonna be subbed because his number was up, I literally screamed *One Kerry Dixon! There's only one Kerry Dixon!* I'm sure several others did at the same time, because it had crossed most people's minds that the substitution was going to happen. The song spread in seconds across our whole end. Hearing over half of Wembley singing it was something else. It was mentioned in the paper, I cut it out and stuck it in the inside cover of my work diary because it was such a special moment.

**Mark:** The last game of the 2003/04 season on 15 May, was also the last match of popular Chelsea manager Claudio Ranieri's Stamford Bridge career. It ended in victory over relegated Leeds United as Jesper Grønkjær scored the only goal of the game.

Ranieri's role as manager at the Bridge was at risk from the minute Roman Abramovich had bought Chelsea the previous summer, and the Russian, aided and abetted by new Chief Executive Officer, former Manchester United supremo Peter Kenyon, had undermined the Italian's position throughout the campaign as rumour and supposition about his impending dismissal grew.

England manager at the time Sven Goran Eriksson had been among the early favourites to replace Ranieri which resulted in another version of *La Donna e Mobile*, *We don't want Eriksson, we don't want Eriksson* being conceived. Maybe the board listened to Blues fans vocal protests, maybe they didn't… but the writing was on the wall for the Italian anyway.

Despite being nicknamed Tinkerman by the media, a criticism of his penchant for constantly tweaking line-ups and formation, Ranieri was well-respected by the Chelsea crowd for bringing through John Terry from the youth team and signing Frank Lampard.

Excluding the Champions League semi-final debacle in Monaco (20 April 2004 3-1 Hernan Crespo) in which he lost the tactical plot, Ranieri deserved better than what he ultimately got from the Chelsea board and at the conclusion of the Leeds game, as part of the end of season celebrations, Ranieri did a lap of honour and was greeted with a lengthy rendition of *One Ranieri, there's only one Ranieri*.

To digress slightly, for those who made it, the Monaco trip was also memorable (perhaps more so) for a whimsical remix of *In My Liverpool Home*. Originally written in 1962 by Pete McGovern, and a set favourite of Scouse folk group The Spinners, for decades *In My Liverpool Home* had seen its chorus twisted on a multitude of terraces to; *In your Liverpool slums, in your Liverpool slums. You root in the dustbin for something to eat, you find a dead rat and you think it's a treat, in your Liverpool slums.*

In the millionaires' playground of Monte Carlo, this became the altogether more humorous and quasi-ironic; *In your Monaco slums, in your Monaco slums. You root in the dustbins for something to eat, you find a dead lobster, you think it's a treat, in your Monaco slums.*

Fast-forward twelve years to 15 May 2016, and Claudio Ranieri would hear the chant sang in his honour once more at Stamford Bridge. Having guided Leicester City to an unlikely Premier League title triumph, Ranieri was warmly applauded by both sets of fans who chanted his name in unison as he led the Foxes out for the final game of what had been an unbelievable season for both clubs. For once the result (1-1, Cesc Fàbregas) didn't matter as everyone in the stadium acknowledged the Italian's remarkable achievement.

On 7 February 2010, Chelsea beat Arsenal 2-0 at Stamford Bridge in a game which is remembered by those who were there, not for the match itself in which Didier Drogba scored a brace, but the unwavering support afforded to Blues skipper John Terry who, in the wake of allegations that he had an affair with ex-teammate Wayne Bridge's former girlfriend, had been stripped by the national boss Fabio Capello of the England captaincy two days previously.

*One England captain, there's only one England captain* was the defiant chant of the day from the home crowd. Thirteen months later, Capello finally forgave Terry for his perceived misdemeanour and reinstated him as permanent England captain. "A year of punishment is enough," said the Italian.

3 February 2012, and in the wake of the racial abuse incident involving Anton Ferdinand which took place the previous October during a game at Loftus Road between Ferdinand's then club Queens Park Rangers and Chelsea (23 October 1-0), Terry was once more relieved of his duties as skipper of the national side. This time it was the FA who made the decision… and five days later Capello resigned his position as manager.

Terry would subsequently be cleared at Westminster Magistrates Court of the charge pertaining to the Ferdinand case, but believing his position with England had become "untenable" given the FAs decision to pursue the case, in September 2012 he announced his retirement from international football.

Later that month, an FA independent regulatory commission found Terry guilty of "using abusive and/or insulting words and/or behaviour" towards Ferdinand, banned him for four matches and imposed a £220,000 fine. The FA Panel said the Chelsea captain, 31-years of age at time, was "not a racist' but they were "satisfied" his comments were used as an insult. Terry did not appeal the FA decision.

On 25 November 2012, Chelsea drew 0-0 with Manchester City at Stamford Bridge where despite the drab football fare on offer on the pitch, the atmosphere was the most toxic many Blues supporters could remember. The reason? Club legend Roberto Di Matteo had just been sacked as manager and replaced by former Liverpool boss Rafa Benitez.

Di Matteo's place in the pantheon of Chelsea greats had already been secured as a Blues player long before he'd guided the club to FA Cup and Champions League glory in 2012. Yet less than six months after this unique double triumph, the stylish Italian was given his P45. The denizens of the Bridge were livid, not only at his dismissal, but at the appointment of Benitez who in the past had made a couple of incendiary Chelsea-related statements which would come back to haunt him.

Speaking in the midst of the Chelsea / Liverpool Champions League semi-final clash in 2007 (25 April Stamford Bridge, 1-0, Joe Cole; 1 May Anfield, 1-0, penalties 4-1, Frank Lampard), Benitez spouted, "We (Liverpool) don't need to give away flags for our fans to wave… our supporters are always there with their hearts, and that is all we need. It's the passion of the fans that helps to win matches… not flags." This comment proved so popular that Rafa's words were inscribed on a plaque which was mounted on the wall at Liverpool's training ground!

When speaking the same year about his thoughts on taking the manager's job at Stamford Bridge at the time of José Mourinho's initial departure Benitez advised, "Chelsea is a big club with fantastic players, every manager wants to coach a such a big team, but I would never take that job. For me there is only club in England, and that's Liverpool."

When Benitez faced the media for the first time having taken "that job", he could have made life easy for himself with an apology to Chelsea supporters or at least a placatory statement… but he chose not to. As the Spaniard emerged from the tunnel for the Blues / Man City game, he was greeted with boos and the familiar *Guantanamera*-based chant from his days at Liverpool of *Fat Spanish waiter, you're just a fat Spanish waiter* which reverberated around the entire ground as gleeful Man City fans joined with their Chelsea counterparts to taunt the portly interim Blues boss.

In the sixteenth minute of the game, a reference to the shirt number worn by Di Matteo during the course of a glorious career which saw him score in two FA Cup finals (17 May 1997 2-0 v Middlesbrough, 20 May 2000 1-0 v Aston Villa) and a League Cup final (29 March 1998 2-0 v Middlesbrough), the vitriol directed at Benitez stopped to be replaced by a reverential rendition of *One Di Matteo, there's only one Di Matteo*.

The sixteenth minute *One Di Matteo* tradition would continue at every game until the end of the season – as would the abuse of Benitez.

As a footnote, Di Matteo's Wembley final goals against Middlesbrough which contributed to the 2-0 score-lines in both games, also brought about a new chant when Chelsea beat Boro 2-0 at Stamford Bridge (26 September 1998 Gary Pallister own goal, Gianfranco Zola) in the Premier League.

Borrowing the melody from Richard Rodgers and Lorenz Hart's classic 1934 pop song *Blue Moon*, a chart hit notably for The Marcels in 1961, (and also the signature tune of Manchester City), Chelsea supporters came up with the dreamily funny, *2-0, we always win 2-0, we always win 2-0*.

# IS THERE A FIRE DRILL?

**Mark:** The World Cup comes around every four years, and, if the truth is told, given the continually poor showing of the home nations, after they have passed there is little that lives on in the memory of the majority of people who are restricted by circumstance to watch the tournaments on television.

Italia '90 is probably the exception to the rule.

On July 4 1990, Sir Bobby Robson guided England to the semi-finals of the competition where they faced familiar foes West Germany in Turin. 26 million people tuned in to the BBCs coverage and the jingoistic chant *Two World Wars and one World Cup, doo-da, doo-da,* which echoed around many pubs and bars where people had gathered to watch the game were silenced following England's 4-3 penalty shoot-out defeat.

*Two World Wars and one World Cup* which borrows the melody from *Camptown Races* would later be annexed by Chelsea supporters when the Blues faced German opposition in Europe. Notably, for the first time since Italia '90.

On 13 May 1998 in Stockholm, Chelsea played VFB Stuttgart in the European Cup Winners Cup Final. Prior to the game, on the heavily-policed streets of the Swedish capital, Blues fans had kept themselves amused whistling and humming American composer Elmer Bernstein's iconic soundtrack to the World War Two movie *The Great Escape*.

Once in the Råsunda Stadium, bemused Stuttgart fans gathered at the opposite end of the ground were greeted by the sight of thousands of Chelsea supporters, swaying, arms outstretched, imagining they were Royal Air Force 617 Squadron Lancaster bombers humming *The Dam Busters March*.

Adapted from the old American folk song, *She'll Be Coming Round the Mountain*, with its verse and chorus following the arrangement of *Ten Green Bottles*, *Ten German Bombers* is right up there with the aforementioned tunes when it comes to reminding the German people about the unwanted legacy bequeathed them by the militaristic ambitions of their bellicose ancestors.

*There were ten German bombers in the air.*
*There were ten German bombers in the air.*

*There were ten German bombers, ten German bombers, ten German bombers in the air…*
*And the RAF from Chelsea shot them down, and the RAF from Chelsea shot them down.*
*And the RAF from Chelsea, RAF from Chelsea, RAF from Chelsea shot them down.*

The chant, with some of its singers brandishing authentic-looking (very authentic after a gallon of Swedish lager) inflatable Spitfire fighter planes continued shooting down German bombers until there were none left.

**Walter:** *She'll Be Coming Round the Mountain* was also borrowed for a little ditty in honour of Jimmy Floyd Hasselbaink, Eidur Gudjonhsen, Mikael Forssell and Gianfranco Zola who scored the only goal of the game in Stockholm.

*IIIIIIIIf Jimmy doesn't getcha Eidur will, if Jimmy doesn't getcha Eidur will, if Jimmy doesn't getcha, Jimmy doesn't getcha, Jimmy doesn't getcha Eidur will. IIIIIIIIf Eidur doesn't getcha Forssell will, if Eidur doesn't getcha Forssell will, if Eidur doesn't getcha, Eidur doesn't getcha, Eidur doesn't getcha Forrsell will. IIIIIIIIf Forssell doesn't getcha Zola will, if Forssell doesn't getcha Zola will, if Forssell doesn't getcha, Forssell doesn't getcha, Forssell doesn't getcha Zola will!* Followed by the classic Chelsea rework of Frankie Valli's 1967 hit *Can't Take My Eyes Off You*: *Gianfran-co Zola, la la la la la la, Gianfranco Zola, la la la la la la…*. Genius!

**Mark:** And another *She'll Be Coming Round the Mountain*-themed banger worth adding in here is the classic… *we're the only team in London with the European Cup, we're the only team in London with the European Cup. We're the only team in London, only team in London, only team in London with the European Cup!* Long may it be sung every time we play rival London clubs!

***Editor's note:*** *Who remembers when George Graham was linked with the vacant Chelsea manager's job not once but twice during the Ken Bates era? Firstly, towards the end of the 1995/96 season when Glenn Hoddle announced he would be leaving his post as Blues gaffer to take up the England job, and secondly after Gianluca Vialli was sacked (12 September 2000).*

*Despite his credentials as a former Chelsea player, Graham had made a name for himself as a player and manager with Arsenal winning trophies galore before getting sacked in 1995 and banned from football for a year for taking a bung. When Hoddle left, Blues fans didn't want him anywhere near the Bridge and* She'll Be Coming Round the Mountain *became* You can stick George Graham up your arse – sideways! *The song was reprised when Vialli was sacked. At that time Graham had* worked his way back into the game via Leeds and Tottenham. It would have been a disaster!

**Walter:** Frankie Valli's *Can't Take My Eyes Off You* / *Gianfranco Zola* song reminds me of a version concocted for Steven Sidwell. I've got to be honest, I thought Sidwell was going to be our next midfield general. His song was even more disappointing than his Chelsea career:

*Oh Stevie Sidwell, you are the love of my life,*
*Oh Stevie Sidwell, I'll let you sh\*g my wife,*
*Oh Stevie Sidwell, I want ginger hair too.*

**Mark:** I still haven't got over the fact Chelsea gave Sidwell the No. 9 shirt. That said, before Sidders it was worn by Khalid Boulahrouz. A more memorable *I'll let you sh\*g my wife* version of *Can't Take My Eyes Off You* was rinsed in honour of David Luiz… particularly during his first stint at the Bridge.

*Oh David Luiz, you are the love of my life,*
*Oh David Luiz, I'll let you sh\*g my wife,*
*Oh David Luiz, I want curly hair too.*

I bought a job lot of brownish ginger wigs to sell on the *cfcuk* stall and there were plenty of takers. Blackpool away on a bitterly cold Monday night (7 March 2011, Blackpool 1 Chelsea 3, John Terry, Frank Lampard x2) went down in history as the night of the wigs. For the baldies among us they provided the means we needed to keep our bonces warm.

*****

Unlike England, who since the fabled 1966 World Cup final triumph have an endured little more than misery against West and the later unified Germany international team, at club level, Chelsea's record against teams from Deutschland is impressive.

Stuttgart were beaten 1-0 (Gianfranco Zola) to bring the Cup Winners Cup trophy back to Stamford Bridge for a second time, and in numerous Champions League encounters that followed, most famously the 2012 final against Bayern Munich, the Blues have come out on top.

To compound the difference between club and country, victory over Bayern came not only in the German club's stadium, but via a penalty shoot-out.

Returning to Italia '90, while penalty miscreants Stuart Pearce and Chris Waddle would go on to feature in a curious Pizza Hut advert six years later which starred another England failure from twelve yards, current national team manager Gareth Southgate (Euro '96, 26 June, semi-final penalty shoot-out loss at Wembley v Germany... again), it was the antics of Paul Gascoigne and Gary Lineker in the Turin semi that have truly stood the test of time.

Gascoigne, who'd already received a yellow card in the preceding game with Belgium, was booked for a foul on Thomas Berthold. Realising he would be suspended for the final should England beat Germany, Gazza's eyes welled up with tears. Lineker, stood nearby, looked at his teammate and turned to the bench pointing at his own eyes while mouthing words of advice to boss Bobby Robson. At the time it appeared he was making a comment about Gascoigne crying, but the England striker subsequently said he was telling his manager to keep an eye on Gazza because of the midfielder's fragile temperament.

Countless highlights that followed set the incident to music, and it was Italian operatic superstar Luciano Pavarotti's emotional and spine-tingling rendition of the aria *Nessun Dorma* which the BBC had chosen as its theme tune for their coverage of Italia '90 that accompanied footage of Gazza's tears.

Grown men wept in shared sorrow, and the nation's women-folk flocked to record shops to buy Pavarotti's single version of *Nessun Dorma* which spent three weeks at No. 2 in the charts (kept off the top slot by the Elton John double-A-side *Sacrifice / Healing Hands*).

On the eve of the World Cup Final on 7 July 1990, in which Germany would defeat Argentina 1-0, Pavarotti as part of the Three Tenors ensemble that also comprised Spaniards' Plácido Domingo and José Carreras, sang *Nessun Dorma* at a concert held at the Baths of Caracalla in Rome.

A recording of the concert would go on to become the biggest selling classical music record of all time. Pavarotti, Domingo and Carreras had found a new audience who weren't wholly interested in full renditions of operas, just the best tunes. Listening to the three acts of Giacomo Puccini's *Turandot* would take 240 minutes, whereas *Nessun Dorma* that nestles in Act III lasts just over three minutes.

The Three Tenors association with the World Cup would continue to USA '94 and France '98.

## CAREFREE! CHELSEA CHANTS AND TERRACE CULTURE

16 July 1994 – on the eve of the Brazil v Italy final of the US tournament, Pavarotti, Domingo and Carreras Opera's staged a concert at the Los Angeles Dodgers Stadium which was beamed live around the globe and watched by an estimated television audience of over one billion! The next day, double that number of people tuned in for the final... a disappointing affair that ended 0-0 after extra time and saw Brazil triumph 3-2 on penalties.

The July final was already long forgotten by the time a live recording of The Three Tenors concert at the Dodgers Stadium stormed to the top of the UK long player charts in September. The penultimate track on the album *La Donna e Mobile* would eventually inspire Chelsea supporters to chant their once reverential support of José Mourinho, but it is the adaptability of the melody that has produced some laugh-out-loud versions that have kept the Stamford Bridge faithful entertained down the years.

The 1996/97 season provided my first real recollection of 'banter' between opposing fans featuring *La Donna e Mobile* when Chelsea played Middlesbrough.

21 August 1996, and the first meeting of the campaign between the two sides took place at Stamford Bridge and there was an Italian flavour to the game which was perfectly suited to *La Donna e Mobile*. Two strikers who just three months previously had won the Champions League with Juventus found themselves in opposition and in the spotlight.

For Chelsea, free transfer bargain Gianluca Vialli was making his home debut while Boro featured £7 million record signing Fabrizio Ravanelli in their starting XI.

*We've got Fabrizio, you've got f\*ck allio,* chanted the travelling Teesiders in the glorious evening sunshine. It was hilarious. Blues supporters had the last laugh though. Chelsea won 1-0 courtesy of another Italian also making his home debut, Roberto Di Matteo. A record signing at £4.9 million from Lazio, Di Matteo immediately endeared himself to Blues fans by rifling home a late winner.

*D.I. MATTEO, D.I. MATTEO* sang Blues fans with a hastily concocted though imaginative vocal tribute to the Italian which reworked Ottawan's 1980 chart hit *D.I.S.C.O.*

Chant-wise, Vialli's time would come soon enough. On 2 November 1996, Chelsea beat Manchester United 2-1 at Old Trafford. Michael

Duberry nodded in a Dennis Wise header to open the scoring in the 31st minute, and Vialli put the game beyond United firing the ball through Red Devils' keeper Peter Schmeichel's legs shortly after the hour mark.

Shortly after a fabulous chant based on Dean Martin's 1953 Italian-influenced hit record *That's Amore*.

*When the ball hits the back of the Old Trafford net, that's Vialli.*
*When his goals light the sky there's a tear in his eye, oh Vialli.*

An alternative second line is occasionally sung, *he nutmegged the Dane, and poor Fergie's in pain, it's Vialli.*

Vialli's ability to cause Manchester United grief didn't stop as a Chelsea player. As manager at Stamford Bridge the Italian masterminded one of the most emphatic Blues victories over the Red Devils in recent history.

It was a brilliant day out on 3 October 1999 – Super Chelsea obliterated United 5-0 (Gustavo Poyet x2, Chris Sutton, Henning Berg own goal, Jody Morris) with visitors' keeper Massimo Taibi enduring a traumatic afternoon. Statistically, it wasn't exactly correct, but the rib-tickling version of *Camptown Races* that the Chelsea choir came up with is still occasionally reprised today.

*Who put the ball in the Man U net? Half a, Half a.*
*Who put the ball in the Man U net?*
*Half a f\*cking Chelsea.*

Exiting Stamford Bridge after the game, Blues supporters bounced down the Fulham Road to the *Hold Tight*-influenced *One, two. One, two, three. One, two, three, four – five nil!*

*****

**Mark:** While Stamford Bridge underwent a phase of renovation in the mid '90s when recommendations of the Taylor Report resulted in all-seater stadia becoming mandatory in the Premier League, in August 1995 Middlesbrough went the whole hog abandoning Ayresome Park for a new purpose-built home the Riverside Stadium. On 26 August 1995, Chelsea had been the first team to play Middlesbrough at their new Riverside ground, losing 2-0. I wasn't at the game, but the following season (26 March 1997) I travelled up to Teeside to watch the Blues lose to a Juninho goal and remember being impressed by the ground and the facilities.

## CAREFREE! CHELSEA CHANTS AND TERRACE CULTURE

The Riverside was the first brand new purpose-built stadium in the English top-flight and a crowd of 29,811, not far off the capacity of 30,000, made for a good atmosphere, better than anything I ever remember at Ayresome Park though self-preservation was more the order of the day than singing at Boro's old ground.

Statistically, The Riverside may have been pretty much sold out, but it didn't look that way… maybe the bean counters massaged the actual attendance figure like they seem to do for some ill-attended Champions League group stage games at Stamford Bridge.

Ten minutes after the game started, a wily Blues wag started singing *Your ground's too big for you* in *La Donna e Mobile* fashion. I cried with laughter and everyone joined in. The chant has gone on to become a staple part of all travelling football choirs' repertoires when they rock up at new venues.

Supporters of Arsenal, Manchester City, Sunderland, Derby County, Southampton, Coventry City, Leicester City, Brighton and Hove Albion, Bolton Wanderers, Stoke City, Hull City, Reading, Swansea City and perhaps most appropriately of all Wigan Athletic have all been vociferously advised by Chelsea supporters that their new grounds are too big for them… and no doubt once Stamford Bridge is rebuilt into a 60,000 capacity stadium, Blues fans can expect the same ironic treatment.

*Your ground's too big for you* is often sang in jest, but the highly amusing variation with the same melody it spawned is usually no laughing matter for opposing fans. Thanks to Roman Abramovich's Roubles, Chelsea began to enjoy a period of dominance in the English game that saw the team suddenly become capable of meting out thrashings of such magnitude that supporters of the teams on the receiving end would leave Stamford Bridge or worst still their own ground early rather than stay to the bitter end. As Chelsea goals went in one after another, opposition seats would empty and the fantastic chant *Is there a fire drill?* would echo around the stadium.

While emphatic home victories over the likes of Sunderland (16 January 2010, 7-2, Nicolas Anelka x2, Florent Malouda, Ashley Cole, Frank Lampard x2, Michael Ballack), Aston Villa (27 March 2010, 7-1, Frank Lampard x4, Florent Malouda x2, Salomon Kalou and 23 December 2012\* 8-0, Fernando Torres, David Luiz, Branislav Ivanović, Frank Lampard, Ramires x2, Oscar, Eden Hazard), Stoke City (25 April 2010 7-0 Salomon Kalou x3, Frank Lampard x2, Daniel Sturridge, Florent Malouda) and Wigan Athletic\*\*, had the desired effect… there was a flat track bully aspect to beating these teams at home by seven or eight goals – and, besides they hadn't sold out their respective allocations meaning the *fire drill* looked as if it had already started.

\* The timing of the 8-0 trouncing of Villa, coming as it did during the festive period, also brought with it the fantastically imaginative and off the cuff *Guantanamera*-inspired *Gone Christmas shopping, you should have gone Christmas shopping*.

\*\* 9 May 2010 It's fair to say that when Chelsea thrashed Wigan 8-0 (Nicolas Anelka x2, Frank Lampard, Salomon Kalou, Didier Drogba x3, Ashley Cole) at the Bridge in the last game of title-winning 2009/2010 Premier League season, the *fire drill* didn't really get going until Drogba completed his hattrick in the 80th minute as Latics fans housed in The Shed appeared to be voyeuristically rooted to their seats while Carlo Ancelotti's men but on a display of total football.

Ancelotti was less than a week away from masterminding an historic Double as Chelsea would go on to beat Portsmouth 1-0 (Didier Drogba) in the FA Cup Final.

Despite being on the receiving end of a serious drubbing, Wigan lived to fight another day in the top-flight… but their season was over. A hasty re-work of the *fire drill* chant resulted in the gem *You're going on holiday, we're going to Wembley*.

\*\*\*\*\*

It was a teatime Saturday kick-off on 5 March 2005 at Carrow Road for a Premier League game between Norwich City and Chelsea, (1-3, Joe Cole, Mateja Kezman, Ricardo Carvalho), meaning that both sets of fans had extra time in the pubs to come up with imaginative chants and the results were exceptional.

*You're not Chelsea anymore*, taunted Canaries followers, a barb related to the money Abramovich had poured into the Stamford Bridge coffers since his arrival.

*We've got Abramovich, you've got a drunken bitch* was the humorous *La Donna e Mobile*-inspired response, germinated by Norwich director, celebrity chef Delia Smith's drunken "where are you? Let's be having you" half-time outburst in a previous televised game with Manchester City. *We've got a super cook, you've got a Russian crook* was the witty reply using the same melody which was batted back with *One Gordon Ramsay, there's only one Gordon*

## CAREFREE! CHELSEA CHANTS AND TERRACE CULTURE

*Ramsay.*

The time-honoured Norfolk remix of the Adams Family theme was also served up by Blues fans to tease the home crowd.

*Your sister is your mother, your father is your brother, you all sh\*g one another, the Norwich family.*

On the pitch, as expected, Chelsea had the final word. And when Carvalho made sure of all three points for Mourinho's men putting the visitors 3-1 up with ten minutes left, the home fans opted to beat the rush home. Cue... *Is there a fire drill?*

*Guantanamera*-themed, culinary-inspired chant again targeted at Delia... *Down with the soufflé, you're going down with the soufflé* also raised a chuckle... and Norwich were indeed relegated at the end of the campaign.

\*\*\*\*\*

Embarrassing West Ham at the Boleyn Ground became a regular thing once former Hammer Frank Lampard had made the switch to Chelsea. Abramovich's arrival at the Bridge ensured further funds were available to plunder the Upton Park academy of its brightest graduates as Glen Johnson and Joe Cole joined Lampard at the Bridge.

*West Ham's our feeder club, West Ham's our feeder club,* teased Chelsea fans on their visits to East London, retaining the *La Donna* melody and then switching the words to; *Is there a fire drill* as the goals went in.

2 January 2006 1-3, Frank Lampard, Hernan Crespo, Didier Drogba; 18 April 2007 1-4, Shaun Wright Philips x2, Salamon Kalou, Didier Drogba; 1 March 2008 0-4, Frank Lampard, Joe Cole, Michael Ballack, Ashley Cole; 11 September 2010 1-3, Michael Essien x2, Salomon Kalou; 23 November 2013 0-3, Frank Lampard x2, Oscar; Fire drills at the Boleyn became a regular occurrence... but are now also a thing of the past. The start of the 2016/17 season saw West Ham move take up tenancy at the former Olympic Stadium in Stratford. The 60,000 seater stadium presents a fantastic opportunity for a *fire drill* unlike any ever seen at the Boleyn... watch this space in future editions of *Carefree!*

\*\*\*\*\*

Three most effective stadium 'evacuations' ever initiated by Chelsea merit closing your eyes and imagining what it would have been like had Pavarotti in his finest hour stood among Blues supporters belting out; *Is there a fire drill? Is there a fire drill?*

For older fans who grew up in an era when a Chelsea victory over Arsenal was a scarce occurrence, recent results have more than made up for what went before. Memories of Gunners' long-term manager Arsene Wenger gesticulating in angst on the touchline as he watches his team capitulate while their supporters leave the stadium en masse will never fade and are always guaranteed to raise a smile.

Go on Luciano my son, sing it loud; *Is there a fire drill? Is there a fire drill?*

29 November 2009 Emirates Stadium: Chelsea's vociferous travelling supporters were singing in the rain which belted down in torrents from a heavy leaden sky throughout this Sunday afternoon encounter in London N5.

A Didier Drogba brace bisected by a Thomas Vermaelen own goal earned the Ivorian man-of-the-match plaudits from the media following the Blues easy 3-0 win.

Fittingly, it was former Arsenal defender Ashley Cole, having spent much of the game being abused by the home crowd, who teed up Drogba for his first goal and supplied the cross that Vermaelen deflected into his own net.

2-0 down at half-time, the Emirates began to empty midway through the second period as Arsenal failed to cope with the tempo of Carlo Ancelotti's side, and the *fire drill* was completed when Drogba lashed home a late free-kick.

Consolation for officials of the home club came from the knowledge that their wonderful still-new 60,000 capacity stadium could be evacuated so swiftly during a game.

With the *fire drill* complete, and only Chelsea fans and the most masochistic Gunners followers remaining in the Emirates, the chant *They're here, they're there, they're every f\*cking where, empty seats, empty seats* which insanely borrows the melody from Scouting favourite *Quartermaster's Store* compounded Arsenal's misery.

Like *Guantanamera*, *Quartermaster's Store* which was previously adapted for

## CAREFREE! CHELSEA CHANTS AND TERRACE CULTURE

Chelsea cult heroes Frank Leboeuf and Joe Cole so they could be *here, there and every f\*cking where* (or *we're not allowed to swear* as the ironic polite version went), and those who *were there* when (Colin) *Pates went up, to lift the* (Full) *Members Cup* (23 March 1986) and (Dennis) *Wise* (17 May 1997, 20 May 2000) and *John* (Terry... 19 May 2007, 30 May 2009, 15 May 2010, 5 May 2012) *went up, to lift the FA Cup*, was brought to more mainstream attention via American folk musician Pete Seeger... a remarkable legacy all things considered.

Back to Luciano's fabulous *fire drill*.

Wenger's 1000th game in charge of Arsenal was on 22 March 2014 at Stamford Bridge. What could possibly go wrong for the Frenchman who had recently been labelled a 'specialist in failure' by his nemesis, Blues boss José Mourinho? Everything as it transpired.

Noisy Gunners' fans who had taken up their full allocation of tickets in The Shed for this early kick off were muted as early as the fifth minute when Samuel Eto'o gave Chelsea an early lead which was doubled a couple of minutes later by André Schürrle.

Shortly after, referee Andre Marriner farcically sent off Arsenal defender Kieran Gibbs for a handball committed by his teammate Alex Oxlade-Chamberlain. Eden Hazard converted the resultant penalty to put the Blues 3-0 up with just 17 minutes played.

The horror-show was too much for many Gunners fans who headed for the exits with the strains of; *Is there a fire drill?* ringing in their ears. More left at half-time following Oscar's goal just before the interval... and those that remained to see the Brazilian make it 5-0 did so mainly to taunt their own manager with chants of; *Sacked in the morning*.

When Oscar's replacement Mo Salah completed the 6-0 rout, the number of Arsenal fans still in the Bridge could be counted swiftly by hand. With the day's *fire drill* successfully completed, gleeful Chelsea supporters turned their attentions to mock Wenger with chants of *Specialist in failure you know what you are* and *Arsene Wenger, we want you to stay* sung to the melody of *Sloop John B* by the Beach Boys a ditty also responsible for *Champions of England* (*Europe* when the mood takes us) *we know what we are*.

And finally Luciano, will you sing an encore? Why not save the best till last.

*Is there a fire drill? Is there a fire drill?*

Wembley Stadium on 15 April 2012. 85,731 spectators gathered for an FA Cup semi-final between Chelsea and Tottenham Hotspur. The Blues had been through the wringer with mid-season managerial change seeing André Villas-Boas sacked and replaced by his already legendary assistant… the fabled Roberto Di Matteo.

Expectations going into the game were mixed. Yes it was Spurs, a side Chelsea had regularly bossed for a couple of decades… but the Lilywhites were going well under popular gaffer Harry Redknapp who was being touted as the next England boss.

When Didier Drogba gave Chelsea the lead just before half-time, there was no inkling of what was to happen in the second period. Jocularity followed Juan Mata's 49th minute ghost goal that referee Martin Atkinson deemed had crossed the Tottenham goal line but clearly hadn't. Spurs fans cursed. A polite translation of their wrath suggested that Atkinson should visit Specsavers for an eye test. Where he might find fellow ref Andre Marriner!

Gareth Bale pulled a goal back for Spurs, but Chelsea were always in the driving seat. When Ramires made it 3-1 in the 77th minute, Lilywhites fans started leaving and the *fire drill* chants started… and grew louder four minutes later when Frank Lampard made it 4-1.

The punishment didn't stop there as Florent Malouda compounded Tottenham's misery by completing the rout with an injury time goal. 5-1 to Chelsea. Another effective fire drill had seen the safe evacuation of over 30,000 Spurs fans many of whom were probably almost home by the time Malouda scored.

Blues supporters of course returned to Wembley the following month to see Chelsea triumph over Liverpool in the final, (5 May, Chelsea 2 Liverpool 1, Ramires, Didier Drogba), as for affable 'Arry Redknapp, his dreams of managing England were left in tatters… and worse was to follow as he was sacked by Tottenham at the end of the season.

There is no doubt that Ramires and his Brazilian countryman David Luiz would have enjoyed the grand sense of occasion thrashing Redknapp's men at Wembley, and it's highly likely they would have reported back to their friends and family at home how Chelsea played *samba-style-soccer* too beautiful to behold for Spurs fans.

## CAREFREE! CHELSEA CHANTS AND TERRACE CULTURE

Little did the boys from Brazil know that the pendulum of fortune would swing brutally the other way just over two years later.

The date was 8 July 2014 and the venue was the Estádio Mineirão, Belo Horizonte. Host nation Brazil 'entertained' Germany in the semi-finals of the World Cup. There was a strong Chelsea flavour to the game with the Seleção managed by former boss Luiz Felipe Scolari, captained by David Luiz and featuring ex Blues Oscar in their starting XI and Ramires on the bench playing a Germany side able to call on super-sub André Schürrle.

Flamboyant central defender Luiz, a huge favourite with the Stamford Bridge crowd, had just been sold by Chelsea for a phenomenal £50 million to Paris Saint-Germain… a move that had incensed many Blues fans still annoyed by then manager José Mourinho's decision to sell former player-of-the-year Juan Mata to Manchester United.

Unfortunately, Luiz had a shocker as Germany took Brazil to the Belo Horizonte branch of Sketchleys, thrashing the hosts 7-1. Schürrle bagged a brace for Germany while Oscar got Brazil's consolation goal. Such was Germany's dominance they were 5-0 ahead inside 30 minutes, a feat that sparked a mass exodus of tearful Seleção supporters. As the seats emptied in the Estadio Mineirao, German fans swapped their *Deutschland, Deutschland über alles* chant for *Gibt es eine Brandschutzübung…* which in English apparently means; *Is there a fire drill?*

Scolari would later lose his job as a result of the humiliation, and few Chelsea supporters would ever question again the merits of selling David Luiz again although there would be a brief flashback when he returned to Stamford Bridge in 2016. Thankfully, Luiz had laid the ghost of Belo Horizonte to rest and he played an outstanding role in the Blues side that went on to win the Premier League title under Antonio Conte a year later.

# CHANGE

**Mark:** The shared experience of watching football has changed significantly from the early days when Chelsea supporters first developed an identity. Plenty of older fans will testify that events that brought about all-seater stadia and the advent of live television and its effect on kick-off times have neutered the atmosphere at games and alienated many to the point of giving up.

Having followed Chelsea through the major shifts that have occurred in football from the mid-60s to the mid-90s, Champagne Les was well-placed to describe to Walter how change had affected him personally.

**Champagne Les:** "League Football was always on a Saturday and a Wednesday. I hate the rearranged kick-off times and the early starts. Us supporters – well, we'll do what they tell us to do because they know we'll always travel. But no-one I know really likes it. It's taking the mick, and it's all because of money. Clubs wouldn't survive without us fans – look at the *Save the Bridge* campaign. (This was founded by Ken Bates in April 1987 to try and raise £15 million in two years to buy the freehold of Stamford Bridge which in 1984 had been sold by David and Brian Mears to Marler Estates plc, later owned by Cabra Estates plc.) Every match I put my hands in my pocket to save the Club. Now the Club take money from SKY and on Sunday it is a 13:30 kick off up at Burnley. It's bad. It's not fair. I should be having Sunday lunch with my family. I also hate no replays in the League Cup!

In regard to the ground redevelopments over the decades – well, I started in The Shed. My mates and I would always meet by the second pole holding The Shed up. If I was in a rush, I'd be coming from Fulham Broadway and go in the Bovril Entrance, and make my way across The Shed to the second pole. If I was on time, I'd go in the main entrance.

When the East Stand was built, we got season tickets in there. They were about fifty quid each, I think. I was in in the lower tier, Gate 13 – and you'd always get a main bulk of chanting in there. I think it was about 1976/77 that we went over to the benches. The Eddie McCreadie era.

Then it was maybe 1981/82 that we left the benches and got seats in the West Stand. We stayed there from right up to 1996/97 before the West Stand was demolished. Some of us managed to take the wooden backs off our seats with the number on – yes, I've still got mine! I've been in the

## CAREFREE! CHELSEA CHANTS AND TERRACE CULTURE

Matthew Harding Upper ever since. That's just reminded me – I was sent an invitation from Ken Bates to go to the opening of the Matthew Harding. I was one of about twenty season ticket holders who were invited. We had a champagne reception, a meal and a Q&A with Mr Bates – his gesture really made me feel a part of the club.

Charlie Cooke remains my favourite player of all time. He was a wizard with a football. He was a dream. I only saw Stanley Matthews at the end of his career so I can't really compare – but Charlie Cooke had everything. I loved him. I took so much pleasure watching him. My song for Charlie Cooke didn't take off like the others. I saw Osgood's first game against Workington in 1964. We had Tambling and Hudson was young and local – me and my mates were all the same age, so we really associated and connecting with them.

I really do believe that Chelsea fans are unique with their sense of humour. I've seen current affairs, pop music and politics all influence and affect songs – and some of them are very clever. Even last night on the TV, I was watching the FA Cup replay between Leicester and Derby – the Derby lot were all singing all our songs with their own twists! Our songs. They had a *Magic Hat* version – Keef hates that song, but I don't mind it.

I couldn't go to Athens in 1971 for the European Cup Winners Cup Final. I was a young married man with a little baby, struggling financially. Football matches like that had to become secondary because of responsibilities and finances. I couldn't afford or justify going to Athens when I've got food to buy and bills to pay. I've been so lucky since, mate – I've been to all the finals. Every League Cup, every FA Cup – all of them. I've been to forty different European away games – others have done much, much more than that, but I'm proud of all the places I've been and gone.

I could talk about *every* season and I'd bore you silly. You haven't got enough paper to write it on, son! There's been lots of ups and downs and journeys and stories.

Firstly, there are people I met when I was working in Grantham still come down for a drink at home games. They really are my Chelsea family. I've got the loveliest friends.

Secondly, right, there's Airport Peter. (He works at the airport!) I met him about, I dunno, a decade or more ago through Keef because Peter is on the away scheme, same as I've always been.

Thirdly, there is Martin and Mick. When I left the old West Stand and went up to the new Harding Upper (1997/98) I'm sitting beside Martin and Mick. They are now great, great friends. I know their family – their wives and their kids and they all know my Val. It's a great family – all because of Chelsea Football Club. Ha, that reminds me, I can't leave out Winnie.

Steve 'Winnie' Winters and me go back all the way. Ah, for example on 1976/77 Chelsea are vying with Bolton Wanderers for top spot. (26 February 1977, Bolton Wanderers 2 Chelsea 2, Steve Finnieston, Kenny Swain.) We get up to Burnden Park on the train and we go in the away end, but it's full of Bolton! Chelsea had already taken the Bolton end. So, in a roundabout way, we'd gone in the wrong end! So, we go to the bottom of the terraces and Keef and Winnie climb the wall and jump off the terrace onto the pitch. But there's like a big moat if you like, and I'm standing on the wall and Winnie and Keef had got across but I'm still standing there! I distinctly remember that the players weren't on the field yet. I'm still up on the wall, I need to jump and get over this moat! Then this copper appears and pointed a stick at me. I try telling him that I'm Chelsea but anyway, I jumped and I swerved him and I ran up the other end with my pals. A few other Chelsea done the same thing. All the stands around the ground booed us – I can remember the booing! They thought we were trying to have a row. But we were simply legging it to the Chelsea end who were in the Bolton end. Winnie says to me, even to this day – "You – standing on that wall!" – and I can still see myself needing to jump!

That match at Hull that Keith mentioned previously, that was an FA Cup replay – Keith's right, we were banned and no tickets and Mickey G sells us some in the pub. The other thing about the game was somehow we're in the ground and we see a door saying PLAYERS LOUNGE and one of us pushed it, and it opened. We walked in, got three beers and sat down. The Chelsea players who weren't playing were in there – Graham Wilkins and Ian Britton signed our programmes. As has already been described, we beat Hull 2-0 and drew Wrexham in the fourth round. (23 January 1982, Chelsea 0 Wrexham 0) That went to two replays! (First replay: 26 January, Wrexham 1 Chelsea 1, Alan Mayes.)

We were still banned from away games, but we went of course and eventually we won the second replay which was also played at the Racecourse Ground. (1 February, Wrexham 1 Chelsea 2, Alan Mayes, Micky Droy.) Keith knew a local MP and he got us signed into the Working Man's Club and we got tickets in there for the game! So, as you can see. I'm so very lucky to have a variety of wonderful, different people from all walks of life that come together – that's what it means to me – my family."

## CAREFREE! CHELSEA CHANTS AND TERRACE CULTURE

Walter prompted Les again about memories of Mickey Greenaway and his renditions of *Zigger Zagger*. Les sighs, and smiles.

**Les:** "Yeah, of course I knew Mickey. I remember one time in The Shed, he was taken out with a badly cut head. Like me, he wasn't a brawler. He came back in with a bandage on his head singing *Zigger Zagger* which caused a big laugh and a cheer.

So much has changed, but that's life.

The pubs have changed, as well. Back in the early days, the pubs would remain like the fans remain. Of course, it's obvious to say it, but the Cock on North End Road was only a few doors away from the Church Hall and Youth Club, so we all drank in there until the lads I grew with up with were getting married and moving away.

Then I started to drink in the Britannia for many, many years until that changed. Over the last twenty years I've had to move pubs regularly. Wheatsheaf, George, Princess Royal (Tommy Tucker), Rose & Crown on Parsons Green – more of a restaurant now. Then the Mitre didn't want us anymore. Now Keef has a reserved table for us at the Malt House. The Guv'nor there told me that Chelsea fans keep him going and he doesn't know what to do when we go to Wembley while the Bridge is redeveloped.

The football world changed again with our all-seater stadia. From a TV perspective – everyone wanted a piece of the action! Look at the world it opened up. Firstly, it's a good thing – sharing cultures, respecting cultures – it's good. But is it too much? If everyone has a slice of cake – what's left for you?

In some respects, the regular supporters have been taken over and pushed out. We should share Chelsea, but we shouldn't give it away – and I think the Board over the years have done that. The local boys and girls in and around South London and West London should be coming to Chelsea, but the reality is the rich tourists from not just Europe, but the world, come to London for a football match on an inflated ticket price. It's happening in our away ends, too. Regulars can't get tickets and you've got a group of tourists at Anfield or Old Trafford in our away section. Madness!

It looks like we'll play at Wembley while the Bridge is redeveloped. After Wembley, my favourite drinking places won't be as they were. Change happens. I don't like change. We have to deal with it because it's what happens.

I love the FA Cup and the FA Cup draw. We used to listen to the radio at school to hear the draw! I had to accept change when it became three points for a win instead of two points – we got used to it. When the goalkeepers couldn't pick up a back pass – I got used to it. The League Cup format changed – I got used to it. The Shed was demolished, Bates built a Hotel – I got used to it. The West Stand was redeveloped – I got used to it. Saturday 3pm kick offs are a rarity these days. It's a terrible thing. However, I repeat – change happens. We have to deal with it because it's what happens."

# ONLY A POUND

**Mark:** Football fanzines form an integral part of many supporters' matchday experience. From a Chelsea perspective no one is better placed to explain their role in football culture than David Johnstone, founder and editor long-running Blues fanzine *cfcuk*.

My interview with David concludes the old-school section of *Carefree!* and forms a bridge with the modern era which Walter focuses on

**Mark:** "Football fanzines first came to national prominence in the mid 1980s with the emergence of *When Saturday Comes*, what are your recollections?"

**David:** "Like most young football fans, I'd grown up with *Shoot!*, *Goal*, *Match* and the like and of course, the back pages of the newspapers but the arrival of *When Saturday Comes* made me aware that there that the people writing about the football were also embracing the 'culture' of those who went to the games.

The late '70s punk explosion had opened the doors to many, particularly those aspiring 'alternative' musicians and writers. Many involved in the punk fanzine scene went on careers in the mainstream media and it has been the same with football fanzines. Some involved in the *Chelsea Independent* fanzine went on the to write for club newspaper *Onside* whilst another who wrote for the 'Indie' is world renowned author John King who, of course, wrote *The Football Factory*.

By the late 1980s, there had been a demise of the music fanzine scene but the football fanzine had grown massively with those involved in the publication and sale were writing articles expressing their particular thoughts on not only the football but also the way in which their club was being run, often openly opposing the person of people who owned the club that they supported, the culture of their own clubs and that of 'the terraces'.

Football and popular music have never been far apart in the lives of many and reports on bands associated with a particular team were featured."

**Mark:** "There were a number of now defunct fanzines associated specifically with Chelsea, the *Chelsea Independent* and *Red Card* being the main ones that older supporters will remember. Tell us about these publications and any others that resonated with you."

**David:** "*Red Card* and *The Chelsea Independent* were established at roughly the same time in 1988 with the latter being the voice-piece for the Chelsea Supporters Association (CISA), the then newly founded supporters organisation whose aim was to improve 'the lot' of those who followed the Chelsea Football Club.

Both were published with a view to holding the club to account over issues that supporters weren't happy with. Whilst both often took a somewhat satirical stance on many topics, the Independent was considered the more 'serious' of the two. Initially, those writing the *Chelsea Independent* got on well with Bates but, comparatively quickly, the relationship deteriorated with CISA eventually publicly opposing him and aligned themselves with Matthew Harding.

There have been a few others over the years... *The Chelsea Historian* was one I enjoyed although only a few issues were published and another was (the first) *Carefree*, edited by Nick Brown and Jim Ross. Unfortunately for them, they were forced to stop publishing after a 'fall-out' with a certain football club owner...

Alan Collis brought out another 'mini' fanzine entitled *Weststanders* with had a particularly satirical slant, which proved popular with some of the older 'old-school' Chelsea supporters."

**Mark:** "What motivated you to publish your own fanzine *Matthew Harding's Blue and White Army*?"

**David:** "I became 'involved' with the *Chelsea Independent* by way of helping to sell it on the Fulham Road before home matches from their stall outside the 'Lost Theatre' which was located where the Fulham Broadway Methodist Church (next to the entrance to the Fulham Broadway Centre car park) stands.

When Chelsea author Mark Meehan took over as the *Independent*'s editor, he gave me the chance to write for it. Although I'd previously written articles for several music magazines, it was the first time I'd put 'pen to paper' to write anything related to Chelsea. I wrote about trying to blag one of Steve Clarke's playing shirts to wear to a recording of *Fantasy Football* hosted of course by David Baddiel and Frank Skinner.

Sometime later, Mark compiled a *Best of the Chelsea Independent* book and I was flattered to see that he'd included my article. Having submitted that first article to Mark, he then offered me a regular column in the fanzine, one that still features today in *cfcuk*.

For various reasons, those individuals who'd been the mainstay of CISA establishing themselves as a credible organisation were no longer involved and the Chelsea Independent Supporters' Association began to implode, whilst the fanzine was, sadly in decline.

Along with several others, I decided to try to keep the 'fight' with Bates going and, as a result, in 1999, the first edition of *Matthew Harding's Blue And White Army* was published."

**Mark:** "Why did you change the title to *cfcuk*?"

**David:** "I chose the name *Matthew Harding's Blue And White Army* primarily in order to honour the memory of Matthew Harding but also to (hopefully) agitate Ken Bates, a man whose was patently aggrieved by the affection that the Chelsea supporters had for Harding, a man who cut his teeth standing in The Shed.

Admittedly, there is a little traction in the argument that Bates 'saved' Chelsea but - in my opinion at least (and those who first helped establish *MHBAWA*) - he'd done and was doing more harm than good. Identity cards, (the threat of) electric fences, an unashamed love of income streams derived from Chelsea's supporters, the treatment of some former players who were, in the eyes of the Blues' faithful, absolute heroes but, in my eyes, his biggest 'crime' was dispensing with the '70s lion', the crest that was undoubtedly up there amongst the most iconic club badges in English football.

The trouble with Ken Bates was that for everything that he did whilst at Chelsea that was liked, he managed to temper it with something that was hated but, despite this, I'm sure that he'll be remembered with at least a little affection by a great number of Chelsea supporters.

When Roman Abramovich took over in 2003, any concerns associated with the direction that Bates was taking the club vanished. The name was changed after Gary Bacchus (now of *Chelsea.vitalfootball.co.uk* suggested using *cfcuk* as a 'fresh start' with the first now renamed edition being numbered 51.

Happy that Mr Abramovich had bought (and saved) the club, the fanzine decided to support the new owner. All in all and although we've managed to upset (more than) a few at Chelsea over the years (more than a few times), I think overall, the overwhelming theme maintained within the fanzine has been positive."

**Mark:** "I may as well nail my colours to the mast here David. I'm in the camp that believes Ken Bates did far more good than harm when it came to Chelsea FC. If he hadn't stepped in to save the club when he did in 1982 and a decade later set up Chelsea Pitch Owners, who knows what might have happened? That's a separate story in itself, so let's park that debate here.

Fanzines can supplement, oppose and complement a football club's official party line and *cfcuk* has never shied away from tackling issues that are important to supporters. Tell us about some of them."

**David:** "Personally, and some those who've known me through the years because of my involvement in the Chelsea 'fanzine' scene will testify to this, I never gave up hoping that the '70s lion would come back and also that we'd one day have a fantastic stadium at Stamford Bridge.

When Mr Abramovich took over, *cfcuk* published a petition requesting that the club reinstate the '70s lion as the club crest, Over the course of the 2004/2005 season, we sent over 20,000 signatures to Chelsea and readers also sent their completed forms themselves. Towards the end of that season, I was chatting with Bruce Buck at a function when he intimated that the badge would once again become the club crest commenting that, "the club had been inundated with petition forms".

Obviously I'm not claiming that it was '*cfcuk* that brought the badge back' but I know for sure we were a major influence on the decision."

**Mark:** "Chelsea players read *cfcuk*, that's remarkable! Why do you think that is?"

**David:** "Over the years, I've got to know loads of the players (and staff) and I always pass them a copy. Those of the players who know me and have read the fanzine realise that it's a publication written by genuine supporters who love the club and are speaking from the heart. The only thing I won't allow in it is slagging off the players and swearing.

A few years, I saw Ashley Cole and went to give him a copy of *cfcuk*. Instead of accepting it, he said, 'I don't read that anymore...'

'Why not?' I replied, somewhat taken aback.

'Because, (the then Chelsea and England left-back answered, "In the last edition, that bloke on page ??? (no clues here I'm afraid...) was coating me off!'

That made me think 'Fair play for saying it straight and yes, you're right – we should be supporting you…'

Since then – and I know that it has been frustrating for one or two of the contributors – there are no negative comments about the playing staff.

The players and the staff who know me trust me and are generally relaxed when I'm in their company. I've been extremely fortunate to have met many of the players over the years but I must say that John Terry, Frank Lampard and Joe Cole in particular have been extremely kind to me over the years."

**Mark:** "*cfcuk* is approaching 200 issues, what do you attribute the fanzine's longevity to?"

**David:** "Fundamentally, I think it's because it's an 'honest' fanzine with all the very excellent contributors often passionately arguing their case for why they hold their opinions on the 'comings and goings' at Chelsea.

The factual articles are well liked by our readership, particularly the 'historical' ones whilst *Geno Blues Guide To Chelsea Skinhead Reggae* is now in its fourth year, whilst those amongst the 'writing pool' who are a bit more 'experimental' in their work - stand up Walter (and protege JJ Reid) – are ever popular.

Were it not for those who put their time into writing for *cfcuk*, it wouldn't exist, as least to the extent of producing a minimum of 10 issues every season."

**Mark:** "Chances are most people who've been to a Chelsea game in recent years will have heard the sales pitch, "It's only a pound now, hurry up!" That's incredible value compared to the matchday programme! With production prices rising year-on-year can we expect an increase?"

**David:** "Thanks to the generosity of an unnamed Chelsea supporter, those who advertise and, of course, those who buy the fanzine, the printing, the running of the stall and all the other associated costs are just about covered so, at the moment at least, I can't foresee a price-rise. That day might come though after 'me old-mucker' R*pert M*rdoch has finally seen sense and bought us out..."

**Mark:** *"Hurry Up!* What's that all about?"

**David:** "That's all about wanting to sell what fanzines I have with me at the time as quickly as possible. Trust me… there are better things to do and better places to be rather than standing about outside an away end or on the Fulham Road after a game. Don't get me wrong, the stall is a great place to be before a game, with loads of faces meeting each other there and there's always a laugh to be had there. However, there are plenty of times when the thought had crossed my mind that, "I've been doing this too long now, it's getting closer to the time I'm going to have to leave." That is sure to come sooner or later but, rest assured (especially the subscribers and the advertisers!) that the intention is to keep going until we reach the 200th issue at least and, the way things are going, that looks like it will be in the middle of the 2018/19 season so it will run to the end of that season at least.

Through coming to Stamford Bridge to watch Chelsea, I've met a lot of nice people and made some very good friends. I've come to know a lot of people because of my involvement with Chelsea fanzines and I've done a lot of things I wouldn't have had it not been because of *MHBAWA*/*cfcuk*. Over the years I've had some proper laughs at football and been to places that I wouldn't have ordinarily considered travelling to and had some proper good nights out and laughs with some top pals, especially whilst abroad.

A long-time mate of mine from Chelsea is Phil Messenger, nephew of the late Ron Hockings. When Ron was ill, Phil, his son Joel (who is also my God son), his young friend and I went to Guy's Hospital to visit him. After Ron had asked him if he'd been to see Chelsea, Joel's friend told him that he hadn't yet but was hoping to go to his first match soon. Ron replied, 'Well… you've got to start sometime…' Thinking further about what he'd just said, Ron continued, 'It's not a bad life following Chelsea…'

Using that logic, I'll have to say that, on the whole, it's not been too bad a life selling Chelsea fanzines…"

**Mark:** "For people who can't get to Chelsea games, is it possible to subscribe to *cfcuk* and is there a digital version available?"

## CAREFREE! CHELSEA CHANTS AND TERRACE CULTURE

**David:** "Email cfcuk@gate17.co.uk for hard-copy *cfcuk* subscription enquiries or try www.ChelseaFan12.com or www.cfcuk.net for digital copies."

**Mark:** "*Carefree!* is based primarily on 'terrace culture' and associated songs and chants. We've covered a broad range across the years, have you got a personal favourite, funny or otherwise that sticks in your mind?"

**David:** "I've got one that's a bit obscure that always makes me smile when I hear the original tracks they were lifted from. In the late 1970s while Liverpool fans on The Kop were singing along to Queen's *We Are The Champions* which reached No.2 in the UK charts in 1977 (a theme copied by fans of every side that has been blessed with glory since), the up-and-coming youngsters in Chelsea's Shed End adapted the flip side of the double A side single *We Will Rock You* and made it their own eagerly chanting *We will ruck you.*"

**Mark:** "There have been plenty of what might be described as 'conventional' songs that have been recorded by Chelsea-supporting performing artists, Chelsea supporters and, of course, a few by the players themselves. You're well-informed in this area what can you tell us?"

**David:** "As has already been described, the most famous of all has to be *Blue Is The Colour,* released in 1972 and recorded by the Chelsea squad of the time. Chosen as a single from an LP of the same name, the song became known to not only Chelsea supporters and fans of other teams but also to a wider listening public due to the fact that it reached No. 5 in the UK charts.

In 1994, the then Chelsea FC squad recorded and released an FA Cup Final single entitled, *No One Can Stop Us Now*. However, it seems Sir Alex Ferguson and his Manchester United team didn't bother listening to the song as they went on to defeat Chelsea 4-0 at Wembley and complete the Double for the first time in their history.

Following the tragic death of Matthew Harding on 22 October 1996, accomplished musician and Chelsea supporter Steve Lima wrote, produced and released a tribute to the former Shed boy. *Matthew's Dream* by The True Blue Crew was a song that encouraged Chelsea supporters to hold to the hope of one-day seeing a 'proper' stadium at Stamford Bridge, rather than the football ground attached to a hotel that had been sanctioned and built by Ken Bates. Thankfully and thanks to Mr Abramovich, *Matthew's Dream* looks like becoming a reality."

**Mark:** "*Matthew's Dream* is a brilliant dance-rock crossover track that stands up on its own as a banging tune. The musicianship and vocals are really strong, it's a shame it never found a wider audience and the same can be said for some more Chelsea-related musical gems that are still well worth checking out. There were a couple of tracks that rode the crest of the popularity wave created by the signing of Ruud Gullit for starters."

**David:** "Yes, that's right. Stamford Bridge season-ticket holder Eddie Levy, the owner of Chelsea Music Publishing – the company obviously named after his favourite football club – released and published a 7" version of *We'll Keep The Blue Flag Flying High* under the name of The Boys From The Shed. At around the same time that Eddie's track was made available, another Chelsea supporter Henry Turtle penned his own version of the song. Keeping the same title, Henry's adaptation appeared on the market with an original song entitled *Ruudy's Rock Steady Crew* written to honour then Chelsea manager Ruud Gullit.

Then in 1997, The Chelsea Punk Rock All Stars put out a 7" single on Blue vinyl entitled *Chelsea's Gonna Win* c/w *(They're All) Chelsea Maniacs*. Featuring Gene Putney on lead vocals and Mark Wyeth on bass, the lead guitar was played by Paul 'Foxy' Fox (RIP) of The Ruts whilst the drums were played by Manic Esso, a musician who made his name with punk band The Lurkers.

In 1998, and following both the sacking of Gullit and the admission price increases to Stamford Bridge courtesy of Ken Bates, members of The 'Punk Rock All Stars collaborated with Gene Blagger (lead vocals) and Trust Me (backing vocals and lyrics) on The Chelsea Bluebaggers' version of The Clash classic *White Riot*, this time releasing the track on the *Stabbed In The Back* (four track) EP with the title *Blue Riot*. Foxy's son Lol, a talented drummer, also featured on the release which also included a version of The Cockney Rejects' track *Bad Man*, the song's lyric being adapted to highlight the inadequacy of Ken Bates' chairmanship of Chelsea.

In 2000, Wyeth – a leading light behind the renowned Club Ska at Rayners Lane and currently the genial host along with John King and Andy Chesham of *Human Punk* (so named after the classic John King novel), an occasional punk rock club night held at Oxford Street's 100 Club – released an FA Cup Final single called *Zigger Zagger* with The Shed Enders, a group featuring Ska legend Laurel Aitken. Based on the chant first introduced to The Shed terrace by Mick Greenaway the track was paired with the original version of *Blue Is The Colour* and released by Cherry Red Records."

**Mark:** "Another Chelsea-supporting singer-songwriter-musician whose had no problems reaching a wider audience is Suggs of Madness. There's a real connection between the band, it's music, and our beloved football club... tell us more."

**David:** "*Blue Day*, written by Chelsea supporter Mike Connaris and endorsed by the then WEA Records Director of Publicity Barbara Charone – a Chicago-born Chelsea supporter – was a club-sanctioned single released in 1997 to coincide with the Blues FA Cup Final appearance and reached number 22 in the UK charts. It was credited to 'Suggs & Co'. (Connaris also wrote *Blue Tomorrow*, another 'official' 'souvenir single' release which coincided with Chelsea reaching the 2000 FA Cup Final. Curiously, like *Blue Day*, the song peaked at number 22 in the charts.)

With lead singer Suggs and drummer Woody being passionate match-attending Chelsea supporters, they both must be extremely pleased that their band Madness has now become a part of Stamford Bridge folklore with the 1979 hit single *One Step Beyond* regularly played after notable victories at Stamford Bridge or after a trophy has been presented. In 2012, the tune was famously heard around the world via television as viewers watched the European Cup being paraded by the players in front of the Chelsea supporters in Munich as they celebrated their side winning the trophy for the first time."

**Mark:** "Phil Daniels has been a household name thanks to *Quadrophenia*, *Parklife* and *Eastenders* for the best part of 40 years, he also an avid Chelsea supporter..."

**David:** "Yeah, Phil's a Lower Matthew Harding season-ticket holder and involved in the *Chelsea Podcast*. He released a 'punk' version of *Blue Is The Colour*, ably abetted by James Stevenson (once of punk band Chelsea) and Steve 'Smiley' Barnard who are currently playing with The Alarm. Phil said, "We have never performed it live but would love to do it on the pitch at Stamford Bridge – I'd even let Tommy Baldwin join in!" – If you ARE reading this Chelsea..."

**Mark:** "Jonathan Kydd is a name known to listeners of David Chidgey's excellent *Chelsea Football Fancast* pod. Actor and sublime voice-over artist, Kyddo's a man of many more talents isn't he..."

**David:** "He is that. In 2008, he released a self-penned single entitled *Chelsea Blue*, a tribute to his boyhood favourite Chelsea players, the like of whom included Peter Osgood, John Bumstead, Mickey Thomas and Kerry

Dixon. Featuring supporter chants including *Carefree*, and *We Will Follow The Chelsea*, the video of the track also includes photographs supplied by Hugh Hastings who has provided the cover photo for this book. Although Jonathan's current band is The Rudy Vees, he recorded the song with his then group the Bay Citee Molars. Jonathan's track can be viewed on his website at jonathankydd.com or on *YouTube*."

**Mark:** "Of all the indie Chelsea music artists out there, my personal favourite is Billy Bluebeat. I thought it was just one mysterious multi-talented fella, but it's actually a musicians' collective isn't it."

**David:** "That's right, they debuted back in 1992 with a version of *The Liquidator* and were involved in the *Blue Riot* recording. As a band Billy Bluebeat has had a variety of musicians credited to its releases including Chelsea-supporting indie band Upper Tier, so named because brothers James and Mike, the groups' guitarist/song-writer and singer, are Matthew Harding Upper season-ticket holders.

Like both Eddie Levy and Henry Turtle, Billy Bluebeat released a version of *We'll Keep The Blue Flag Flying High* but with the title *Blue Flag*. The band then went on to release three versions of the track, as they did with *Pride Of London*, the latest versions being available on a limited edition CD single that was made available to coincide with the 2007 FA Cup Final.

In 2015, Billy Bluebeat released a download single entitled *96-97*, a song dedicated to Chelsea hero Robbie Di Matteo whose goals not only helped win Chelsea two FA Cups and a League Cup but who also led Chelsea to perhaps their greatest triumph so far, the Champions League, in that memorable final of 2012 in Munich."

**Mark:** "Is it still possible to get hold of or listen to any of the indie material readers may be less familiar with?"

**David:** "Yes, many of the songs listed above are featured on the Cherry Red album *Blue Flag* which can be purchased from the Chelsea Megastore or via download from Cherry Red Records, Amazon and iTunes. A search of the internet will also unearth many videos which make use of the tracks I've mentioned and a plenty more that I haven't. There's probably a separate book on its own to be written to do all the musicians and their songs justice."

# PART TWO

## WALTER'S CHELSEA JOURNEY

# WHERE IT ALL BEGAN FOR ME
## Tottenham, Sheffield United and Ruud Boy

**Walter:** I was born on the 25 June 1975. I share a birthday with a diverse bunch of characters including Jamie Redknapp, Ricky Gervais and Alan Green. Oh – and also George Michael. George released *Careless Whisper* in July 1984. Over 31 years later, Chelsea fans returning to London on the train from an away game with Manchester City (3 December 2016, 1-3, Willian, Diego Costa, Eden Hazard) 'serenaded' a busker at Euston Station who was playing the tune on a saxophone. As is the way of things these days, someone filmed it and the clip went viral on social media. It took a week to get the tune out of my head. Sadly, George Michael died several weeks later on Christmas Day. I wonder if he ever saw the clip for himself and, if so, what he made of it!

My Grandfather (Walter) was born on 13 October 1908 in York, Toronto, Canada. He travelled to England on the Canadian Pacific shipping line, docking in Southampton on 24 September 1938 and settled in Thames Ditton, Surrey. I don't remember him ever being particularly affectionate with me, but I do remember his love for golf. He scolded me for not wanting to learn how to play – I always preferred kicking my football on the green in front of his flat where he lived with my Granny Doris. I also have an inkling that he played ice hockey for the Toronto Maple Leafs – I have no idea if this is true – I mean, it's true that he played ice hockey – I'm just unsure if he really did represent the Maple Leafs.

I don't know if he was winding me up or not, but once he told me he saw a pal's fingers sliced clean off after he fell on the ice and another skater went straight over his hand. Picture that. Imagine the screams of pain, the blood spilling on the cold playing surface, and the hockey game stopping immediately as four fingers lay detached on the ice. My Granddad was proper sporty, and I inherited his genes. My own father however, by his own admission, couldn't be less sporty if he tried. As I grew up, I soon discerned that he had no connection, interest or enthusiasm at all when it came to sport or to football.

I loved Primary School, but I absolutely hated Secondary School from the age of about thirteen upwards. I did like my Art room though as you'll find out in the *English Civil War* chapter. My school was located on the Chessington / Surbiton border in Surrey. I remember there were a few Chelsea fans in my year, but we never went to games together. I imagine most of the school these days are Chelsea supporters.

One week, a lad in my class said he was going to Derby. His Dad was driving and they invited me along too. My parents refused to let me go. Chelsea won 6-4, (15 December 1990, Kerry Dixon x2, Gordon Durie x2, Dennis Wise, Graeme Le Saux), I had missed a classic!

I've never held it against my parents. I honestly understood completely where they were coming from.

For example, in March 1985 when I was nine-years old, Chelsea played Sunderland in a second-leg semi-final tie of the League Cup at Stamford Bridge – (4 March, Chelsea 2 Sunderland 3, David Speedie, Pat Nevin) – the match was marred by serious crowd disorder that saw over a hundred people arrested and forty injured.

*Editor's note: Former Blue Clive Walker over-celebrated as he scored a brace for the Black Cats, his second goal in the 70th minute sparked a pitch invasion! Such perceived treachery saw Walker targeted by a loan intruder who scaled Chairman Ken Bates' famous perimeter fence and attempted to assault him. Chelsea defender Joey Jones got in the way until the miscreant was apprehended by the police and bundled off the pitch accompanied by the chant* loyal supporter, loyal supporter.

**Walter:** Imagine my Mum watching the news or reading the paper the next morning. She's never been inside a football ground in her life, but she's got a football-mad son kicking the ball against the wall in the garden and she's aghast at the violence surrounding not just Chelsea, but both English League football and England Internationals.

A little under three months later (29 May), my Dad let me stay up to watch the European Cup Final between Juventus and Liverpool. Like his wife, he had never set foot in a football stadium. We witnessed the Heysel disaster unfolding. I remember feeling sick. And that was that – there was no chance of me ever going to a football match.

The violence associated with the Middlesbrough v Chelsea relegation / promotion play-off in 1988 which the Blues lost 2-1 on aggregate, (25 May, Boro 2 Chelsea 0. 28 May, Chelsea 1 Boro 0, Gordon Durie), probably set me back too and then the Hillsborough disaster happened less than a year later on 15 April 1989. Ninety-six Liverpool supporters perished as a result of gross police negligence, though it would take twenty-seven years to establish the truth about what really happened on that fateful day.

As has been documented and verified by Blues supporters who were there at the time, Filbert Street, where Chelsea were playing Leicester City in a Division Two fixture (lost 2-0) on the same afternoon as the shocking events at Hillsborough were unfolding, could have been the scene of another tragedy. With just a point required to secure promotion, circa 10,000 Chelsea followers made for the game to see if the boys could do it. Herded into a pen far too small to accommodate their increasing numbers, fortunately, before kick-off, an adjacent empty section of terrace closed off to segregate supporters was opened up to help relieve the crush. Had that not happened, the consequences could have been dire. Even with the additional pen being made available, the cramped, over-crowded environment was nowhere near safe.

Then came the World Cup, Italia '90. I remember watching loads of games on television during the previous tournament, Mexico '86. Every lad I knew tried to replicate Manuel Negrete's scissor kick for Mexico against Bulgaria. Four years later there was a definite shift in things, me being a bit older, a penny dropping for my parents maybe? They began to relent. My Dad was still proper strict, but he was certainly softening.

We had one TV in the house, and we would watch Italia '90 games together. Back then there were only four channels, and BBC and ITV both had World Cup matches on, so he didn't have much choice. BBC2 was probably showing a load of old flannel – programmes like *Tomorrows World* or *Gardeners World* and that.

The BBC's opening sequence with Pavarotti singing *Nessun Dorma* was genius, clearly stirring emotions for all and sundry, Des Lynam's presenting and Barry Davies' simple commentary gave the viewer the complete package. And my Dad *got* it. Albeit briefly, he got into football. (Plus, maybe it gave him something in common with others in his office, so he had something to talk about, I don't know!)

On my fifteenth birthday, Eire beat Romania on penalties and later that evening Italy beat Uruguay 2-0 and Barry Davies described something almost romantic about Salvatore Schillaci's Sicilian eyes. Davies also commentated about *dancing feet* when Claudio Caniggia of Argentina skipped through most of the Brazilian team.

Years later, when The *Daily Telegraph*'s *Fantasy Football* game first exploded on the scene, about eighty of us from the pub, church and work were in a league. Each month I produced a four-page fanzine (sponsored by West Ham Biggles's *Hair To Go* mobile barbers business) with the Fantasy League table printed in alongside various quips and anecdotes, and I titled it

*Dancing Feet.*

The day after the Eire and Italian victories, Bobby Robson's England beat Belgium 1-0 with a wonderful strike by David Platt after a ball in by Gascoigne to put them in the quarter-finals against Cameroon. A nation was gripped. It really did feel like that – maybe more so because my Dad was bang into it. That summer, Chelsea signed Dennis Wise and Andy Townsend. My Dad was even aware of Big Nose – not only because he has a massive hooter himself, but because Townsend had played for Eire in the World Cup.

I had to wait a few more months, but it wasn't long before I made my debut in The Shed. My Dad's pal from Church was taking his sons to Chelsea against Spurs. I knew these lads back from when we were toddlers at Sunday School, we'd practically grown up together.

Another older lad called Tall Paul was a Chelsea regular with his Dad, and they had sorted the tickets. My Dad relented in letting me go, probably because he knew I'd be in safe hands with his pal and Tall Paul taking me. But he did say I had to pay for the ticket myself. It was seven quid. My paper round paid £1.48 per week. I raided my copper collection, stashed under my bed in a big ice-cream tub, tipped the one and two pence pieces out all over my floor and counted them out into piles. I had enough money. I can still remember handing Tall Paul seven quid in coppers and him cracking up affectionately. I was in business.

Usually nobody in my house was permitted to watch TV on Sundays, but Chelsea were up at Old Trafford on *The Big Match Live* on Sunday 25 November 1990. My parents let me turn the television on. Hallelujah, it was a miracle! Chelsea won 3-2 thanks to a Gary Pallister own goal, an Andy Townsend solo effort and a Dennis Wise penalty. Damien Matthew made his debut. I loved watching the away fans tumbling and celebrating, singing and giving it to the Mancs – and I only had six sleeps until my first game.

Saturday 1 December 1990 – a day I have never forgotten and will never forget.

All those years kicking a ball against a wall, (I should add that I wasn't allowed to join a football team when I was a kid either), and now I was able to go to watch Chelsea.

All those Saturday mornings buying Panini stickers with my pocket money, racing home, laying on the carpet and slowly and expectantly opening the packet and cherishing the smell of the stickers, and now I was going to see players in the flesh.

All the times I got high on the anticipation of a silver sticker or a rare player being inside the packet, and now I could see Kerry Dixon with my own eyes on the pitch.

All the occasions I had to listen to the kids in my class talk about their trips with their Dads and Uncles to Manchester, Highbury, White Hart Lane or wherever and swallow it down.

All the times I had to listen to the radio for updates or watch Teletext scores unfold. I could go on and on – I was a football addict who had been in a strait jacket, and now the chains were off and I was finally going to Stamford Bridge.

Tall Paul said we'd stand in a particular section of the Shed with his cousins where he always met them. My Dad's friend John told me and his son to always remain within eyeshot if we got separated on the terrace. It's a cliché to say that I remember it like it was yesterday, but I do – and not just the way the match unfolded on the pitch, but the smells and the songs and the feelings and all that made up the experience – it was a day as memorable as when I first met my wife, as significant as finding out I was going to be a Father myself, and more life changing than being in Stockholm, Wembley or Munich – and I have no hesitation in writing that because that's how it was for me – it was my first time – none of those finals had happened then, they were all in the future – I was a fifteen-year old kid who finally got to go to Chelsea!

On reflection my life had meaning for the first time.

I wasn't some invisible kid at church, I wasn't the bullied little teenager scared about going to school. In a funny kind of way I had both lost my virginity and been re-born. I was somebody and I was part of something now – a new community that did not judge me.

I was a fan like everyone else; standing in The Shed like everyone else; supporting my team like everyone else; singing vociferously like everyone else – I loved to sing – I really loved to join in – it was mad – I could sing with hundreds of other lads and I loved it and craved it, it was a release – and I knew immediately that is was a release I needed – no-one knew my name but being an individual that made up a group that made up a crowd meant I was accepted, I was liked, I had identity.

My big sister (who fancied the pants off Tall Paul – they now have three children!) got me a Saturday job in a pharmaceutical warehouse on Chessington Industrial Estate. I'd work from eight in the morning until midday then shoot off to Stamford Bridge – I was an addict. I had my routine, I loved my life for the first time in years, at least since my childish innocence was lost I reckon – oh, and about that first match of mine? Chelsea won 3-2 (Kerry Dixon, John Bumstead, Gordon Durie) and Gary Lineker missed a penalty! Up yours, Tottenham!

As time went by I became Tall Paul's little mate. I was in the away ends at White Hart Lane, Loftus Road, Highbury then further afield to Villa Park, Old Trafford, Anfield, Hillsborough, Bramall Lane – I dared to write in to fanzines (*Red Card* and *The Chelsea Independent*) where my pseudonym and nickname Walter Otton was born.

I began collecting programmes (I've since given most of them away), I visited the Club Shop when I had an inset day at school and brought a T-Shirt. I have since found out that Matt Lucas and Kenny Rice worked together at the Club Shop back then. Matt (Arsenal fan) went on to be a nationwide celebrity, and Kenny went on to find stardom on *Twitter* as Nice Guy King Kenny of the Shed Upper. He's lucky enough to be nicknamed Kenny Christmas by me because he's like Santa Claus sorting out tickets for people like me or my mate Smiffy.

The following season, I brought a Club Membership – absolutely enthralled that by doing so, Mr Kenneth Bates personally guaranteed me a ticket to be at Wembley should Chelsea get there – due to my upbringing regarding matters I have already explained – I had missed out on the ZDS final the season before (25 March 1990, Chelsea 1 Middlesbrough 0, Tony Dorigo) by months.

When I turned sixteen, I went to Sixth Form College and I got my ear pieced. My Dad went potty, so I went back out and got three more piercings – also in my ears. On the school field one lunchtime I smoked my first spliff and passed out. I've never touched weed since. A new confidence had slowly taken over me. The lads who bullied me had moved on to jobs or other colleges, but this fresh assurance of mine was more to do with football bringing me out of my shell. In no other environment could I shout and swear and sing a rude song about John Barnes, or chant about, *Arsenal running too,* even though I hadn't had a proper fight since I was eleven. I'd been on the pitch after Chelsea beat Graeme Souness's Liverpool 4-2, (4 May 1991, Kerry Dixon x2, Dennis Wise, Gordon Durie), when The Shed poured over the advertising boards and I legged it on with

## CAREFREE! CHELSEA CHANTS AND TERRACE CULTURE

Tall Paul, I put some grass from the pitch in my pocket, then I joined the throes of blues taunting the Scousers, *Where's Your Title Gone?* repeatedly, and I felt a million dollars.

I went to games as much as I could afford to. I begged Tall Paul to drive to away games and take me. Nothing has changed! In season 1991/92 our FA Cup run started with a 2-0 Third Round win away at Hull City, (4 January 1992, Vinny Jones, Dennis Wise), the tricky away fixture had been hurdled. The same day, Arsenal (the Champions) lost their tie at Wrexham who had finished bottom of Division Four but incredibly escaped relegation because Aldershot had been expelled from the league. Ex-Chelsea player Mickey Thomas scored Wrexham's winner.

The next Chelsea game was a week later – a 2-0 win against Spurs (29 January, Clive Allen, Dennis Wise) – and the crowd jubilantly sang, *Wrexham Two, Arsenal One, Hallelujah!* to the tune of *Michael, Row the Boat Ashore*, a negro spiritual first noted during the American Civil War, 1861-1865.

*Michael row de boat ashore, Hallelujah!*
*Michael boat a gospel boat, Hallelujah!*
*I wonder where my mudder deh.*
*See my mudder on de rock gwine home.*
*On de rock gwine home in Jesus' name.*

Occasionally, to this day, I find myself singing it on the walk home from the boozer.

**Editor's note:** *The Highwaymen took a commercialised version of the song to the top of the UK charts for one week in October 1961. Everton supporters purloined the melody in the mid '60s and came up with the chant* Send St John to Vietnam, Hallelujah! *A barbed reference to Ian St John who played for rivals Liverpool and the Vietnam War. Why Vietnam? No idea. Funny though, and worth a mention. Tim Rolls also recalls another entertaining concoction which celebrated Tottenham Hotspur's relegation from the old First Division in 1977... and Chelsea's promotion back there...* Chelsea Up, Tottenham Down, Halleujah! – *Brilliant!*

**Walter:** In the next round of the Cup, Chelsea were set to play Everton at home. The BBC moved it to a Sunday to show the match live, (26 January, Chelsea 1 Everton 0, Clive Allen), and things had progressed with my parents so, not only was I allowed to watch the TV on Sunday's, I was now permitted to physically go to the football on Sunday's. Maybe they saw that I was genuinely happy for the first time in about five years – they got it that football had become my medicine cabinet.

As I grew older it became my garden shed, too – something that occurred to me when chatting to a young lady after Wigan away one season which is covered in *The Wigan Train* chapter. A rendition of, *Jimmy Hill is a w\*nker, is a w\*nker* resounded around Stamford Bridge as the crowd knew he was up in the commentary box with good old Desmond Lynam. It wasn't a sell-out, but the noise was tremendous. The place went mental when Kevin Hitchcock saved Tony Cottee's penalty meaning Clive Allen's volley was enough to see us through to the next round. I remember seeing a minibus load of Evertonians urinating up against a wall near Parsons Green and thinking how disgusting it looked as a flow of piss ran down the wall, onto the pavement and into the gutter – but then at the same time it had a certain romance about it as they'd driven all the way down from Merseyside, lined up along the wall as best mates and emptied their bladders in unison.

And then it was the Fifth Round and we were drawn at home to Sheffield United. The game was played on 15 February 1992. I'll never forget that day because I started a song completely by accident and when I think about it I realise that I have been buzzing off it ever since.

I didn't care that I didn't receive any Valentine's Cards (okay, maybe I did) but my love was Chelsea FC anyway. The match was significant for several reasons. After four seconds, Vinny Jones went in on Dane Whitehouse and was shown a yellow card. Vinny had broken his own record set when playing for Sheffield United, when he was booked after five seconds for taking out Peter Reid of Manchester City at Maine Road. (Funnily enough, Dave Bassett's Blades had been given a Fair Play Award before this match!) Chelsea won 1-0 with a brilliant individual goal by Graham Stuart, probably my favourite player at the time. His nickname was 'Bobby Dazzler', soon to be shortened to just Bobby, and at full time the place went mad – we were in the FA Cup quarter-finals – belief and euphoria swept across the ground – and from my place in The Shed, for some reason, without any deliberation or anything like that, I blurted out, *Blue is the Colour* and everyone around me continued, *football is the game*, and then it felt like half The Shed sang, *we're all together* and then it felt like the majority of The Shed sang, *and winning is our aim*, and then it felt like the whole end roared, *so cheer us on through the sun and rain*, and then the West Stand joined in, *coz Chelsea, Chelsea is our name*, and then the tannoy blasted out the first bars of the song and the whole ground sang from the top as one, *Blue is the Colour*, – at least that is how I remember it anyway. It all unfolded from my spontaneous blurt.

## CAREFREE! CHELSEA CHANTS AND TERRACE CULTURE

By the time I was seventeen I had met Smiffy and Big Chris and we'd become firm friends. A quarter of a century on, and we still go to matches together and always will, until death us do part. I went to the 1994 FA Cup Final (14 May, Manchester United 4 Chelsea 0) with Tall Paul. Neither Smiffy nor Chris were members, so they couldn't get a ticket.

Inexplicably, I only went to one match in the 1994/95 season. I went in the West Stand to watch a 3-0 win against Manchester City. Gavin Peacock, Denis Wise (with a magnificent chip over Tony Coton) and an own goal by Michel Vonk sealed the win. The old away end was being built into a new stand, and The Shed had temporary uncovered seating. It was always strange to me that the plastic seats were bottle green in colour rather than blue. Maybe Ken Bates had got a cheaper deal on green seats.

That summer my parents had moved up to Nottingham, and I moved into a mate's spare room in Worcester Park. I was working in a grey office with dirty walls and tired people. There must be more to life. I'd decided to take up an opportunity working for a charity – it was a voluntary, unpaid position in a local Church called *Generation*. In return, I'd live rent free in my accommodation, get trained in all kinds of skills such as Youth Work and Public Speaking, I'd run assemblies and lessons in schools, coordinate and train kids in Football Clubs across three Primary Schools, and have the opportunity to work abroad for two weeks. (I went to Marseille and nearly drowned in the Med.)

I took the job and as a result I had to knock Chelsea on the head for that 94/95 season.

I couldn't bring myself to sing, *We're All Going on a European Tour*, because, well, I wouldn't be going on a European Tour. Despite losing the FA Cup Final to Man U, Chelsea qualified for the European Cup Winners Cup by virtue of the fact that United won the Double. It was the same for Tall Paul – he wasn't going on a European Tour either, but a tour of a different kind. He had decided to jack in his job, move out of his parents and go to Australia. He'd been saving for years. He left soon after the 1994 FA Cup Final and he didn't come back until 1998.

In an incredible turn of events, the next game we attended together (close to being exactly four years apart) was travelling to Stockholm for the European Cup Winners Cup Final, (13 May 1998, Chelsea 1 VFB Stuttgart 0, Gianfranco Zola), along with Den and Jervo the Pervo. As sick as I was to miss Chelsea for the 94/95 season, it was, at the time, the right decision. Looking back, though, I wish things had played out differently. I wish I had dug in, borrowed some money, gone to a few games. You don't know what you've got until you lose it, and hindsight is a wonderful thing.

I didn't even go to the home leg of the Cup Winners Cup quarter-final with Bruges – what was I thinking? It was 16 March 1995, Chelsea 2 FC Bruges 0, Mark Stein, Paul Furlong, Chelsea won 2-1 on aggregate. I remember Smiffy took some sort that he was seeing at the time, and I was working. I was working? On reflection – my head had gone.

That season we went out of the FA Cup to Millwall on penalties after a replay (8 February 1995, Chelsea 1 Millwall 1, Mark Stein, penalty shoot-out Chelsea 4 Millwall 5, Mark Stein ✓ Dennis Wise ✓ Craig Burley ✓ David Lee ✓ John Spencer oh dear!) I can remember listening to the first game, (28 January, Millwall 0 Chelsea 0), on Capital Gold. I was preparing for a big youth event. I was half way up some scaffolding tying a projector screen to some tri-light in Tolworth Recreation Centre while Jonathan Pearce was roaring, *"Chelsea supporters are Frisbeeing their broken seats into the Millwall end!"* Great stuff.

In July 1995, I was offered a job after my voluntary placement, and I took it. I was on a meagre wage, and most my pay went on rent and bills. I was also working most weekends, because that was the nature of the work. As the 95/96 season unfolded, I managed to get to a few more matches, but nothing too significant.

In January 1996, I went to Loftus Road in the FA Cup Fourth Round, (29 January, QPR 1 Chelsea 2), Chelsea were wearing the now classic tangerine and graphite kit. (Not orange and grey, okay – it is tangerine and graphite.) I adored watching Ruud Gullit – what a player. What an influence. What a man. Gavin Peacock put us 1-0 up, but I missed Paul Furlong's goal right before half-time because I was going for a piss. I can't ever remember missing a goal before. However, it was the start of a trend. I don't think I've seen any Chelsea goals since that have been scored between the 41st and the 50th minutes because I'm either in a queue, boozing, or urinating. Up the Chels!

They say you shouldn't have any regrets. I'll tell you something, I have plenty of them. Loads. If I could turn back the clock I would've made some other choices, done things very differently when it came to Chelsea.

The Blues hadn't been in Europe for twenty-three years, but I threw myself into work for two years. The least I should've done was get in a bit of football. I could've done both, especially in that 95/96 season. I turned down paid work because I felt obliged to continue various voluntary commitments – I felt I owed the people who had trained and mentored me and the organisation that had invested in me. A foolish decision, though I thought it was the right thing to do at the time.

I watched Chelsea play Man United at Villa Park in the FA Cup semi-final, (31 March 1996, Manchester United 2 Chelsea 1, Ruud Gullit), on the TV. It really hit me then. Why the hell wasn't I in the Holte End? What has happened to me? I'd slowly let it slip away. I was fuming with myself. I was working six days a week, and most evenings too.

From a personal perspective, my parents had moved to Nottingham with my little sister, my big sister and I (at the time, not now) were fairly removed from each other, my dear Granny Doris had passed away, I'd had my heart broken by a treacle from Molesey and although I didn't recognise what it was at the time, I was full of anxiety, grief and depression with no appetite for food. One morning, I collapsed in the shower. Later on, that day, I passed out again. A pal of mine I'd confided in, insisted on driving me to the Doctors. The Doctor signed me off for three weeks and prescribed me anti-depressants and medication to build myself up. I weighed eight stone. I went to live with my parents for a fortnight. I slept and ate, ate and slept. I was twenty years old.

*You are my Chelsea, my only Chelsea!*

In June 1996, for my twenty-first birthday, my parents bought me a season ticket in the West Stand. Terracing had long gone across football grounds in the top divisions, we were in a new era. I was sitting on my own. Tall Paul was in Australia. Smiffy and Big Chris went to games when they could. Jervo the Pervo and Den had memberships, but weren't able to get season tickets yet.

You couldn't just turn up with your mates anymore. People were spread out across the ground. The atmosphere suffered. My season ticket wallet was burgundy in colour – I loved and treasured it – even all the vouchers it was full of for away games that I couldn't afford to go to so I rarely used – but at least I had my Chelsea back. Things had gone full circle with my Dad, I guess. The season ticket cost him £421. I was completely bowled over that he would do this for me. Maybe in some ways it was an olive branch – an apology for not taking me when I was a kid, or not being a sporty hands-on Dad. And maybe in some ways it was an award – go on, Son, you're twenty-one now – do what you love to do best – go to Chelsea. And maybe it was because he saw his boy in pieces – skinny and burnt out, depressed and grieving – and he wanted to fix things and make life better. Maybe it was a mixture of all these things. I've never really reflected on it until now as I'm writing it all down.

I vowed to never burn out again. This was another promise I ended up breaking – but that came years later in 2012 – and my kids, my wife, my football mates and my Church pals pulled me through that too.

After a 0-0 draw away at Southampton (18 August), the first home match of the 1996/97 season was on Wednesday 21 August (Chelsea 1 Middlesbrough 0, Roberto Di Matteo) and I was about to take my new seat – my first seat – my first season ticket, upgraded from membership, a new me, less work, more football, new pattern, fresh journey, slower pace, trepidation at who I'd be sitting next to – or between – on my own, no mates around me – what will be, will be.

The bloke to my left was a lorry driver from Preston. Bald and stressed, full of expletives and anger. He didn't like me, I could tell. He seemed suspicious of me. I wondered if the seat that I was sitting in was the seat that his mate used to sit in, or his ex-wife, I don't know. The man to my right was big. Too big for his wooden seat. Good job I was a skinny lad. On the other side of him, at the end of the row, sat his mother. They shared a small, transistor radio. I wondered how long they'd been coming to Chelsea. For the entire season, I only remember him speaking twice. Firstly, during the winter weeks, he looked up at the freezing cold sky and remarked, "They're snowy clouds, they are!" The second thing he said was a passionate exclamation aimed at our left-back, "Come along, Minto!" he yelled. I burst out laughing, so he looked at me and I replied, "Yeah, too right, come along, Minto!" And that was that.

In front of me were the benches. Every match I'd observe this one bloke, he fascinated me. He wore the same blue Chelsea top every game, with *RUUD BOY* across the back and the white 1970's crest stitched in the front. He had short, dark hair and a decent sun tan and was probably a good twenty years older than me. The veins in his neck would stand out when he got agitated. He had fists that, for sure, had fought for the cause in the name of his team. I haven't seen him since the end of the 1997 season – maybe he is one of the hundreds that are either banned, priced out, disgusted at the gentrification of his Club or a blend of all these things.

When there was a significant dip in the atmosphere or when the chips were down, when the players had to dig in and the crowd had to dig in too, he would stand on his bench, put his back to the pitch, face the West Stand

above him, take a very deep breath and let loose:
*Oh, Why Don't You Just Give Me A –*
*C (C!)*
*H (H!)*
*E (E!)*
*L (L!)*
*S (S!)*
*E (E!)*
*A (A!)'*
Then he would look to the Heavens and roar:
*Who Do You Love?*
*CHELSEA! (CHELSEA!) CHELSEA! (CHELSEA!) CHELSEA! (CHELSEA!) CHELSEA! (CHELSEA!)*
Repeat to fade.

What I learnt from Ruud Boy is that it takes one person, one voice to start a chant. You just need some confidence twinned with being able to gauge the right moment. Or, in simpler terms, you require bollocks and decent ingredients. I'd been drinking in The Cock since I was eighteen – if I wasn't on my own I'd be with Smiffy, Den, Big Chris, Taxi Alan and Tall Paul. Other times I'd drink down The Wheatsheaf with Vastly Intelligent Keith, Tax Dodging Tommy and Champagne Les. After the internet became a thing and social media came alive, I met other people and drank in other pubs and many have become firm friends.

So, that in a nutshell is my journey. After 1996/97, I transferred my season ticket to the Matthew Harding Upper when I sat between Paul the Postie from Kent and Untitled Roger, who never had a proper nickname, so *Untitled* works quite well, I think. I left working for *Generation* in 2000 to work part-time setting up Youth Work for Smiffy's new charity *Regenerate* in London SW15. I also got a part-time job in Wandsworth selling CCTV and packaging my sales in a tiny warehouse in All Saints Passage SW18. I gave my season ticket up in 2001/02 because I moved down to the south coast to work for *Spurgeons*, a children's charity. I was made redundant ten years later in 2012.

I currently live near Worthing. I am married with two children. I struggle to afford to take myself to matches, let alone pay for my kids too. I literally cannot take them! But I go as often as I can. I have made many, many friends. Friends that were there for a season, and friends that will be there until the end.

*OH, WHY DON'T YOU JUST GIVE ME A C!*

# ENGLISH CIVIL WAR

**Walter:** I started Secondary School in September 1986 – an all-boys school with an ageing Headmaster who would wear a long flowing black gown. When he walked into the assembly hall, absolute quiet would instantly envelop the room as if a few hundred lads had all become monks and taken a vow of silence. The only sound to be heard came from his shoes click clacking on the wooden floor as he strode to the front of the hall and went up the steps to the stage. *Click-clack, click-clack.*

In the summer of 1986, the cane was abolished. Do I think that was a good thing? Yes, I do, because of abuse of position, power and responsibility. The venom in the swing, the swish of the stick, the brutality of the action, the pain and the shame. However, I do believe that this was a watershed moment.

Fast-forward seven years and I left school (after staying on for Sixth Form), and it was obvious to me how respect for elders had slowly diminished, an air of fearlessness prevailed amongst many pupils – I believe that they believed they were untouchable and could get away with scoffing at authority and behaving badly – after all, now the cane was gone, what was the worst that a teacher could do?

The art classrooms were right up on the fourth floor. The art teachers who took our lesson were either Mr Rayner or Mr Armstrong, and they were both well all right. Mr Rayner had a little earner on the side – he was a barber. At lunchtimes he'd charge a few quid, get his clippers out from his desk drawer, and cut pupils hair. No way would he get away with that now. (Though, I must be honest, when I was in Sixth Form I went to see him for a trim and he really messed my hair up. Suffice to say, those of you that know me are probably asking why I continue to let him still cut my hair, then?!)

My class had our double art lesson on a Friday after lunch – the last lesson before the weekend. It became apparent to a few of us that a pattern had emerged. Mr Armstrong would've been in the pub over the road for his lunch and had a few whiskies. It must've been hell to drag himself away from the boozer, climb up all those sodding stairs to the fourth floor, walk to the end of the corridor and teach thirty boys – half of which would have been playing football all lunchtime and had no enthusiasm or motivation to work, to draw, to paint, to sketch or to learn. The Graveyard Shift. Looking back now, I can still remember the layout of the art classroom and, most of all, the fascination I had, as an eleven-year-old, with a huge painting on the wall that dominated the room.

I used to stare at this painting. I would get lost in it. It made me think, it made me dream, it made me wonder, it did something to me – it was the front cover of an album and I knew that I couldn't sing or play any kind of instrument – but, it didn't matter – this art work ignited something in me – like the flick of a Clipper lighter to spark up a flame – something glowing within that I couldn't articulate – I proper loved this painting – it meant something but I didn't know what this meaning was – flick, spark, ignite – it was ridiculous really because at the time I didn't even know what songs were on the album or if it was any good. I'd heard of the band, but that was it – and I wasn't very good at art either – but here I am and this is what it is – flick, spark, ignite – I stared at this powerful image of a man smashing his prized guitar – it grabbed me and shook me and I liked that – a blend of inspiration and intrigue – and even when I wasn't studying it because I was drawing some fruit in a bowl or something – it was there – the bassist swinging his instrument like an axe – and looking back I reckon I probably asked older lads or even Mr Rayner more about the album cover that an older pupil had painted both magnificently and perfectly over the entire wall – and I couldn't wait to listen to the song, the album, maybe even get the T-shirt – flick, spark, ignite.

It was the front cover of *London Calling* by The Clash.

Fast-forward to 2014 or so and two Clash-related Chelsea stickers were doing the rounds – they were stuck on tubes and trains and concourses and seats and pub walls and toilet doors and in some cases on the back of stewards or the Old Bill. Though neither of these two stickers were a mock-up of Clash bass player Paul Simonon smashing his guitar on the stage in an explosion of anger and frustration – they did however specifically mention LONDON CALLING alongside the Union Jack with the Chelsea crest, and my favourite – the second sticker, had a London skyline with LONDON CALLING at the top and the lyric TO THE FAR AWAY TOWNS at the bottom.

*Over Land and Sea. Chelsea away. London Calling.*
*I live by the River.*

I love the River Thames. In 2004, I walked most of it. I think I might walk it again one day – but this time all the way. Maybe in 2025 to celebrate my fiftieth birthday or something. It'll take a week, maybe more. The River is like fire to me – I can watch them both for ages. River and fire. They are nature's television. The flow of the River, the sound of the water, the power to captivate, the possibility to destroy. The flames that dance, the cracking of the wood, the power to give warmth and light, the potential to wipe out countryside and life.

As I grew older I read about Joe Strummer being a Chelsea fan and how racism and violence troubled him. I read that the Clash members, when working on *London Calling* would play football with each other, and kids from the area in Islington would join in after school. (*London Calling* was recorded at Wessex Studios located in Highbury New Park – flats now, like a certain football ground that was also nearby.)

Many times, in interviews, band members have alluded to the fun, the unity and the significance of those moments. I read that the reason why the bassist smashed his guitar wasn't a display of bravado or rock and roll, but a spontaneous act of rage because security wouldn't let the audience out of their seats during a gig, they had to stay sitting down.

*London Calling* was released in December 1979 when I was only four-years old. It was many years later, bowled over by the painting in my art classroom, that I eventually purchased the album on tape. In 1990 when *Beats International* (featuring Lindy Layton) released *Dub Be Good to Me*, I remember saying to my big sister that the bass line was lifted from *The Guns of Brixton*. (I don't think she took any notice!) My favourite songs were *Lost in the Supermarket*, *Rudie Can't Fail* and *Train in Vain*, and the lyrics of *Spanish Bombs* nudged me to take an interest in history for the first time in my life and research about the Spanish Civil War.

Which brings things nicely onto the English Civil War.

The Clash's version of *English Civil War* was on their album *Give Em Enough Rope*, released a year before *London Calling* in November 1978. The village I currently live in is surrounded by other little villages. There are memorials to those people who had died during wars. Recently the school my kids (at the time of writing, aged seven and nine) go to were focusing on the Poppy Appeal. I explained to them how men went to fight and many didn't return, and pointed out the memorials.

My kids are familiar with Clash songs (they grab chopsticks and drum along to *I Fought the Law* – well, who doesn't?) and I played them *English Civil War* after explaining the meaning behind it. As it blared from our old, dusty stereo in the kitchen, my daughter picked up on the tune, recognised it and sang, *And that's why we love Salomon Kalou!*

We all burst out laughing and sang the Kalou song. It got me thinking about how the traditional anti-war song *Johnny Comes Marching Home* evolved into Mick Jones and Joe Strummer composing *English Civil War* and the tune and lyrics have also evolved into various football chants – a few of which I'll focus on now.

### 3 July 2007 Fernando Torres leaves Atlético Madrid.

Fernando Torres signed for Liverpool from Atlético Madrid. He later stated that he turned down the chance to join Chelsea after the World Cup in 2006. Chelsea pursued him during the 2005/06 prior to their bid, the transfer didn't happen and Roman signed Andriy Shevchenko instead.

The following summer, in July 2007, Torres signed for the Scousers, and they sang: *His armband proved he was a red – Torres, Torres. You'll never walk alone it said – Torres, Torres. We bought the lad from sunny Spain, he gets the ball he scores again, Fernando Torres, Liverpool's number nine.*

Liverpool supporters staked their claim to first use of the tune – especially after John Arne Riise's miraculous own goal in the Champions League semi-final First Leg match at Anfield sparked Chelsea's version about loving Salomon Kalou (22 April 2008, Liverpool 1 Chelsea 1). They reckon we nicked it, but the truth is there was a Kalou version doing the rounds four months prior to Torres signing for Liverpool – and here's how it all unfolded.

That said: In the end, the argument from Chelsea supporters' perspective would prove futile as Liverpool fans were proved right! But it was nothing to do with Fernando Torres, they had a version dating back to 1965! It's explained at the end of this chapter.

### 11 March 2007 FA Cup quarter-final
### Chelsea 3 Tottenham Hotspur 3
### (Frank Lampard x2, Salamon Kalou)

Unbelievably, Chelsea were 3-1 down. Then Petr Cech made an incredible double save and belief spread across the Bridge like wild fire. Just get one back and we'll see – just get one!

Sir Frank Lampard rippled the net from two yards to make it 3-2. Everyone roared the team on even further – and then Salomon Kalou scored the equaliser in the 86th minute – a stunning brilliant volley after a Didier Drogba knock down.

Kalou's cult status was growing. He got his fair share of grief from the crowd, a scapegoat for many. Unfortunately, there is always one player that sections of the crowd pick on and moan at, but what a finish by him against our rivals.

It was now seventeen years since Spurs last won at the Bridge. According to the BBC, the referee blew for full time at 1448. At around 2000 hours, a massive riot kicked off in nearby Parsons Green resulting in ten people being hospitalised with stab wounds.

A police spokesperson said, *"Clearly there was a degree of organisation. These guys had not turned up with sticks and bats to play a game of hockey or baseball. We are trying to establish whether it was a pre-arranged fight or if it was one group of organised hooligans setting upon another."* No sh*t, Sherlock! Give him a promotion!

The replay would be in eight days. The Old Bill would need to be right on top of this one. To flex their muscles in preparation to combat inevitable disorder, the Metropolitan Police released a statement banning celery for the replay. Not hockey sticks with nails in them – not baseball bats with nails in them – but celery… without nails in them. I kid you not. On 16 March, Chelsea released their own statement to remind fans that lobbing the vegetable in question was a criminal offence: *"The throwing of anything at a football match, including celery, is a criminal offence for which you can be arrested and end up with a criminal record."*

## 19 March 2007
## Tottenham Hotspur 1 Chelsea 2
## (Andriy Schevchenko, Shaun Wright-Philips)

Chelsea supporters of a certain vintage have articulated the 'celery' phenomena much better than I could. Personally, I love it. Not the vegetable itself to consume, but its place in Chelsea history and its prominence in pubs, concourses, grounds and public transport – especially in its traditional appearance at Cup away games.

Back in 2002 at White Hart Lane at an FA Cup game that Chelsea won 4-0 (10 March, William Gallas, Eidur Gudjohnsen x2, Graeme Le Saux), I had seen the Old Bill violently eject a Chelsea fan in front of me to my left for picking up a piece of celery and throwing it in the air. Not aimed at anyone. Certainly not at the opposition fans. Just tossed in the air. The poor supporter in question was a middle-aged, bespectacled replica-shirter with a matching scarf. He was obviously causing no harm and clearly not a threat. This is the police at the football for you. They man-handled him down the steps and kicked him out. They knew he wasn't a face, but they still did what they did anyway and to make matters worse for the poor fella they also broke his glasses.

Tensions were higher than usual because of the Parsons Green episode.

Back to the 2007 Cup replay, it was a after a goal-less first half when Shevchenko masterfully opened the scoring. Alan Shearer loved the strike – he mentioned that Sheva didn't even look up, *"the goal posts don't move"*, Shearer said, explaining that the Ukrainian instinctively knew how to hit it. Brilliant analysis. SWP made it two nil with a Mark Hughes-style half-volley after a chest-pass-knock-down from Drogba. Now that is an assist. Robbie Keane scored a penalty for Spurs, (Carvalho should've been sent off), and Chelsea were through to the FA Cup semi-finals.

At full-time, then manager José Mourinho steamed onto the pitch, fists pumping, screaming with passion. What a win. John Terry, Frank Lampard and Ashley Cole led the celebrations giving it the big one as they marched towards the euphoric away support. At that moment, a Spurs fan ran on the pitch and swung for Lampard. Drogba took him down before the stewards could get there – another fan had followed but lost his bottle.

As the stewards took down the bloke who'd gone for Sir Frank, both Drogba (a kick) and Mikel (a stamp) gave the berk what he deserved – maybe he wanted revenge for his Granddad who lay in hospital with a rusty nail stuck in his bum cheek after his arse was hit with a hockey stick the week before in Parsons Green.

Salomon Kalou was a sub, coming on with four minutes to go. The support hadn't forgotten his contribution eight days previously, though.

Since the turn of the year in 2007, things had been mental in my household. The Doris gave birth (at home, all planned) on 20 January and life changed inconceivably as a baby girl came into my world on the bedroom floor of my rented flat, three floors up.

I realised that for the rest of my days on planet Earth I would be a father to my daughter and I'd never felt love like it. I hadn't been to a match since late December (30 December 2006, Chelsea 2 Fulham 2, Liam Rosenior own goal, Didier Drogba), but my next game would be Watford away at the end of March. For the remainder of the season I adjusted to life with a baby girl and I didn't make any games in Europe or the FA Cup – though I did go to the League Cup Final in Cardiff, beating Arsenal 2-1.

What a day that was, and a great day for celery too, loads of the stuff getting launched at Cesc Fàbregas (who loathed Chelsea back then) when he went to take a corner down our end. Fàbregas these days, of course, wears a magic hat. (Well, he does at the time of writing!)

Anyway back to Watford away, Salomon Kalou and the English Civil War!

**31 March 2007 Premier League**
**Watford 0 Chelsea 1**
**(Salomon Kalou)**

Man United are top of the league six points ahead of us, their match versus Blackburn is on the big screens in Wetherspoons Watford. The pre-match atmosphere is brilliant. *Chelsea Allouette, You Are My Chelsea, We Hate Tottenham* – I've missed this. *Celery* does the rounds again and again, and as we discuss the ban and the Tottenham FA Cup games, a bloke called Dave butts in and introduces himself. He said he was ejected during the replay for throwing celery at the Lane – and, get this, a 'Chelsea fan' had grassed him up. He was banned but is here at Watford anyway.

Our conversation is interrupted because everyone goes bananas. Blackburn score to go one up through Matt Derbyshire. The place goes mental. Electricity shoots through the air around the pub and fists shake at the screen in defiance, belief and jubilation and *Who the f\*ck are Man United?* resounds.

Champagne Les turns up – it's great to see him. I love it when this happens. I don't think I've seen him since Fulham away last September! Les says what we're all thinking, that United will come back, and they do, they end up winning 4-1.

So, onto Vicarage Road. After a dull, uninspiring first half, José took off Claude Makélélé and brought on Salomon Kalou who headed the winner in injury time. Michael Ballack won a ball in midfield, Andriy Shevchenko whipped it in and there was Kalou! Goal! Our end fell. The final whistle.

One of the chaps behind the original 'Chelsea Stickers' phenomenon is Callum. When I told him what that I was writing about Kalou, he told me that he and his mates were down the Big Chill House in Kings Cross the week after Watford away drinking before Chelsea's next match. Together they composed, to the tune of *English Civil War*, the chant: *He can't finish but we don't care, Watford away we were there, Salomon Kalou, Chelsea's 21!* So, there you have it. A pub chant that grew momentum amongst mates and mates of mates, but sadly never transitioned to the grounds. There are loads and loads of songs like this that never made the jump, and many are mentioned in this book.

Callum went on to tell me, "There was also one my friends and I made up to *21 Seconds* by So Solid Crew. There genuinely was 21 seconds to go when Salomon buried that header: *There was twenty-one seconds to go, when Kalou scored the goal, cross from Shevchenko at Vicarage Road, there was twenty one seconds when Kalou scored the goal.*"

The original Kalou song grew a little in stature, and it had enough of an influence to morph into the *Riise* version over a year later and went onto to become a Chelsea classic.

## 22 April 2008 Champions League semi-final, First Leg
## Liverpool 1 Chelsea 1
## (John Arne Riise own goal)

Celebrations were afoot at *Walts Towers* as the Doris found herself pregnant again. We were looking for a new place to live, work for me was mental, picking and choosing my Chelsea games were now the norm and Chelsea were away to Liverpool in the semi-final first leg of the European Cup.

I wrote this a week later:

I arrive back home from work bang on half seven, popping on ITV and popping open a bottle of Miller Gold at the same time. I'm tempted to mute the television so I'm not subjected to more Scouse bias, but in the end, I don't, and as the game unfolds my fears grow and I have no confidence at all that we will progress to the final.

Michael Ballack wins the ball and the ref blows for a foul. It was never a foul, and the free-kick is taken from completely the wrong place by Xabi Alonso. I'm up out my seat and almost know what's coming as Alonso's delivery creates panic in the Chelsea penalty, ricochet's back and forth eventually falls to Dirk Kuyt. My, '*no... no NO!*' getting louder and when the ball hits the back of the net I scream, '*f\*ck it*', and slam my hand down on the sofa and my fifteen-month-old daughter jumps and whimpers and then cries at my outburst as she's never seen aggression like that from me, and my pregnant wife storms off to bed saying she's got a headache, which leaves me on baby duty while the semi-final first leg unfolds.

I've rarely doubted God's existence (although I've had my moments) and I certainly believe wholeheartedly He exists now. You know what's coming. The 94th minute, The Kop singing their anthem, Salomon Kalou crosses the ball and John Arne Riise scores the most incredible own goal in the history of football. I go spare. Who doesn't? I am convinced that no-one in my block of flats is spared from my celebratory outbursts. My daughter wakes up screaming, the Doris screams at me some more from the bedroom. I go and pick her up (my daughter, not my Doris), I've got stars spinning round my head, the *Rivals* message board open on my lap top crashes due to the huge volume of traffic and posts, because they are pouring in. Mark Hughes defends us in the ITV studio with a wry smile on his face and a euphoric spark in his eye, yes, we have actually done it, not only an away goal – but the sweet, beautiful way in which it came was just miraculous. I settle my daughter back down in her cot and attempt to sleep on the sofa but I'm buzzing so much I can't sleep with the adrenaline overload.

A new chant was born. The *Johnny Come Marching Home / English Civil War* song had evolved again:

*He came from the Ivory Coast, Kalou, Kalou.*
*He don't do coke like Adrian Mutu, Mutu.*
*He crossed the ball from the left, it landed right on Riise's head,*
*And that's why we love Salomon Kalou!*
*La La La La La La La La La La La La!*

Oh, good Lord. The 94th minute! YNWA silenced by John Arne Riise – I really don't have the words. It took a few days for the own goal to sink in. It does on Saturday night at my pal Al's fiftieth birthday party. The DJ plays, *Wonderful World, Beautiful People* by Jimmy Cliff, and the Doris comes over and takes my hand to lead me to the dance floor, and I know she's forgiven me. We watch our daughter toddling around. She is dancing in front of disco lights and trying to catch bubbles from the bubble machine and I feel conscious about my 'dancing' feet as the Doris leads me. Before the night ends, *One Step Beyond* is pumped out. The party is reaching a climax, I have my wife's forgiveness, I have a daughter that likes reggae and *Madness* are bringing the party to an end. It's all set up for the second leg. Come on, Chelsea!

**Mark:** Major Tom Broderick and myself 'somehow' found ourselves sat in the wrong section of the Centenary Stand at Anfield on what became known as Riise Night. We were almost level with the Norwegian when Kalou crossed the ball, and both of us would testify in court to the fact that the stereo effect of The Kop to our immediate left being muted and Chelsea's travelling support housed to our right in the Anfield Road end going ballistic was 'proper Dolby'. Trying to disguise our delight at what had just happened proved tricky, but on this occasion fortune favoured the brave.

The recent *Sloop John B* recreation that was *F\*ck your history, we're going to Moscow* was sung with more conviction on the way home from Anfield thanks to Kalou's assist, and just over a week later (30 April) Chelsea beat Liverpool 3-2 at Stamford Bridge (Didier Drogba x2, Frank Lampard) to win the tie 4-3 on aggregate.

**Walter:** *The Entertainer* then formed the basis for this jewel.

*Tell everyone you know that Chelsea are going to Moscow!*
*We'll be flying from Gatwick coz tickets are hard to get,*
*Chelsea are going to Moscow!*

## John Arne Riise

The 1962 hit *Hey! Baby* by Bruce Channel was covered by Austrian DJ Ötzi in 2000 and served as the tune to commemorate Riise's own goal:

*John Arne Riise, ooo-ah!*
*I wanna know, how did you score that goal? You ginger c\*nt!*

Good old John Arne signed for Fulham in July 2011. On 9 April 2012, I went to watch Chelsea play Fulham at Craven Cottage (Fulham 1 Chelsea 1, Frank Lampard). Standing in the wooden away end at Craven Cottage, the sound reverberating across the Thames and Bishops Park, West London's finest reminded Riise time and time again that Kalou crossed the ball in from the left, and also that he was a ginger so and so!

## Fernando Torres again.

Torres signed for Chelsea on 31 January 2011. Despite hit and miss form for the Blues, our crowd supported him relentlessly unlike poor Salamon Kalou who was barracked by sections of our support.

The Spain international's arrival at Stamford Bridge saw the *English Civil War* ditty transition once again. The Kop's version was meaningless, as was the *Carragher's bit on the side* homophobic shocker that was widely sung by fans of opposing club's including Chelsea's when Torres had featured for

Liverpool against their team. Now he was <u>our</u> number nine.

*He's now a blue he was a red, Torres Torres.*
*He left The Kop to join the Shed, Torres Torres.*
*He used to go out on the rob, but now he's got a proper job!*
*Fernando Torres, Chelsea's number nine.*

If I look carefully, I still think I can see the bruises all over my legs from going bananas in the Nou Camp in 2012. (24 April 2012, Champions League semi-final, second leg, Barcelona 2 Chelsea 2, Ramires, Fernando Torres). No further explanation needed! By way of a curious coincidence, both Torres and Kalou came on as second-half substitutes in this game and both would play a part in the final.

**The Clash:** *Live at Shea Stadium* **New York City, 13 October 1982.**

While researching this piece to I stumbled across a live version of the *English Civil War* and I am utterly perplexed as to how I had not heard it before! The intro is brilliant, the MC screaming, *"So will you welcome all the way from Ladbroke Grove London W10 – The Clash! Come on!"* Give your ears a treat, if you fancy it, it's on Spotify! Me? I'm still singing; *There was 21 seconds to go, when Kalou scored the goal, cross from Shevchenko at Vicarage Road, there was 21 seconds when Kalou scored the goal.*

21 seconds to go. Squad number 21. God Bless Salomon Kalou.

**Finally:**

I was thinking bragging rights were secured for Chelsea regarding 'first use' of *English Civil War*, right up to the moment the editor of this book read this chapter and told me that, in truth, Blues supporters were forty years behind their Liverpool counterparts.

As has been noted in earlier chapters, in March 1965 Liverpool beat Chelsea 2-0 in an FA Cup semi-final at Villa Park. The Kop reworked *Johnny Comes Marching Home* and came up with:

*While on the bus to Villa Park haroo, haroo.*
*I heard my mate make this remark, haroo, haroo.*
*We made poor Chelsea weep and ill, it's Liverpool two and Chelsea nil,*
*And we'll all get blind drunk when Liverpool win the cup!*

Like it or not, Reds supporters had a version years before Salamon

## CAREFREE! CHELSEA CHANTS AND TERRACE CULTURE

Kalou or Fernando Torres were even born. Joe Strummer, lead singer of *The Clash*, was only twelve-years old, and chanting on the terraces had only just started to organically blossom, let alone be as creative and symbolic as this from the Scousers.

Like a wonder goal from the opposition, sometimes you've just got to sit back, nod your head and admire it.

# THE WIGAN TRAIN

**Walter:** *The Lion Sleeps Tonight*, also known as *Wimba Way* is a song written and recorded originally by Solomon Linda for the South African Gallo Record Company in 1939. A while back I was sent a link of a clip of an inebriated Villa fan on a train singing a song about their striker Christian Benteke to the tune.

*There was a striker, a Belgian striker called Christian Ben-tek-e.*
*There was a striker, a Belgian striker called Christian Ben-tek-e.*
*Two, three, four…*
*A Ben-teke, a Ben-tek-e, a Ben-teke, a Ben-tek-e*

It made me laugh and shake my head both at the same time. Gone are the days when you can have a drink and a sing on trains, in pubs and on concourses without the world and his wife filming.

Whether they're desperate for *YouTube* hits or to gain respect for being there when 'it' happened, (whatever 'it' was going to be), I don't know. But elements of your whole day out are filmed by various random people at different stages. It's part of the package now. This takes out the spontaneity of the day out for me, probably spoiling the experience. I think it keeps people on edge as they're more likely to feel judged or not want to risk being humiliated if something goes amiss. I mean – if you've ever been there when a *Chelsea Alouette* goes wrong the last thing the choirmaster wants is to be mocked on social media.

Don't get me wrong, sometimes it is brilliant – a solid memory never to be erased of a significant moment following your team, for instance the fifty-second clip from March 2009, *We are Chelsea in Turin*, brings goose bumps – the chaps on the Perspex fencing arms aloft applauding their team is what it's all about.

I also love the Coventry supporters at half-time against Arsenal in the FA Cup (January 2014) – 2-0 down on the concourse and singing *Twist and Shout* – one supporter has a pint in one hand and is using the bin as a drum with his other hand, it could be one of my mates or one of yours. Sadly, in these times, he could quite easily be ejected for being drunk, fined for damage to property (denting a bin) lose his job if he got grassed up to his employers and, as a result, get banned by his Club from going to games.

The Villa fan singing about Benteke in 2014 was mocked and adored in equal measure. Ten years previously in 2004, he probably never would've been recorded.

Train journeys have the potential to be the highlight of the day. The way up to the game with beers and mates, photos and laughter. Catching up with your friends, forging memories and moments, a break from work coupled with the anticipation of the match to come, combine to give you that comfortable buzz that you really wouldn't want to be anywhere else at that moment in time.

The train journey back can be messy, funny, tiresome, annoying, stressful, forgettable or memorable – or a little bit of all these things! Best of all, songs can be forged. Time needs to be killed. To quote lyrics from *Oom-Pah-Pah* on the *Oliver!* Soundtrack; *There's a little ditty, they're singing in the City, espeshly when they've been on the gin or the beer.* When you mix in the ingredients of friends, football, travelling and above all alcohol, what else are you going to do?

When the Club announce a dry train, then that obviously means no alcohol allowed. But booze is an essential ingredient to bonding with pals and creating chants. As the seasons have rolled by and Club trains have become more regular, smuggling booze on has become more creative, and crackdowns have become more military.

At first it was both obvious and simple – prepare a bottle of Coke and fill it with rum or whiskey, or mix vodka and lemonade to replace the water in your bottle of Evian. (As is detailed in the story below.) Soon, the stewards were on the platforms, bottle tops were being removed, drinks sniffed and ditched in the bin before being welcomed aboard. Then, in some cases, soft bottles were only allowed on if the seals were unbroken. I went to Ewood Park one year (2008 I think) and met Cathy McDonnell in the pub who was feeling slightly unwell. She'd filled a Frijj chocolate milkshake with Bailey's, drank it on the dry train journey, and now was on pints of cider. Curdle o'clock! Fans started buying up miniatures and storing them in knickers, bras, socks and boxer shorts.

As often happened, the unofficial Chelsea website *Rivals'* message board was a place of inspiration. As cfcww writes: "A number of *Rivals* regs could be found in O'Neill's prior to a 'dry train' away day, busily hollowing out bread rolls to lay small miniature vodka bottles in, covering them up with token ham and salad, then wrapping them up in cling film. British subterfuge at its finest!" This spurred a memory from mhl_pete regarding beating the booze ban: "The *'Eine Baguetten Special'* was, I believe, a midweek trip to Hull. The booze was inside the baguette. I remember thinking there's no way I'll get it on – the steward checked the carrier bag from the bottom and it weighed a f*cking ton, but he didn't pick up on it."

This journey also featured a magnificent *'Pork Pie Salad Surprise'* from PeterCFC and a four pack of a panda pops type drink, one of which contained a little more than the stated ingredients. I also had a bottle of refreshing *'chocolate milkshake'* for dessert."

Preston North End away in the FA Cup in January 2010 (23 January, Preston 0 Chelsea 2, Nicolas Anelka, Daniel Sturridge) saw a new level of cunning. MHLPisshead's wife was inspired by Jamie Oliver, a watermelon and chi chi barbecues. She adapted the idea and provided her husband with syringes from her veterinary supply, the two fattest oranges that money could buy, and half a bottle of vodka. The vodka was injected into the oranges at home, carried onto the dry train, and consumed by the time the train had reached Preston. This surely must win some prize!

*****

3 November 2007, Chelsea played away at Wigan Athletic and won 2-0 (Frank Lampard, Juliano Belletti) with the Wigan chairman Dave Whelan only charging away fans £15 a ticket. He understood that he'd rather have a sold out away end buying his pies and booze, (and an odd matchday programme), than not. Other clubs should have taken note. Which of course, they didn't. I couldn't find any evidence to support this, but I'm fairly certain that Whelan also stated that with Christmas approaching, it was a time for budgeting, especially for football supporters. (Later that season, Chelsea repaid Whelan's generosity by charging Wigan fans a whopping £48 to come to the Bridge!)

For the game at the JJB Stadium, Chelsea laid on supporter trains for only a tenner a ticket which we happily snapped up. While going through my personal archives looking for inspiration and ideas for this book, I came across an article I'd written about this trip. It was never published in *cfcuk* due to an administrative error, so here it is in all its glory. It really was the funniest train journey I have ever had. I have no idea if you will relate to this as a reader, but I do hope it conjures up memorable moments from your travels far and wide to support the team.

Interestingly enough, a chap called Stephen (The Sherman Chef) and his son Simon were on our carriage on the journey back to London, both of whom are now good friends. When I plan to take in a home game, I always try and meet up with The Sherman Chef and his now grown up lad for a pre-match drink. Indeed, their circle of pals have become good mates too – it's funny how things turn out sometimes.

## TICKER TACKER, TICKER TACKER – OI OI OI!

I'm standing in the kitchen with a carving knife in my hand and a roast chicken in front of me feeling like my Dad as I slice off the skin and pop it in my mouth – I'm remembering as a kid how I used to watch the old man with awe doing the same thing as he expertly carved the roast up and stole pieces of skin on the way, grinning at me and flicking chicken skin in his mouth.

He'd tell me it was the carver's privilege to eat the extra skin, and now here I am doing the same, turning into my Dad as I carve and munch the golden skin, listening to my wife educating me that chicken skin has got more fat in it than an entire roast lamb – *you won't want any then*, I tell her with a grin – while slicing off a bit more and trying not to burn my mouth.

When I saw my Dad last week he asked me what I wanted for Christmas. I replied he could pay for my Blackburn away ticket (23 December 2007, Blackburn Rovers 0 Chelsea 1, Joe Cole), he grumbled a response about how some things never change, and now I listen to him moaning about the football and the players' salaries and how his council tax will probably go up again. So, I tell him he'll have a free bus pass in less than three years and he half swings for me, so I dodge the palm of his hand to escape a clip round the ear.

"You're not too young for a slap," he says – how many times have I heard that – and he doesn't get football, or any other sport for that matter – he thinks that because I'm going to Wigan for a match in November there's no need to go to another game in December.

The Wigan chairman deserves huge respect for his cheap ticket prices and the £10 train from Roman was incredibly well received. I can't say I blame them for not allowing booze on the train, but where there is a will there is a way as far as me, Big Chris, Tall Paul and Smiffy were concerned.

At Euston on the platform, standing by the doors to our carriage, two stewards with a clipboard take our names and tick us off. After taking our seats on the train, two different stewards with a clipboard approach us, take our names, tick us off, and move down the carriage.

A few minutes later, another steward bursts into the carriage all hot and flustered and flapping his arms. He has a massive go at everyone in the carriage for jumping on the train without getting ticked off first. He starts shouting about what will happen if the train crashes, that he won't know who is present or who is missing. Everyone looks at each other in bemusement. Firstly, because we have all been ticked off twice already, and secondly because if the train crashes it'll be every man for his mates and himself to get away safely, no clipboard in sight – the fuming steward in front of us continues to shake his finger at all in the carriage, everyone bursts out laughing.

When the train leaves Euston, I've hardly got the lid off my rum and coke when the guard makes a special announcement over the Tannoy that a certain fanzine seller will be making his way down the train selling the latest edition. A huge cheer went up, and Dave done a good bit of business that day selling a copy of *cfcuk* to nearly every supporter on the train.

The first laugh of the journey up to Wigan came when Tall Paul opened his litre Evian bottle filled with vodka and lemonade. As he twisted the lid, the pressure from the gas and the fizz blew the lid off and a wealth of his carefully concocted beverage splashed all over the table and down his jumper.

The second laugh of the journey came when the trained slowed to a halt just past Rugby. Everyone looked out the window, as you do when the train is stationary, and we were alongside a traveller site. All the kids out playing looked up. They stopped kicking and bouncing their balls, got off their bikes grimaced at us with their unique snarl and gave us all the finger until the train started to pull away. Well, it would have been rude of them not to.

It was one of those away day moments to cherish when stepping off the train and a song erupts. It gathered momentum as the multitudes left the platform, became louder as we headed for the exit – *Hello! Hello! We Are The Chelsea Boys!* It echoes off the roof and reverberates around the station, onlookers no doubt feeling a mixture of surprise, fascination and slight intimidation as over five-hundred thirsty supporters explode onto the High Street – most of them dying for a pint – it's Saturday afternoon and it's a traditional 3pm kick off; none of us would rather be anywhere else.

We walked to the ground and got drinking in the Marquee and there's a father and son that I don't know by name, but I recognize from the Cock when I started drinking in there circa 1993. (Note: 9 March 2016 before the 2-1 home Champions League defeat to Paris Saint Germain, Diego Costa,

I'm formally introduced, after all these years, to Mark and Wayne.)

Then I find myself chatting to a fella I haven't seen since pre-match at Watford, (31 March 2007, Watford 0 Chelsea 1, Salomon Kalou), we get into our seats and stand all game. Chelsea are dominant with goals from Super Frank and Juliano Belletti before twenty minutes is even on the clock.

As we made our way out the ground, I stop on the bridge over the canal and stand and ask everyone down below to, *give me a C!* and everything in the world felt so good. Back onto the High Street, with less than half an hour until our train, we decide to split up. Tall Paul and Big Chris reckon the stewards won't be checking for booze, so they nip to the off licence for supplies. Me and Smiffy go to the kebab house for a takeaway for everyone and we agree to meet back at the station. Luckily it all worked out.

It's proper chaotic at the train station so we pile on any carriage and manage to get around a table, all four of us sitting together. There had been no checks for booze and everyone has piled loads on. I reach into my takeaway bag and toss my three pals a large chicken kebab each with salad wrapped up in paper rather than packed in a polystyrene box. We are all ravenous, destroying our dinner in a matter of minutes. While we eat a bit of drunken post-match singing begins up and down our carriage. I honestly cannot remember such a blinding kebab. It's on a different level. First one I've had without pitta, but wrapped up in a naan type bread, it was incredible. I guess that it's all right up norf, sometimes.

Before long the stewards stepped into the carriage with a large clipboard in hand. Instantly, groans went up from everyone, followed by a round of laughter, because everyone had groaned simultaneously when the stewards had walked in. Our table was first in the firing line. With a dramatic swing of his arm, the steward plopped his clipboard down with a thump on our mayonnaise and chilli sauce stained table. He grinned widely and asked us for our names. Smiffy leans towards him and says loudly: "Gianfranco." The steward repeats the name under his breath, muttering, "Gianfranco, Gianfranco, Gianfranco", while tapping his biro on his clipboard and studying the paperwork. The steward looks back at Smiffy. The steward doesn't realise that he has the focus of the whole carriage. He looks up and says to Smiffy: "Gianfranco? Um, surname please?" Smiffy looks up at him, smiles, and says in a louder voice: "Zola."

As one, the whole carriage absolutely cracks up. And so, it began. Someone on the adjacent table points at the steward and starts singing: *Sign on! Sign on! With a pen in your hand, and you'll never tick us off, you'll neeeever tick us off!* The whole carriage joins in. To be fair to the steward, he was actually alright. He took it all in good spirits. Big Chris was holding his belly, trying to keep his kebab down and not be sick with laughter, happy tears streaming down the stubble on his cheeks. The scene was set.

Song after song ensued. Here's a selection of the Chelsea songs the carriage sung that were reworked to embrace 'ticking':

*Tick us off, tick us off, tick us tick us off. We're the boys in blue in Division Ttwo and you'll never tick us off!*
*Get your ticks out, get your ticks out, get your ticks out for the lads!*
*One man went to tick, went to tick us off, one man and his clipboard (and pen!) went to tick us off!* (Yes, we went all the way up to ten men.)
*You won't tick us off! You won't tick us off! You won't tick us, you won't tick us, you won't tick us off!* (Tune: *Knees Up Mother Brown!*)
*You will never tick us off, over land and sea, and Leicester! You will never tick us off, onto victory! Altogether now!*

It all died down after maybe half an hour, there were other songs sung with the same theme that I can't even remember now. And just when everyone thought that was that, wiping their eyes and feeling exhausted from a long, boozy day out, embracing few welcome seconds of silence, a young lad (Simon) suddenly piped up:

*TICKER TACKER, TICKER TACKER!*

And the whole carriage replied, *OI! OI! OI!* And off we went again.

It was one of those moments where I was crying with laughter. And it didn't end there. At the other end of the carriage was a bunch of lads, probably aged between fifteen and seventeen years of age. For some reason, they stood up and started to do the Conga, singing: *Do do do! Come on and do the Conga! Do The Conga* was a UK chart hit for Black Lace in 1984 which made it quite bizarre and rightly, the poor bastards got absolutely slaughtered for trying to get that going!

***Editor's note:*** *Weirdly though, a couple of years later, The Conga would provide the melody to the popular Nicolas Anelka tribute chant, Nicolas Anelka... do, do, do. Maybe these lads were responsible for it.*

**Walter:** *What the f\*ck, what the f\*ck? What the f\*cking hell was that? What the f\*cking hell was that?* Followed by, *You what? You what? You what, you what you what?*

But, fair play to them, they retaliated with:
*Back for the bingo! You're getting back for the bingo!*

And it continued going back and forth between the yoof and the olds:

**Olds:** *We were here, we were here, we were here when you were sperm! We were here when you were sperm!*
**Yoof:** *Put your slippers on, put your slippers, put your slippers on.*
**Olds:** *ASBOs, ASBOs, ASBOs.*
**Yoof:** *Ovaltine, Ovaltine, Ovaltine.*
**Olds:** *Does your mother, does your mother, does your mother know you're here?*
**Yoof:** *Werthers Originals, Werthers Originals, Werthers Originals, Werthers Originals!*
**Olds:** *You watch CBeebies, la la la la la la, you watch CBeebies.*

**Walter:** Then somehow, the mention of *CBeebies* made the jump to the topic of nursery rhymes. The next thing I can recall was Big Chris standing up and singing at them: *If you're happy and you know it clap your hands!* And, well, the whole carriage clapped. And Big Chris carried on. And, no word of a lie, I then unbelievably witnessed an entire carriage of mostly well pissed, or in some cases very sober, Chelsea fans old and young singing together *and* doing the actions to: *If you're happy and you know it, pat your head,* while patting their head. Incredible.

Then one of the yoof who had waited for his moment belted out *Chelsea Allouette*. Respect. I can't see myself attempting that one. When the song was finished, he got a huge round of applause and a standing ovation. I walked to their end of the carriage and extended my hand and the lot of them greeted me with: *Are you Wenger in disguise?* B*stards! They certainly had the last laugh, but they didn't leave me hanging, we all shook hands.

It had been a train journey like no other, and jumping on the tube back to Wimbledon an Australian lady sat next to me and instantly struck up a conversation with me, asking about my day. In my younger years, I was always unnerved by Australians or New Zealanders chatting away or striking up conversations. It wasn't until I went to Australia myself in 2005 for a few months that I realised it's what they do. It's natural.

(On my first day near the town of Mooloolaba, I was in the supermarket looking for decent bacon. I was told it didn't exist, but I had to find out for myself, and I can clarify that it doesn't exist, all the bacon is like cardboard, well it was in 2005. Other customers choosing what yoghurts to buy on the adjacent shelf would ask me, "how you going mate? What you up to later, mate?", and I was completely taken aback. I realised then that's how it is with them, and I had to get used to it.)

So – I tell this young Australian lady sitting next to me on the tube to Wimbledon that I've been to the football and had a great day out. She winked at me and told me every man needs a Garden Shed. I smiled back and told her she didn't know how right she was. I then got all reflective about terrace days. As she stepped off the tube I blew her a kiss goodbye and sang, *We're the middle of The Shed* to myself.

At Wimbledon, Smiffy left to get a bus home. Me, Big Chris and Tall Paul waited for the train to Worcester Park. My Doris and our baby girl were staying over Paul's, and I couldn't wait to get back. When all is said and done, I just want to see my baby. We get in and I sink a pint of water, and refill my glass. I quietly open the door to Tall Paul's spare room and close it behind me. I looked at my ten-month-old daughter sleeping soundly for a while and thanked God for her. I lent down into her travel cot, drew her blanket up and over her shoulders and tucked her in. I sat on the edge of my bed, took off my socks and shoes, and then pulled my top over my head. The Doris stirred. I turned to look at my wife. Eyes closed, she mumbled at me not to be a sex pest. Well, you can't blame a man for trying, not that I had even got around to the trying! I hadn't even got my kit off and climbed into bed. Who needs sex anyway? I've just had a banging time going Chelsea away. Brilliant!

# IVANOVIĆ

*Ivanović! Der-der-der-der-der.*
*Ivanović! Der-der-der-der.*
*Ivanović! Der-der-der-der-der, der-der-der, der-der-der, der-der-der-der, Chelsea's number two!*

**Walter:** I first met Stan in the flesh at the Arkles pub by Stanley Park, Liverpool L4. At the outset I struggle to remember who and when, then the more I think about it the more I'm sure it was away to Everton in the FA Cup Fourth Round 29 January 2011 (Everton 1 Chelsea 1, Salomon Kalou).

I'd gone up in the motor with Taxi Alan, Champagne Les and Smiffy. I remember a group of pissed-up younger lot falling into the Arkles half-cut singing about *Josh McEachran having a party*. At the queue for the turnstiles Smiffy and I both had large quantities of celery confiscated, but Smiffy still managed to smuggle a load in. Don't ask. The match was a draw, Everton won the replay via a penalty shoot-out (19 February, Chelsea 1 Everton 1, Frank Lampard, penalties Chelsea 3 Everton 4, Frank Lampard ✓ Didier Drogba ✓ Nicolas Anelka oh dear, Michael Essien ✓ Ashley Cole oh dear).

Stan and I, amongst several others, had communicated a lot over the years on the *Rivals* message board. We exchanged phone numbers over email. After I arrived in the Arkles he texted me: *"I'm over by the pool tables under a poster of Gerrard with the European Cup. Boooooo."* Over I went, we met, and the rest is history.

Stan, a Matthew Harding Lower season ticket holder, is the *Ivanović!* song creator.

The big-bummed Serb, (Branna, not Stan), arrived in January 2008 for £9 million. To quote @JakeFCohen on *Twitter*: "In 9 years with Chelsea, Ivanović managed 68 goals and assists (34 each). That's over 7.5 per season coming from a RB/CB." Jake continues: "In Steven Gerrard's last five seasons at LFC, he scored 28 non-penalty goals. Guess how many Ivanović scored over that same period? 28."

It's been a couple of weeks since Branislav was sold to Zenit Saint Petersburg (31 January 2017). I'm sitting with Stan in the Pembroke in West Brompton London SW5, tucked up in the corner with my back to the door. We're drinking with Scott and Johnny before the home game with Swansea (25 February, Chelsea 3 Swansea City 1, Cesc Fàbregas, Pedro, Diego

Costa) – also *Rivals* regulars who I met through the message board.

**Stan:** "I was born in 1981 in Westminster Hospital and lived in Pimlico. My older brother and my Dad were Chelsea regulars – but they would mostly go mid-week because Dad worked a lot of weekends. I was conscious of them leaving the house together to go the football, so I would nag them – beg them to let me go with them – but they never took me.

Finally, they relented. My first game was Palace at home in the semi-final second leg of the Full Members Cup – sponsored by Zenith Data Systems. I can remember the date – it was 3 March 1990. My Dad took me, I remember going up to the main gate by the old Club shop entrance – we arrived and the gates were shut! That has always sat with me – it's a distinct memory. I bought a programme and then we were told that the game was called off because of high winds! Match postponed! I couldn't believe it.

The game was re-arranged for 12 March and I bought another programme because on the cover it said it was re-issued and updated – but it was exactly the same one! It cost a pound. Chelsea won 2-0 (John Bumstead, Gareth Hall). The attendance was 15,061, my brother and I sat in the posh seats (East Middle), which back then cost a dizzying £12.50 or so.

We were already two up from the first leg (21 February, Crystal Palace 0 Chelsea 2) – I remember Kerry Dixon and Kevin Wilson scoring in that game. This sticks out in my mind because we wore a white kit. It was our third kit – a Commodore sponsored V-neck with a blue trim. I can't remember us wearing the kit again. The next match I attended after that was Sheffield Wednesday in the League Cup semi-final first leg (24 February 1991, Chelsea 0 Sheffield Wednesday 2)."

**Walter:** I remember that kit. I think loads of fans kicked off because it looked like a Tottenham shirt. I was at that Wednesday game. There was a feeling in the air we'd lose. I remember they packed out the away end and every man and his dog had balloons. They were everywhere. I thought to myself that I wish our fans had done that. There'd been such a massive build up because we hadn't won a major trophy for twenty years.

We'd done Spurs 3-0 in a replay at The Lane in the quarter-finals, (23 January, Andy Townsend, Kerry Dixon, Dennis Wise), but we were terrible against the Owls. The fans froze and so did the players. I thought I'd never get to see Chelsea at Wembley, let alone lift a Cup. They were a division below us but were flying high. They had David Hirst, Trevor Francis, Chris

Waddle, Carlton Palmer. In the second leg, we wore a red kit. I don't remember us wearing that ever again.

**Scott:** "I was at the Bridge for the Wednesday game, too. I was in the family section in the East Lower. There were two of their fans in front of me, a mum with her son. He looked about thirteen-years-old. Thing is, he was completely blind. She talked to him the whole game. Not only did I have to deal with getting well beaten at home in a cup semi, I had two Wednesday fans in front of me and I had to endure a f*cking running commentary."

**Walter:** We all fall about laughing. Sheffield Wednesday went on to beat us 5-1 on aggregate (second leg, Wednesday 3 Chelsea 1, Graham Stuart) and in the final, they beat Man United 1-0.

I ask Scott if he has any other stand out memories from his youth.

**Scott:** "When I was about nine-years-old," he says, necking some more lager before carrying on, "I asked my Dad why fans had inflatable celery. It must have been about 1989 when inflatables were all the rage for a bit. My Dad told me to ring the Club shop to find out. So, I did. The bloke who answered laughed and said the inflatable celery was obviously because of the celery song – and then he sang the song down the phone to me!"

**Walter:** As mentioned previously, Matt Lucas was working in the Club shop around that time with Kenny Christmas. It would be hilarious if it was Matt or Ken that had serenaded young Scott, but they both would've been too young.

"What was your first game?" I ask him. He looks as me and finishes his drink. His answer is brief. We all know the game he refers to – Easter Monday 1986 (31 March).

**Scott:** "Lost 6-0 at Loftus Road. Drink anyone?"

**Walter:** Off Scott goes to the bar. I prompt Stan to explain how his chant for Ivanović came about.

**Scott:** "I was sitting on the khazi at work and it came to mind. At first, I didn't realise it was the theme tune to *The Muppet Show*, I was simply working on the fact that the syllables fit. *I-van-o-vić!* I sang it to my pal Brad – he loved it. Others I sang it to just told me to f*ck right off! Brad and I first tried it at West Ham away (25 April 2009, West Ham 0 Chelsea 1,

Salamon Kalou).

It was the game when Gianfranco Zola was their manager, and Petr Cech saved a penalty from Mark Noble. Ivanović played the full match, previously he'd been more of a bit part player really. Well, we try to get it going, and Doug shouts at us: "What the f*ck are you pair of c*nts singing?" and that was that.

It became a bit of a challenge to me and Brad – we tried it mostly at away games. Then someone said to us, "I heard that in the boozer" and so it was then that we realised it had enjoyed a bit of success – another group of fans we didn't know had been singing it in a pub. The first time it took off was Arsenal away (29 November 2009, Arsenal 0 Chelsea 3, Didier Drogba x2, Thomas Vermaelen own goal). The thing is, it was mad because someone else started it! Brad was like, "F*ckin' hell, that's our song!" We both had a sense of surprise and bewilderment. It started off as a bit of a joke, people seemed confused, and then, yeah, it took off.

That game is also memorable because the next time we went to Arsenal we got spanked 3-1 (27 December 2010) and Brana scored our goal! We had a fight in KFC after and then later on it all kicked off again in a gay bar in Leicester Square. Don't ask.

Over time, the song morphed. For me, it was supposed to go on and on – that was the point. Then at some stage people started going, *Sssshhh*, after, *Chelsea's Number Two,* and then another fan would start it again. To be honest, I don't like how it morphed."

**Walter:** Hilariously (well, I thought so, anyway) the *Mah Nà Mah Nà* song written by Piero Umilliani debuted as part of a soundtrack for a 1968 Italian film titled, *Svezia, inferno e paradiso* which translates as: *Sweden: Heaven and Hell.* It is a documentary film about wild sexual activity and other behaviour in Sweden. The song accompanied a scene in the film set in a sauna which was originally titled, *Viva la Sauna Svedese* which means, *Hooray for the Swedish Sauna.* It was performed by a band called Marc 4 and the lead part was sung by Italian singer/composer Alessandro Alessandroni and his wife Giulia.

Many versions followed and via *Sesame Street* and *The Benny Hill Show,* the most famous performance of all, Ivanović excepted, came in the first episode of *The Muppet Show* that first aired on TV in 1976. As a result Piero Umilliani's original version of *Mah Nà Mah Nà* was re-released and reached was a top-ten hit in the UK the following year!

## CAREFREE! CHELSEA CHANTS AND TERRACE CULTURE

I explain to Stan that I like how the Ivanović chant morphed. For me, it still fits, he disagreed – which is fine, I can see why. We go on to discuss other songs – songs for past players.

**Stan:** "Dennis Wise in the San Siro is historic. We must have had 10,000 out there (26 October 1999, Champions League, Round One Match Five, AC Milan 1 Chelsea 1, Dennis Wise)."

*Oh Dennis Wise,*
*Scored a f\*cking great goal,*
*In the San Siro, ten minutes to go.*

***Editor's note:*** *The Dennis Wise chant borrows sections of the melody from the Pat Boone version of Speedy Gonzales, a song about the fastest mouse in all Mexico that charted in 1962.*

**Stan:** "*His Name Is Tommy Baldwin* and *Osgood Osgood* are songs that have stood the test of time, and rightly so. It's proper that we should acknowledge former players and their contributions. I don't like the *Gerrard / Demba Ba* song (See *Best Of The Rest* chapter). That didn't benefit us. It's about a moment in time. I don't like the *Lampard 200* (excluded from this book) song either. I just associate that with Rafa Benitez being our manager.

I love what I call *The Comeback Song* – it gathered momentum over the summer of 2014 on *Twitter* and that – and then we played Burnley away (18 August 2014, Burnley 1 Chelsea 3, Diego Costa, André Schürrle, Branislav Ivanović) – our first game of the season and everyone got on it: *Olé, Olé, Olé, Olé! Chelsea, Chelsea!* This was a perfect example of how social media can be quality. Everyone was behind it. The chant had phased itself out over the late 1990s for some reason, it was great to have it back."

**Walter:** Several hours later after this initial chat and the match itself, we end up post-match in the Rose (which I still call the Tup) and a few more *Rivals* message board regulars are in tow. Six Nil Kez has an unlit Benson dangling from her mouth, arguing with Giant Jon about something while Campo and Stan watch on laughing.

Two Pints rolls his eyes and gets his phone out, scrolls through his gallery and shows me photos on his phone (taken of his original photos) from the early 1980s tour to Sweden. He tells me he's got some old posters in the loft that were put up around the towns before pre-seasons in Sweden and in Aberystwyth.

Scott chips in and says he's been thinking about songs since our chat this morning. He talks about the Chelsea players version of *Chelsea Alouette*, the final track on *Blue is the Colour* that Mark references earlier in this book. He tells me that it is available on iTunes and I should have a listen. (So later that week, I do!)

Scott and Two Pints explain that the track is introduced by Eddie McCreadie featuring David Webb as the lead singer and it is the original song with its original lyrics, and it was often heard in pubs regularly lead by fan Billy Bond.

Scott holds his hands out, palms up, ready to educate me. Two Pints smiles and nods, the Guinness making his eyes twinkle, backing Scott up all the way.

**Scott:** "Thing is, Walts, this is different to the sub-par egg-chasing version that seems to be the most prevalent today. I'm not sure when or where or why it changed, but these are the key differences: treble chin, wilky eye, hare-lip, slim skim waist, knocky knees and pigeon toes."

**Walter:** "Seriously? What about VD and hairy arse?"

**Two Pints:** "Na! Slim skim waist and knocky knees mate!"

**Walter:** I knock my head back and shout to the roof; *Oh, she had a hairy arse!* We all have a laugh and then Campo leans in and anounces he's getting another round in for everyone. Bottoms up!

**Two Pints:** "The only song that I miss singing is one that we used to sing every Boxing Day back in the early 1980s when we nearly always played Queens Park Rangers away. (26 December 1981, QPR 0 Chelsea 2, Clive Walker, Alan Mayes: 27 December 1982, QPR 1 Chelsea 2, Clive Walker, David Speedie: 26 December 1984, QPR 2 Chelsea 2, Kerry Dixon x2) The reasons I think this died out was because we got promoted and didn't play them that often and because of our connection with (Glasgow) Rangers in Scotland.

> *Hark now hear the Chelsea sing. The Rangers run away.*
> *And we will fight forever more, because of Boxing Day.*

It used to boom around Loftus Road in the old days from all sides of the ground and used to send a shiver down me as it sounded like the whole ground was singing it! Although, it was probably because I think QPR had their own version of the song with different lyrics. Nonetheless, as a teenager travelling away, to me it was f*cking brilliant and stuck with me. I tried to get the song going recently when we played them in the cup but just got a load of weird looks!"

**Walter:** The chant is based on the 18th Century *Hymn for Christmas Day* by Charles Wesley. Wesley's original hymn began with the opening line *Hark how all the Welkin rings* – this was changed to the familiar *Hark! the Herald Angels sing* by George Whitefield in his 1754 *Collection of hymns for social worship*.

The hymn later took on different versions and recordings. One of the best-known cover versions of the song is by disco-group Boney M from 1978, *Mary's Boy Child – Oh My Lord*. This version returned the song to the top of the UK charts and given the timing of the Chelsea version (there were/are plenty sung by other clubs) was probably the catalyst for the terrace songsmiths to do their stuff.

Capitalising on his reflective mood, I encourage Two Pints to continue, prompting him with questions about his recollections regarding the origins of *Zigger Zagger* and the like. He nurses his pint, those pupils of his twinkling some more, the creases on the side of his eyes become more apparent as he screws his face up, digging deep into his Chelsea memories.

**Two Pints:** "I can just remember Mickey Greenaway and his famous *Zigger Zagger* chant. I could clearly hear it from The Shed, later on in the Benches and on many away trips when he used to sit in the seats. The chant was hugely impressive to me as a youngster because Mickey used to be in the opposite side of the ground to me.

If he was in the lower tier of the East stand (next to the away fans) I could hear him! It went on forever – getting faster and faster in a high pitch scream – I will never know how he managed to keep it going for such a long time! I didn't really know him myself but saw him on many home and away matches – just a normal bloke with a receding hairline working for British Rail.

These days I very rarely join in with the *Zigger Zagger* chant because Mick was unique – these days as no one has even come close to replicating the sheer noise and length of that chant he used to produce out of his lungs. Plus, I suppose it seems a bit of an insult sometimes to his memory."

# WILLIAN

**Wednesday 21 August 2013**
**Willian has a medical at Spurs**

**Walter:** It's all about Tottenham Hotspur in the paper and on the radio. Gareth Bale is probably on his way to Real Madrid, and Anzhi Makhachkala midfielder Willian is having a medical at White Hart Lane. The Brazil international played twice against Chelsea in the group stages of the Champions League for his previous club Shakhtar Donetsk and looked the dog's bollocks to be honest. When scoring a brace at Stamford Bridge, (7 November 2012, Chelsea 3 Shakhtar 2, Fernando Torres, Oscar, Victor Moses), he was particularly impressive.

Spurs have already signed Étienne Capoue, Roberto Soldado and Nacer Chadli but I'm on way to see the Blues who have got Aston Villa at home tonight and José is back in charge. We've won back-to-back European trophies and all this Tottenham talk is all standard early season transfer window waffle – *Champions of Europe, You'll Never Sing That!* Up the Blues.

I was killing two birds with one stone. I'm not working today. I'm collecting my UEFA Super Cup tickets and then we play Aston Villa. Making my way down the Fulham Road I turned my face towards the blue sky. The sun was shining, a beautiful day. A great summer evening for football. I counted four ticket touts out doing business, two on each side of the road. It was only 1pm in the afternoon. I was so astonished, I double-checked the time on my phone. I look back at the four touts – yes, it was only 1pm in the afternoon. Seven hours until kick off. Mental them being out already. Or was it? I had half an hour to wait before I met No Beans Kenny, so I decided to watch the touts in action.

I sat down on the pavement and leant against the wall of the West Stand. I spent half an hour observing tourist's clutch their blue, plastic Megastore carrier bags, pass by the wall, turn right onto Fulham Road and straight into a tout. You had to hand it to them. They made six sales in the thirty minutes I watched. I don't know how many tickets that was – all the tourists were in pairs, at least.

A CFC security officer sat in his CFC security booth ignoring everything unfolding before him. I thought to myself that he must be on commission. At 1.30pm I got up and walked to the Osgood statue to meet No Beans Kenny. He was bang on time. I was happy. I don't cope well with

## CAREFREE! CHELSEA CHANTS AND TERRACE CULTURE

those who are not punctual.

No Beans Kenny got his nickname in Monaco last summer (31 August 2012, UEFA Super Cup, Atlético Madrid 4 Chelsea 1, Gary Cahill) when telling the waiters and waitresses he wanted no beans with his breakfast. He must've repeated himself ten times.

Kenny is retired and has a bad knee. A really bad knee. In Basel in April (25 April 2013, Europa League, semi-final first leg, Basel 1 Chelsea 2, Victor Moses, David Luiz), I had to help him up the steps into the ground. The stewards and Swiss Old Bill refused to open the gate to allow him to walk into the ground at the away end and sit in a seat. So, he was forced to walk up about one hundred steps and then walk down to his seat. Also, Kenny has never used a computer. The sales for Super Cup tickets were online only. The Box Office (originally) weren't that helpful. They simply shooed him away, instructing him to get online. Kenny has been going to Chelsea since 1960/61. He is a home and away season ticket holder. He is on the UEFA away scheme. He is computer illiterate. And Chelsea won't sell him a ticket because it is ONLINE SALES ONLY – so time for me to have a wee chat with the Box Office.

Credit where credit is due – the employee listened, empathised and apologised for any miscommunication. They still wouldn't sell him a ticket though. In the end, I had to go online and add Kenny to my 'friends and family' on my account and buy him a ticket that way.

Eventually we sorted No Beans Kenny out – but it shouldn't be like that, should it? I think it's disrespectful. We went our separate ways. I crossed the road to the Butchers Hook. I noticed the touts were still going strong – in fact, they had increased in number. Now there were six of them.

The Megastore tourists were still in full flow – coming out of the Megastore with their blue bags, passing the CHELSEA v ASTON VILLA 'SOLD OUT' sign, staring at it mournfully before turning right and straight into a tout. How convenient. The CFC security officer continued sitting unmoved in his CFC security booth.

In the Butchers Hook the barrel of IPA was being changed. The IPA sign on the pump handle was reversed. The sticker on it read: NORMAL £3.40. FOOTBALL £3.90. I mentioned it to the barman. He smiled, reversed the sign back to its usual position and asked me not to tell anyone.

I sat down with a pint and whacked this information straight on *Twitter*.

After a few minutes, I went out for a cigarette and once more took in the sun on my face. I need to give up. Again. Problem is, I love to smoke. When I re-entered the pub, one of the touts was in and had sat down. He drank a pint. Then ordered another. Then the barman returned to him with a large tray of various dips and a pint of prawns. A pint of prawns! My brain struggled to digest this. It just seemed strange. I don't know why. I guess he would look more at home with a mess of a bacon and egg on a plate with yolk and ketchup smeared over his face, wiped off with the back of his hand. But, a pint of prawns it was! King Prawns in a pint glass! With a tray of various dips!

Supply and demand. Inflated booze prices. Inflated ticket prices. £3.90 a pint in the Hook. Could always have eight cans for £6 instead. In Prague where Chelsea will play Bayern Munich in the Super Cup, it will be a London price for my Czech pint in my Hotel. Or I could walk half a mile to a gaff where a pint is only going to cost a nugget. Mere shrapnel. The Megastore tourists can clearly afford the money for a touted ticket. If they couldn't, they wouldn't. Touts would argue they are making a living. They don't force anyone to purchase. They set a price. I might not like it, but it is what is. A tourist makes a demand. The tout supplies the ticket. Chelsea staff clearly turn a blind eye. Too much hassle otherwise. Should I be bothered? I should when the law states I can't sell a ticket to a mate face value. If I am caught, I am banned. Sodding joke. I'd better not get caught, then.

A couple of hours later I walked down to the *cfcuk* fanzine stall. I picked up a hundred fanzines. Hurry Up Dave had counted them into four groups of twenty-five fanzines and packed in a Sainsbury's bag. Standard. I took my place by the green box just down from the West Stand. The touts were still about. Seven times people stepped towards me to ask me if I had a spare ticket. Seven times each voice asking me was a foreign one. Seven times I nodded towards the touts. One foreigner came back. He told me he wasn't paying over £200. I guess all the others were paying it. Likewise, it was obvious now the Megastore tourists before them in the 1.00pm to 1.30pm slot that I witnessed were happy to pay it, too.

It was interesting selling fanzines. I talked to a few people who passed me that I knew. I received the middle finger off some white lad in a black hoodie. Straight in my face. I shouted after him that "there's no need for that, you stroppy prick." He kept walking. In less than an hour I offered at least fifty Megastore tourists (still leaving the ground clutching their blue, plastic bags) the opportunity to buy a Chelsea fanzine. For only a pound. I did not make one sale. I even expressed to them that there was a special message to them, the reader, from Frank Lampard, printed inside. (Which was true!) They looked at me disdainfully. They walked on.

My cousin (well, my Doris' cousin really) cheered me up as she walked down the Road. She gave me a hug. I kissed her cheek telling her sorry we couldn't make her wedding. We were away in France. She asked after the kids. I asked after her parents. Then she went to work. She's a hostess in the West Stand. She welcomes the prawn sandwich lot, pops them in a lift to elevate them up to their corporate area, and smiles a lot.

Then my phone rings, and it's the Doris. She's not been well lately, so I answer it. I'll cut to the chase – she needed me home. I went back to the stall to return unsold fanzines, sold my ticket for face value. Luckily the Old Bill weren't watching – if they were I would've got lifted to boost their arrest statistics at the football, justifying their role. No doubt I would've then received a ban. I walked to West Brompton to connect to go home. Family first and all that – and we're off to Prague next week, so it ain't all bad, missing Villa at home isn't a big deal as things stand. (Chelsea 2 Villa 1, Antonio Luna own goal, Branislav Ivanović.)

### Friday 23 August
### Abramovich rings Kerimov

All this paper talk about Spurs takes another turn. It's reported that Willian had a medical at the Lane but never signed. This is apparently because Uncle Roman made a personal call to his fellow Russian oligarch Suleyman Kerimov who owns Anzhi and the player did a U-turn and signed for Chelsea. Can you believe it? Levy must've been fuming. The Spurs chairman allegedly refused to sell Luka Modrić to Chelsea in a £40 million deal in 2010/11, instead selling him to Real Madrid a year later. Ha, if this is true then this is so, so sweet.

### Sunday 25 August
### Willian signs for Chelsea

Willian has signed for Chelsea for a reported fee of £30 million. From one Russian billionaire to another. The deal is, however, subject to a work permit hearing on Wednesday 28 August which will go through because of Willian's time in Europe already and his caps for Brazil.

## Wednesday 28 August
## Done deal

Willian is duly granted a work permit, a five-year contract with Chelsea football club and the number 22 shirt previously worn by Ross Turnbull. *Ross Turnbull's won the European Cup, the European Cup, the European Cup.*

## Later the same day

The Doris and I parked up at my in-law's place in Cobham at practically midnight. I carried my sleeping kids one after the other out of my car and into bed at their grandparents. Then, the Doris and I jumped in the minibus with Smiffy, Big Chris and their respective wives, Clare and Esther who were waiting for us. Beds were made up across the seats in the back. The adventure began. We had a late ferry to catch from Dover to Calais and then a drive through the night taking us through Belgium to Cologne, Frankfurt, then on to Prague to check in any time after 2pm on Thursday – approximately 1,500 miles.

The Super Cup match against Bayern was on Friday evening. The five-star Hotel cost forty notes a head. Peanuts. Big Chris is incredible at finding these deals. Previously, when travelling with work, I have paid more than that for a night in a Travelodge in idyllic Milton Keynes. And Birmingham. And Luton. And Liverpool.

## Thursday 29 August
## The road to Prague

It was about 4am when the ferry docked and we hit the road in Calais – the fog was some of the worst I've ever seen. Visibility was probably twenty yards or something. Smiffy volunteered to do the first stint – driving for five hours, with me navigating as the co-pilot. All the others were sleeping in the back. I've said it before and I'll say it again – I find that there's something significantly therapeutic going on a road trip – especially when the football is involved with mates, and I have the added bonus that I don't have to go to work for a week – I'll be starting a new job in fact, but I'll cross that bridge when I get there.

Breakfast was had in a lovely little town – I just have no idea where, and frustratingly at the time of writing, none of us can remember. We could've been on either side the Belgian / Germany border or further into Deutsch land on the road to Cologne. We devoured great coffee, croissants, ham, cheese and managed to swerve anything alcoholic. I ordered more coffee and smoked cigarettes in the sun, everything seemingly a hundred times better because I'm not sitting on my doorstep outside my front door, I'm al fresco on the way to Chelsea with my Doris resting her hand on my shoulder and Big Chris doing some lunges to get the blood circulating around his giant frame. Esther and Clare were stretching aching arms and legs, fishing out travel toothbrushes from their handbags and working out how many hours were left until they could have a hot shower in the Hotel at the end of the day. Prague was not yet on the horizon. The next leg of the journey was all about the girls. Clare was driving, with Esther and the Doris up top navigating – no doubt they'd talk about make-up, shoes, periods and the upcoming spa day tomorrow.

I've often reflected at how lucky we are, because our respective partners are all good mates. As we grew up (my father still thinks I haven't) and met our girlfriends, (who eventually became our wives), it was great that all our spouses bonded, too. So, it was only natural for us to ask them if they wanted a weekend in Prague in late August – all six of us. They jumped at the chance. We did mention that us lads would have the small matter of a football match to attend on the Friday night. Naturally they put their hands on their hips and tutted a bit, but deep down we ALL new that was lip service. Part of the required reaction. Part of the game. In reality, the girls would be glad to see the back of us for an afternoon and evening so they could enjoy a beautiful meal, a litre of local wine then chill out in a sauna in the Hotel and discuss how lucky they are to have such amazing husbands.

Groggy from being awake all night, and content with a belly full of breakfast, I fell asleep in the back of the minibus. The lads woke me up hours later – we had stopped for lunch in a town called Würzburg. We gathered on a pedestrianised bridge over the River Main – a local chap agreed to take a photo of us all and then he thankfully returned the phone and didn't run off with it.

We enjoyed lunch and freshened up. For the final push to Prague, Big Chris would be behind the wheel with Smiffy navigating as co-pilot, the girls would sleep in the back. I sat behind Smiffy, took out my pen and pad and jotted down some thoughts and feelings… and soon drifted off… but their singing and laughter kept waking me up. Pair of idiots!

I'd float back off to sleep, and their chanting would wake me up once again. I sat up and looked to my right, all the girls were dozing across the seats in the back. Smiffy and Big Chris were trying to pen a song about Willian's U-turn to sack off Spurs and sign for Chelsea. I pulled a pillow over my head to try and drown them out. They were like two teenagers with an Attention Deficit Hyperactive Disorder.

**A song for Willian**

We've all been here so many times before – working out songs and laughing and playing with the words and laughing some more – with little or no success. But we keep doing it anyway. And, with a pillow pulled down over my head, of course they kept doing it anyway. For about an hour I'd intermittently awake with them chopping, changing and 'perfecting' their number.

I was desperate for more shut-eye, but the more I fought against the noise they made composing their song, the harder I pulled the pillow over my face and around my ears, the less chance I had of sleep enveloping me. Annoyed at my pals for having no pity on me as I tried to kip, I had to admit they had summed up the situation surrounding the Willian transfer from Shakhtar perfectly.

They finally settled on this:

*The sh\*t from Spurs, they bought his flight, but Willian he saw the light.*
*He got a call from Abramovich, and off he went to Stamford Bridge.*
*He hates Tottenham, he hates Tottenham, he hates Tottenham and he hates Tottenham!*

The tune for the Willian song is a song called *Tom Hark*. I first heard the melody on the terraces as a young 'un to the chant: *I've got this feeling, I don't know why, after the match, you're gonna die.*

First released as an instrumental in 1958 by Elias & his Zig Zag Jive Flutes, in August 1980, a Ska band from Brighton called The Piranhas who featured Zoot Alors, Dick Slexia and Boring Bob Grover among their number covered *Tom Hark* and enjoyed top ten UK chart success. The melody subsequently became widely used by supporters of just about every British football club as the base for a chant or two or three or more and retains widespread popularity today.

We arrived at the Hotel. It was magnificent. I'm not used to these types of places. Nearly four years on and I've still got the slippers I took from the bedroom wardrobe. (I'm wearing them at this moment while I type.)

We arranged to meet at the Hotel bar in an hour. Smiffy said he only needed fifteen minutes. Our wives gave us a stern, knowing look each that needed no accompanying words: Keep it clean, no visiting the Hotel casino (I promised the Doris), no power drinking and certainly no more bloody singing.

**Friday 30 August**
**Matchday**

On the morning of the game the Doris aroused me awake (ahem) at 8am. We made our way up to the twenty-fifth floor where we swam in the pool before breakfast. Our view was glorious – we looked out the windows across the City of Prague. Not bad. The Eden Stadium was only two miles away. I'd be walking back from that stadium to the Hotel with the lads at around midnight, hoarse from singing and dehydrated from boozing. It played with my brain a bit that we were twenty-five floors up and swimming in a pool. The stash of meds I had bought with me helped to block out anxious thoughts of getting into lifts. They help quell rising panic that infiltrates my mind – thoughts like what happens if there's a fire and how will I get out, sh*t like that.

After our swim, we dried off and changed and went to meet the others for breakfast down on the second floor. And then, the Doris and I returned to the twenty-fifth floor. She'd booked me in for a forty-five minute full body massage. I felt a little uncomfortable as we rode the elevator once again to the top floor wearing only my boxers under a bathrobe and a pair of slippers on. I felt even more uncomfortable when I was introduced to my masseur.... a brute of a man named Ivan.

He was over six foot, built like Jean-Claude Van Damme and spoke like a James Bond villain. He shook my hand, absent-mindedly (I hoped) crushing mine in his. I'm sure he took great pride in watching me visibly wince. He led me up some stairs, telling me he was ex-military, and massage was purely his side job. I hoped this was the only type of job I'd be receiving from him on the massage table. I started praying that I wouldn't have a panic attack as he covered my back in oil. It was a distressing time being oiled, kneaded and pulled around by Ivan, though of course the wives and the lads found it hilarious as I told them about it over lunch later in the day.

Lunch was a fidgety affair for the lads. We just wanted to eat and then get to the boozer with our Chelsea pals who had travelled. The girls sensed it, took the piss out of us for a bit, and then we were off. It doesn't get much better than this – the boys, a massive thirst on, the back streets of

Prague and a date in a small but perfect boozer to meet Big Garry. A seasoned traveller home, away and in Europe – Garry has spent thousands of pounds following the team all his life – and now the Club have banned him for persistent standing. Even though he was banned, he has still travelled. And I had a ticket for him in my back pocket. You can't ban a Chelsea fan!

Big Garry took us to a couple of cheap bars down side streets and then we all gave into the demanding texts on our respective phones – every man and his dog was drinking in and outside The George – so off we went. It was one of those rare and brilliant occasions where many people you knew had gathered in the same place.

Suddenly I was grabbed from behind (no, it wasn't Ivan with a bottle of massage oil), and I was delighted to see Champagne Les. Like me, he doesn't like to fly, I had no idea he was coming! And how here we are in The George. In that moment, Cathy McDonnell took a photo of us that we weren't aware of and she later sent it to me. It's a photo I'm very fond of. One of the best.

I hadn't seen Les since Saints away in March (30 March, Southampton 2 Chelsea 1, John Terry) – five months ago – and we had a lot to catch up on. Before we could get started, Smiffy and Big Chris appeared with a tray of beers and started singing their new Willian song. I joined in and we got it going a bit. On and on it goes.

Champagne Les chortled and took a photo. Big Chris was conducting everyone. Phil the Butler laughed his head off and joined in. To our surprise the song caught on in the boozer beer garden and was heartily sung for a solid ten minutes or so, and I honestly thought that would be that. I was aware of a group of younger lads all enjoying the booze, the sun and the singing. I didn't realise they'd filmed it on their phones. I found out later their names were Russell, Brad and Jack.

At the match, we tried in vain to get the Willian song going again. It failed. Oh well, we were all used to it. Two mates at the front of a minibus and flooring it to Prague laughing at Willian mugging off Spurs and signing for Chelsea then turned into a funny, spontaneous moment outside on a pub on a Euro away and the chant had failed, once again, to make the jump to the match itself. Oh well, such is life. It was the trip that mattered the most. Bayern Munich 2 Chelsea 2 (Fernando Torres, Eden Hazard) Bayern win 5-4 on penalties (David Luiz ✓ Oscar ✓ Frank Lampard ✓ Ashley Cole ✓ Romelu Lukaku oh dear!)

# CAREFREE! CHELSEA CHANTS AND TERRACE CULTURE

**Saturday 31 August**
**The drive home**

We got up, checked out, and began the 1,500 miles drive back. We'd lost the match on penalties to the Germans but yeah, you win some, you lose some. Young Lukaku had a nightmare – Mourinho lost the plot with him on the touchline because he clearly wasn't doing what he should've been doing, especially because we were down to ten men.

We arrived in Calais and got on the ferry, boosted by the signs saying there was free Wi-Fi available. We all needed our social media fix. It had been nearly four days. We all turned our phones on and tuned in. We'd had no internet access for the entire journey – and fifteen hours worth of notifications exploded into mine, Big Chris and Smiffy's mentions. The song about Willian had gone viral!!!

This morning, as we begun the fifteen-hour journey to Calais, the little ditty we'd been singing in the City was put on *YouTube* and *Instagram* by Russell and Brad. Most significantly, perhaps, was that it was 'liked' by Willian himself on Brad's *Instagram* post, thus increasing its popularity to Chelsea supporters worldwide and further infuriating our rivals from North London. My Doris rolled her eyes. I went to the bar and got a round in. I looked at my watch – it was gone midnight.

**Sunday 1 September... and beyond**

By the time I'd got back to my in-laws in Cobham in the very early hours of Sunday morning, the various clips had amassed over 100,000 hits. A new song was born, and Willian hadn't even kicked a ball for Chelsea yet. To put that into context, legendary Blues goalie Petr Cech didn't have a proper song!

In this moment, I understood how powerful social media can be – not only because Willian hadn't even made his debut, but also because there were comments suggesting discrimination was involved – it wasn't. I've also had cowardly, personal derogatory comments made towards me for no reason other than standing with a pint in my hand singing a song.

Willian played against Basel (18 September, Basel 2 Chelsea 1, Oscar) and Steaua Bucharest (1 October, Steaua 0 Chelsea 4, Ramires x2, Daniel Georgievski own goal, Frank Lampard) in the Champions League and Swindon Town in the League Cup, (24 September, Swindon 0 Chelsea 2, Fernando Torres, Ramires), but his debut in the Premier League for

Chelsea was away at Norwich City (6 October). He scored a beauty in the 86th minute to seal a 3-1 win (Oscar, Eden Hazard, Willian) and the jubilant away end broke into his new song.

After the match, Neil Barnett interviewed him for Chelsea TV (with David Luiz translating the lyrics) and it became apparent that we had pronounced his name wrong. It's pronounced Willy-en, not Will.I.An. Ha, ha – you've got to laugh.

A few weeks later, Chelsea Historian Rick Glanvill said that Chelsea TV were keen to do an interview. Big Chris was working, so Smiffy and I went up. It was a very bizarre yet incredible experience for me to be sitting in the East Stand reception awaiting to be taken for a tour and then an interview.

It was surreal standing in the changing rooms, looking at all the kits hanging up, the squad numbers and players names almost illuminated before me. Scratching my head, I turned to Smiffy and burst out laughing. We walked up the tunnel and out into the pitch. It was the first time I'd been on the turf since Gavin Peacock's goal, 13 March 1994, saw us beat Wolves 1-0 in the FA Cup Quarterfinal. Pitch invasion! We sang and danced under the massive Pride of London flag. We were in the semi's and off to Wembley. I was nineteen-years old. Nineteen years later and I was on the pitch again. It all got a bit too much for me to comprehend, so I had a quick lie down across Steve Holland and Mourinho's seats in the dugout. Smiffy took a photo.

I've always maintained – to whoever asks – and in the Chelsea TV interview, that it was never my song – it was all to do with Big Chris and Smiffy – I was trying to sleep in the minibus! I was there at The George in Prague for its virgin birth. There is a second verse that I first saw *theblueman2000* write as a *YouTube* comment which I love. I've adapted it slightly and given it an airing a few times which results in me getting some helpful feedback from my peers. These constructive comments are usually: "Oh shut up, Walts", "Go home, Walts", or usually, "Walts – this isn't a singing pub."

> *He went to Spurs for a medical.*
> *He passed the tests but he signed f\*ck all.*
> *Doctor Eva checked and she said he's fine. So, Willian signed on the line.*
> *He hates Tottenham!*

There's actions as well, you know. Ask me nicely and I'll show you.

# KANTÉ

**Walter:** Chelsea signed N'Golo Kanté on 16 July 2016. My Foxes pals Leicester Chris and Ann D were quick to tell me how gutted they were to lose him, what a humble man he is and that he drives a Mini Cooper. They weren't wrong.

I first saw him play in the flesh against Watford at Vicarage Road (16 August, Waford 1 Chelsea 2, Diego Costa, Michy Batshuayi) and he certainly did the work of two players, no doubt. Incredible. I'd never seen a performance with so much hustling, harrying, tackling and determination. I was knackered just watching him – though I was at the tail end of a bout of gastroenteritis – so I was well drained anyway. I'd been on the toilet for four days. I was in a bad way. I flew back from a holiday in Spain after popping six Imodium and went to see the Doctor. She told me to rest. I said I'm off to Watford v Chelsea, love.

Ten days after Kanté signed, I flew to Romania with Smiffy and Big Chris and my family. We landed in Târgu Mureș, picked up a minibus to begin the drive to Cristuru Secuiesc, a town in Harghita County, eastern Transylvania. Smiffy was driving the sixteen-seater, with Big Chris in the passenger seat and me behind.

There was a massive sense of déjà vu for as all regarding the Willian song, so it was only right that the boys in the front came up with a song for N'Golo. They settled on singing, *Come on Kanté*, to the tune of *Come on Eileen* by Dexy's Midnight Runners. It sounded bloody brilliant at the time (my kids, who were in the back of the minibus, still occasionally sing it) and even my Doris was amused. However, the song peaked at that moment, and it never developed any further, plenty of the lads raising their eyebrows in the boozer pre-Watford in mid-August despite Big Chris' protestations that it would sound the dogs if everyone got it going.

Fast-forward to 13 March 2017, and Chelsea are at home to Manchester United in the FA Cup quarter-final. I spent a couple of days working on a tune for N'Golo to *Ring of Fire*, Johnny Cash's global smash hit from 1963, and my co-author Mr Worrall printed off a Kanté mask and we filmed pre-match at the *cfcuk* stall. (You may be bowled over by the admission that I did the trumpet noise myself.) In the following weeks, it amassed over 12,000 hits, though once again it failed to make the jump to the pubs, concourses or grounds – *Well, thank the Good Lord for that*, I hear many of you cry. Here it is anyway, because I'll be sure to be singing it on my own *(On your own, on your own, on your own!)* when I'm in a pub before the game. It can be viewed on the Gate 17 Chelsea *YouTube* channel, the tune is *Ring of Fire* by Johnny Cash (1963) and, incredibly, after falling asleep on the train home after the game, I was saved from missing my stop by a busker jumping on the train after Hove and waking me up by singing *Ring of Fire*. I sang my N'Golo Kanté song back at him. He wasn't impressed, but I bunged him a quid anyway.

> *He covers every inch – N'Golo Kanté!*
> *Of every football pitch – N'Golo Kanté!*
> *Covers every blade of grass – N'Golo Kanté!*
> *And he'll leave you on your arse – N'Golo Kanté!*
> *Thirty-two million pounds – N'Golo Kanté!*
> *Drives his mini to the ground – N'Golo Kanté!*

During the match, itself (Kanté got the winner!) chants of *N'Golo, N'Golo, N'Golo* to the tune *En-ger-land, En-ger-land, En-ger-land* emanated from the Matthew Harding Lower Stand.

**Editor's note:** *Bizarrely, the melody originated from a patriotic American march entitled Stars and Stripes Forever which was composed by John Sousa on Christmas Day 1896!*

**Walter:** It looked like *N'Golo, N'Golo, N'Golo* might be it song-wise for our soon to be crowned Player of the Year, London Player of the Year and Football Writers Player of the Year. However, young Bartholomew 'Bart' Barrett and his pals had other ideas, though.

Bart was born in 1997 in Chelsea and Westminster Hospital. His Dad took him to his first match when he was six-years old – a 1-0 win at the Bridge against Aston Villa (27 September 2003) – Jimmy Floyd Hasselbaink banging in the winner.

**Bart:** "He scored the first Chelsea goal I saw live, so I've loved Jimmy Floyd ever since. I lived in Wandsworth with my Dad and he got us season tickets together in 2004/05 in the West Lower – it was the only part of the ground we could get two together. We have the same seats still. When it comes to my favourite songs I love the Salamon Kalou chant. It was such a great moment. I was too young to go to Anfield, but Riise's own goal is etched in my memory. I loved the Mutu song, too. I've got to honest, I don't like the Eden Hazard chant, he deserves a better one because he is so important to us and to the team."

## CAREFREE! CHELSEA CHANTS AND TERRACE CULTURE

*Editor's note:* Having failed to lure teenage sensation *Wayne Rooney to Stamford Bridge, Chelsea made do instead with Romania international striker Adrian Mutu who cost £15.8 million from Fiorentina. Mutu wasn't up to much and it soon transpired that he liked to powder his nose in his spare time which made his* Chim Chim Cher-ee / Mary Poppin's-themed chant Chim Chim-in-ey Chim Chim-in-ney Chim Chim Cheroo – Who needs Wayne Rooney when we've got Mutu? *all the more entertaining as Rooney went onto be a superstar and Mutu got the sack, had a tryst with a porn star and was chased by the police.*

Eden. Eden, Eden. Eden, Eden. Eden, Eden Hazard *sung to the melody of Dutch Eurodance outfit 2 Unlimited's No. 1 UK chart hit from 1993* No Limit *has endured as the Belgium international's Chelsea chant of choice. Early versions incorporated the creative midfielder's brother Thorgen who was once on the Blues books. Truthfully, Bart's right about Eden deserving better, especially given the fact that Manchester City banging* Kolo / Yaya Toure *is viewed as the definitive take on* No Limit.

**Walter:** I ask Bart how it's worked out that he sits in the West, but social media seems to indicate that the Kanté song came from the crew who run The Shed Atmosphere group.

**Bart:** "Although I don't sit in the Shed, I met a guy called Alex who plays for my team at Uni up in Manchester. He has a season ticket in The Shed and we've become firm friends. Alex has always been involved with the fellas who organise the flags and banners to boost the atmosphere in the Shed. I met his mates, including Rich who runs the @WeAre_TheShed *Twitter* account, and it was after the Arsenal game (4 February 2017, Chelsea 3 Arsenal 1, Marcos Alonso, Eden Hazard, Cesc Fàbregas) in the pub that I started playing around with a song for Kanté.

I mean, he's so good, isn't he? It was a tragedy that he didn't have a song – he needed one. I remember going to Watford once, and they had a song for striker Odion Ighalo to the tune of *Gold* by Spandau Ballet. I went to the Arsenal game by myself, and to be honest I got well pissed. I went to the Finborough Arms and started thinking of words to sing to the tune. I played about with it a bit – you know what it's like when you've had a drink – and Rich put the lyrics on *Twitter*. It got a few likes and retweets, but nothing more."

*N'Golo, oh! Kanté will win you the ball, he's got the power to know.*
*He's indestructible, always believe in.... N'Golo, oh!*

**Walter:** I tell Bart that I hadn't known about the Watford version for

Ighalo, but I know West Ham sang it to Carlton Cole when they weren't getting the hump with him for being ex-Chelsea and not as good as Sir Geoff Hurst.

**Bart:** "I tried to get it going at Burnley away (12 February 2017, Burnley 1 Chelsea 1, Pedro) but had no luck. It was a bit of a miserable day up there, to be honest. A long time passed really and then we kind of hit the jackpot before United away (16 April 2017 Manchester United 2 Chelsea 0) in the pre-match pub.

Loads of us were in the Piccadilly Tavern next to station. It really got going – there were about fifteen in our group who all knew each other, and then it caught on. There must have been about fifty other Chelsea in there joining in – it was filmed it and uploaded to *Twitter*. The song then successfully made the transition from the pub to the away concourse as everyone was singing it, but people were getting the words wrong. We lost 2-0 and everyone was worried about the league – but the only positive thing coming out the day was the hits it amassed on social media – it looked like we finally had a song for Kanté.

Our next game was down to Wembley for the FA Cup semi-final against Spurs (22 April, Chelsea 4 Tottenham Hotspur 2, Willian x2, Eden Hazard, Nemanja Matić.) We all piled into the beer garden at the Green Man. I ended up going to meet my Dad to sort out our tickets, but Alex stands up on a table and starts the song. It gets filmed and tweeted instantly. He got a bit of stick, but he doesn't mind getting it, he can handle it.

Later on, he climbed up on the roof and started up *Chelsea Ranger* and got the lyrics wrong. Ha! When I was queuing up with my Dad at the Wembley turnstiles, people behind me were singing the Kanté song – it was a mad feeling – but I didn't hear it in the ground."

**Walter:** As Bart pauses, I tell him about my experience at Goodison (30 April 2017, Everton 0 Chelsea 3, Pedro, Gary Cahill, Willian) when Big Chris and I got in the ground about an hour before kick-off to have a beer and a sing-song. I've always liked going to Everton. There's a few songs going back and forth – the small concourse with the low roof is quickly building up with fans. Someone starts the Kanté song up, and the beer chuckers are in full flow and the place is bouncing. During the second half, at some point, supporters at the back of the lower tier got it going, but it soon got drowned out as the away end was in such a buzzing mood, songs starting from all over both tiers.

**Bart:** "I was right at the front of the lower, so I never heard it that day. I didn't get to the ground until right near kick-off. It's mad to think everyone was bouncing to it on the concourse."

**Walter:** I ask Bart to tell me about West Brom away – the match that clinched Chelsea the Football League (West Brom 0 Chelsea 1, Michy Batshuayi) on 12 May 2017.

**Bart:** "Obviously West Brom was a top day. I got to Birmingham about midday – drinking in the Briar Rose and then in Sun on the Hill. I got a cab to the ground – and then it felt all a bit nervy and a bit twitchy because so much was riding on the game. The Albion fans were quite loud and then naturally, everything went mental after our goal went in.

Full-time was amazing. It will stay with me for the rest of my life.

People were on the pitch. All the players got a song – our crowd was amazing – we were going through them player by player and singing their songs – but of course Kanté wasn't playing, he was carrying a knock and he'd been on the bench for the whole game. When he came over to our end, everyone went mad cheering him. We were situated at the back of the stand, we started his song and it spread over the whole away end. It seemed like the players recognised it and started throwing him in the air and the whole end was singing it.

I found out later, that the official Chelsea *Twitter* had tweeted out a clip of all of this. Oh, it felt brilliant! We'd won the league and the whole end was singing my song! I guess I'm still surprised it's taken off! I should give credit to Alex and to Rich, too. Sometimes chants have a fashionable period and they die out. I want it to be the 'go to' song in the pub, you know?"

**Walter:** "Yes, Bart mate – I certainly do know."

# PART THREE

BEST OF THE REST

# BEST OF THE REST

*Editor's note: With so many chants to choose from it was impossible to retain a sensible structure for* Carefree! *and embrace every song sung in the eras this book covers. What follows is a personal selection of oddities and favourites that Mark and Walter felt also merited inclusion. The original songs would make for a truly bizzare* Now That's What I Call Music-*style compilation and underline the diversity of source material. Nothing is sacred and everything is fair game. Pick a melody, write some words and off you go!*

## Cwm Rhondda

**Walter:** Traditional songs, Christmas Carols and Christian hymns have featured widely in *Carefree!* Whatever your stance or your beliefs, the Christian faith in the UK and the evolution of football since Clubs were formed are bound together by community and history. Songs sung to this day have stood the test of time through the ages.

*Cwm Rhondda* or *Bread of Heaven* is a hymn written by John Hughes (1873-1932) – Cwm Rhondda is the Welsh name for the Rhondda Valley. The first verse will be familiar to those who follow rugby union as it is has been sung passionately by Wales supporters for decades.

*Guide me, O thou great Redeemer, Pilgrim through this barren land;*
*I am weak, but thou art mighty; Hold me with thy powerful hand:*
*Bread of heaven, bread of heaven*
*Feed me till I want no more. Feed me till I want no more.*

The tune has been adapted by football fans variously singing, *We'll Support You Ever More! – You're Not Singing Anymore! – Is That All You Take Away? – We Can See You Sneaking Out! – Where Were You When You Were Sh\*t?* and the increasingly popular *Your Support Is F\*cking Sh\*t!*

23 January 2002 Tottenham Hotspur 5 Chelsea 1, Mikael Forssell

Spurs beat Chelsea for the first time in twenty-seven games. It was a League Cup semi-final. Chelsea were 2-1 up from the first leg (9 January, Jimmy Floyd Hasselbaink x2) but were torn apart in the second leg in which Hasselbaink was sent off. This was a case of mistaken identity, it should have been Mario Melchiot.

Less than a month later, the draw for the FA Cup quarter-finals took place – and Chelsea drew Tottenham away!

Everyone was bang up for it. In an extra twist, the match was moved for TV meaning we played on the Sunday. It was the 10 March 2002 – Chelsea FC's birthday! (Tottenham Hotspur 0 Chelsea 4, William Gallas, Eidur Gudjohnsen x2, Graeme Le Saux).

The violence before the game was the worst I'd personally witnessed. It was like a war zone. It seemed to me that half the Chelsea firm came out of Bruce Grove main line station, the other half had gone on the underground – the two mobbed up as one, and met the Spurs firm in the street. Wallop! The hate in the air was tangible.

I'd been to a lot of games, I'd been to White Hart Lane several times before, I'd seen trouble spark all over the place – but nothing like this. I drew on the experience (many years later) to use in a chapter of my novel *Poppy* where two of the characters Frank and Harry are having a row on the Seven Sisters Road.

The game was memorable for several reasons, not just for the two chants that erupted. The ref (Andy D'Urso) couldn't lose his grip on the game, because he never had one. In all honesty, the players never helped him.

The fight on the London N17 concrete transcended to the pitch. Dean Richards (after six minutes) and Les Ferdinand both should've seen red. Graeme Le Saux eventually did – but by then Chelsea were 4-0 up.

At times like this, everyone loved Le Saux or 'Bergerac' as was known. He was born in Jersey in 1968, scouted by John Hollins in 1987, and made his debut for Chelsea in 1989 (13 May, Portsmouth 2 Chelsea 3, Kevin McAllister x2 Clive Wilson.)

Between 1981 and 1991, actor John Nettles starred in eighty-seven episodes as Detective Sergeant Jim Bergerac – a BBC drama set in Jersey. Hence, Le Saux's nickname *Bergerac* was born. The Shed used to sing, *Bergerac, Bergerac, Bergerac,* to the tune of *The Stars and Stripes Forever.*

At 4-0 up and coasting through to the semi-finals of the FA Cup, Le Saux still had the motivation to go in two-footed on Spurs lippy and unpleasant Argentine substitute Mauricio Taricco. Wonderful! That's what it's all about. (The fact that after Le Saux resigned for Chelsea in 1997 and the song never made a comeback, shows you how much the dynamics of our support had shifted as the ground continued its redevelopment.)

## CAREFREE! CHELSEA CHANTS AND TERRACE CULTURE

In response to Bergerac's red card at 4-0 up, the Chelsea end roared, *Ten men! We've only got ten men!* Then Claudio Ranieri substituted Eidur Gudjohsen for Slaviša Jokanović and the crowd groaned, and then laughed, and then some clever dick started up, *Nine men! We've only got nine men!* and the whole end sang it laughing, and if you ever saw Jokanović play then you'll know why.

I can't remember when the chant started, I'm guessing when either our third or fourth went in, because essentially the game was safe – Tottenham were beaten. Each goal was obviously celebrated with limbs flying everywhere. I do remember the chant spreading along the upper tier (I was in the lower) and then down across the lower tier, and soon the entire away in their thousands, arms outstretched stood singing this *Cwm Rhonda*-themed chant over and over and over again:

*Normal service, normal service.*
*Normal service has resumed.*
*Normal service has resumed.*

To top it all off, three days later, (13 March), we beat Spurs 4-0 *again* at the Bridge in the league game – three goals and the match ball for Jimmy Floyd and a goal for Frank Lampard. The chant, as they say, has gone down in Chelsea folklore. *Normal service has resumed.*

**Mark:** Tarrico was sent off in this match for a revenge tackle on Le Saux. He left the pitch to a standing ovation from travelling Spurs fans! This was the last of five bitter encounters between the clubs during the 2001/2002 season. The first (16 September 2001 Tottenham Hotspur 2 Chelsea 3, Jimmy Floyd Hasselbaink x2, Marcel Desailly) had seen Frank Lampard sent off in what was only his fourth appearance since joining from West Ham.

A shift in the demographic of Chelsea's match-going support associated with rising prices coupled with the Roman Abramovich takeover in 2003 presented rival fans with the opportunity to dig out Blues followers. Man United's lot were quick off the mark with the *Cwm Rhondda*-based *You're Not Chelsea Anymore!*

At that time, many Chelsea supporters conceded that they had a point!

More recently (6 March 2017, West Ham 1 Chelsea 2, Eden Hazard, Diego Costa), at West Ham's new-fangled London Stadium home, Chelsea supporters (being used to frequenting the tight, claustrophobic away end at

Upton Park, a brilliant old-school football ground) jeered their rivals, *You're Not West Ham, You're Not West Ham, You're Not West Ham Anymore!*

Sympathy is due to Hammers supporters who have every reason to feel aggrieved at the way their club's owners have ridden rough shod over a century plus of tradition for the sake of progress and chasing a pound note.

**Walter:** The Chelsea career of Alexandre Rodrigues da Silva aka Pato didn't amount to much. The Brazilian striker came to the Bridge on loan in January 2016 when the Club was still in its post-Mourinho-sacking shambles phase. Rumour had it that he was signed despite failing his medical!

"I am so happy to sign for Chelsea. It is a dream for me," quipped Pato who went on to make just two appearances for the Blues before returning home when the season ended. His debut came against Aston Villa at Villa Park (2 April, Aston Villa 0 Chelsea 4, Ruben Loftus-Cheek, Pato, Pedro x2) when he replaced Loïc Rémy who was injured (again).

Pato won a penalty, got up… and scored it himself… immediately inspiring a *Cwm Rhonnda*-themed chant of *We were here! We were here! We were here when Pato scored! We were here when Pato scored!*

It was the first Chelsea match since ex-player Ian Britton had passed away. Over a ten-year period, Ian played 289 times for Chelsea, scoring 34 goals. *Ian, Ian Britton! Ian Britton on the wing.* (*Ging Gang Goolie*) got an airing by the old-timers. It was a sad day for Smiffy, Big Chris and I as we went to Villa Park – the day before we'd been at our close friend Taxi Alan's funeral. I miss him dearly.

**Mark:** 19 May 2012! Their country, their city, their stadium… our trophy. Moments after Didier Drogba peeled away from the Bayern Munich end having scored the most important penalty in the history of Chelsea Football Club, my mate Russell De Rozario who was going mental a couple of rows away started the *Cwm Rhonnda*-based chant *Are you watching White Hart Lane?* This was a dig at the fact that news had spread that desperate Tottenham fans had been buying Bayern shirts to wear as they watched the game. Had the German side won then Spurs would have qualified for the following season's Champions League competition. I still cry laughing about it now… so does Russell. Sky TV were so impressed, they actually filmed Russell talking about it as part of their advertising build-up to the 2012/2013 campaign.

## CAREFREE! CHELSEA CHANTS AND TERRACE CULTURE

*When The Saints Go Marching In*

**Walter:** Keeping with the Christian theme, Bacon Roll Campo reminded me of a game up at Villa Park. It had an 1130am kick-off, (21 March 1999, Villa 0-3 Chelsea, Flo x2, Bjarne Goldbæk), and the Chelsea choir taunted the opposition fans with: *You Should've Gone to Church!* It's the only bit of the game I can remember! There's been a few variations of the song *Oh When the Saints Go Marching In* on the terraces. The origins of the song evolved in the early 1900s. It is of course, the anthem for Southampton Football Club, a team whose roots are firmly 'Jesus-based' – the club was founded by members of the St Mary's Church of England Young Men's Association. Following a *Zigger Zagger*, Chelsea of course sing:

*Oh When the Blue's Go Steaming In, Oh When the Blue's Go Steaming In. I wanna be in that number! Oh When the Blue's Go Steaming In. Oh When the Blues! (Oh When the Blues!) Go Steaming In! (Go Steaming In!)*

Oh, and are you even a proper supporter if your Mum hasn't, at some point, told you off for singing this?

*Oh West London! (Oh West London!) Is wonderful! (Is wonderful!) Oh West London is wonderful! It's full of tits, fanny and Chelsea – oh West London is wonderful!*

*Brown Girl in The Ring*

**Mark:** There's no particular story associated with this 1978 Boney M chart-topper-themed tribute to Didier Drogba, but since his finest moment in a Blues shirt has just been referenced, it can go in here. *Didier Drogba, tra la la la la Didier Drogba, tra la la la la la.*

*Who Let The Dogs Out?*

Similarly, *Who let the Drog out? Who? Who? Who?* was a very popular take without a yarn on the Baha Men's chart hit from 2000.

***Editor's note:*** *Two unlikely stars of the 2012 Champions League final were John Obi Mikel and Ryan Bertrand. Both deserved recognition in song... and got it, Mikel more so... though that was a steadily evolving thing because he was a Marmite-type player. Supporters either loved him (both the authors firmly in this camp) or somewhat bizarrely hated (and it really felt that way sometimes) him. In the modern era, no other Chelsea player divided opinion quite the way Mikel did.*

**Walter:** Sometimes with Mikel you felt he was the reincarnation of

Eddie 'sideways pass' Newton, and at other times he'd shield the ball turn his man in a tight spot, shimmy and ping the ball off like an African Zinedine Zidane.

Signed by José Mourinho in July 2006, by the time he was sold in January 2017, Mikel had played 374 times for Chelsea and been capped 78 times by Nigeria. As the seasons went by, it slowly dawned on supporters that he had been picked game in, game out by Mourinho (both stints) Avram Grant, Guus Hiddink (both stints) and Bobby Di Matteo who, it has to be conceded, know more about football than Big Bazza who sits in the Matthew Harding Upper and thought Mikel was rubbish. Rafa Benitez also picked Mikel, but Big Bazza probably does know more about tactics than the Fat Spanish Waiter. The Super Eagle superstar, (Mikel, not Big Bazza), had a few songs coming his way.

*Blue Moon*

**Mark:** The Rodgers and Hart classic penned in 1934 has been popularised in football by Manchester City. As far as John Obi was concerned it resulted in *Mikel. There's only one Obi Mikel* The chant didn't have the legs that some say it deserved.

*Cotton Eye Joe*

**Walter:** My John Obi tribute effort to the 1994 cover of 19th Century American Country folk song *Cotton Eyed Joe* by Swedish group RedNex was scorned mercilessly by all who heard it:

*Nigerian Super Eagle, playing for Mourinho.*
*Where did you come from, where did you go?*
*Where did you come from Obi Mikel.*

I'll get my coat. (Well, to be honest I got it back in 2007!)

*Seven Nation Army*

**Mark:** The White Stripes track was first purloined by football fans in 2003 when a group of Club Brugge KV supporters gathered in a bar in Milan prior to watching their team's Champions League clash with AC at the San Siro. Hearing the song which had only recently been released belting out of bar's sound system, they picked up on the riff-laden opening and hummed along noisily, continuing at the match and then back at their own stadium where eventually it would be played after every goal. It went viral from there.

Chelsea supporters first embraced it for cult hero right-back Juliano Belletti who joined the club in August 2007 and went on to make 94 appearances for the Blues scoring five goals.

*Juliano Belletti, Juliano Belletti.*

Now (2017) it's a case of *Oh Pedro Rogriguez, Oh Pedro Rogriguez.* Mikel's version was simply *John Obi Mikel*

### Let It Be

**Walter:** The real winner here in the Mikel chant stakes is good old Stan, (creator of the Ivanović song), who composed this delight to the 1970 hit *Let It Be* by The Beatles:

*When we find ourselves in times of trouble, José plays a 4-3-3.*
*He's not quite Makélélé, John Obi, Jon Obi.*
*John Obi! John Obi! John Obi, John Obi.*
*He's not quite Makélélé, John Obi, John Obi.*

Sports Journalist Henry Winter in a column for *The Times* gave it a mention once. Fame at last for young Stanley.

**Mark:** There's a bizarre version of *Let It Be* which gloats about the Double Steven Gerrard might have won had he signed for Chelsea. You'll find it on the Gate 17 Chelsea *YouTube* channel. Sung by the mysterious Stone Island Singer who was apparently playing the old Joanna as well, the chorus goes: *Stevie G, Stevie G, Stevie G Oh Stevie G… You could have won the Double at Chelsea.*

### Iron Lion Zion

**Walter:** The first of two Bob Marley tracks in our compilation, Iron Lion Zion, which dates back to 1973, was used as the base melody for the Ryan Bertrand tribute chant *Ryan like a lion in Bayern. Ryan! Lion! Bayern!*

### Three Little Birds

**Mark:** The second, *Three Little Birds*, often thought to be named *Don't Worry About A Thing* or *Every Little Thing Is Gonna Be Alright*, is reprised by Chelsea supporters every time things go a little pear-shaped on the managerial front and results go awry. Best sampled away from home, the whole Blues end tends to get right behind it and the vibe really is uplifting.

*Sing Hosanna!*

**Walter:** I remember being in school assembly belting out *Sing Hosanna* or *Give Me Oil In My Lamp* when I was a young kid in 1980. Interestingly, it was a hit in Jamaica in 1964 for Ska singer Eric 'Monty' Morris.

Here's the first verse and chorus:

*Give me oil in my lamp, keep me burning*
*Give me oil in my lamp, I pray*
*Give me oil in my lamp, keep me burning*
*Keep me burning 'til the break of day*
*Sing hosanna, sing hosanna*
*Sing hosanna to the King of Kings*
*Sing hosanna, sing hosanna*
*Sing hosanna to the King of Kings*

The word *Hosanna* is a shout of praise, and was yelled by the people to Jesus Christ as he rode on a donkey into Jerusalem. This event is remembered in our calendar as Palm Sunday, falling the week before Easter. The country goes mad buying Easter Eggs, Easter bunnies and hiding eggs for a treasure hunt around the garden for the kids to find. In reality, it is the time of year when Christians reflect on Jesus being murdered on a cross (Good Friday) and celebrate him rising from the dead (Easter Sunday).

During Chelsea's triumphant Europa League run in 2012/13, a different version of *Hosanna* began bubbling away as we advanced through the knock-outs, ultimately hoping to get to Amsterdam where the final was to be played on 15 May:

*Amsterdam, Amsterdam, we are coming!*
*Amsterdam, Amsterdam, I pray.*
*Amsterdam, Amsterdam we are coming!*
*We are coming in the month of May.*

**Mark:** 7 March 2013, (two months before the final), a group of 100-plus Chelsea supporters (myself included) from London and from Sweden congregated in Amsterdam's city centre bars to watch the Blues in Europa League action.

## CAREFREE! CHELSEA CHANTS AND TERRACE CULTURE

Unfortunately, we had to watch the game on television as Chelsea were playing 1,400 miles away in Bucharest! (Europa League Round 2, Steaua Bucharest 1 Chelsea 0). In the preceding round, Ajax of Amsterdam had beaten Steaua 2-0 in the first leg and were hot favourites to progress to play Chelsea.

Given the fact that airlines and hotels notoriously hike prices as soon as they become aware of fixtures, I and many others thought we'd gamble on strongly-fancied Ajax going through as there was bound to be a mad scramble for flights and accommodation with the Chelsea world and its collective wife likely to be keen on the trip to Holland.

Nothing like a bit of glorious unpredictability though eh. Steaua won the reverse leg 2-0 and beat Ajax 4-3 on penalties. If it had been any other city, there might have been a clutch of cancellations, but the lure of Amsterdam, with its obvious temptations, proved too much.

*Amsterdam, Amsterdam we are coming! We are coming in the month of March,* was sung in a fug of herbal cigarette smoke... confusing locals and police alike.

Proper Chels! as some might say.

**Walter:** In the return leg at the Bridge against Steaua Bucharest, (Chelsea 3 Steaua 1, Juan Mata, John Terry, Fernando Torres), I was touring the boozers of West Brompton selling copies of *cfcuk*. At every turn, (The Wee Imp, The Atlas, The Prince of Wales, The Lilly), I kept bumping into pockets of Ajax supporters! They had done the reverse as Mark and 100 plus other Chelsea, and booked up a trip to London anticipating a game with Chelsea that never materialised. As kick-off approached, I took them into The Slug, (Is it called the Grill now? I lose track), to watch the game, but security kicked them out after ten minutes because one of them had an Ajax shirt on.

**Mark:** A year later, as Chelsea looked to be on the march to the Champions League Final in Lisbon, the chant was reprised with *Portugal* replacing *Amsterdam*.

*Portugal, Portugal, we are coming!*
*Portugal, Portugal, I pray.*
*Portugal, Portugal, we are coming!*
*We are coming in the month of May.*

Unfortunately, Atlético Madrid halted the Blues progress at the semi-final stage of the competition. Favourites to progress after a 0-0 first leg draw at the Vicente Calderón (22 April 2014), José Mourinho's side took the lead through Atléti old-boy Fernando Torres in the second leg (30 April) at Stamford Bridge but went on to lose 3-1. Diego Costa was among the scorers for the visitors. Costa's reward for being a thorn in Mourinho's side was a move to the Bridge to join him a couple of months later.

## *Auld Lang Syne*

**Walter:** Scottish poet Robert Burns wrote these famous words in 1788, it later evolved into a song. The phrase 'auld lang syne' roughly translates as 'for old times' sake', and the song is all about preserving old friendships and looking back over the events of the year. To this day it's sung by drunken hordes at midnight as New Year's Eve ticks into New Year's Day.

*For auld lang syne, my dear, for auld lang syne.*
*We'll take a cup of kindness yet, for auld lang syne.*

I don't know why, but the simple Chelsea version to this chorus is one of my favourite chants. I've never really analysed as to why – until now! I mean, I don't have any Scottish blood and if I'm honest, New Year as always been a massive pain in the arse.

Maybe it's because the main lyrics are reflecting on times gone by – the old times – it's something sentimental, it touches on the romantic – running around the slopes (the countryside) and picking daises – paddling in the stream until dinner time.

You had good times together. You grew apart for whatever reason. But let's have a hefty drink and take each other's hands and remember those special moments, for old times' sake. Themes of connection, kindness, the human spirit, loyalty, friendships and binding together are explores through the main lyrics. Or maybe I'm reading too much into it, I don't know.

*Come on Chelsea, Come on Chelsea, Come on Chelsea. Come on!*
*Come on Chelsea, Come on Chelsea, Come on Chelsea, Come on!*

For me it sounds best when sung slowly. This is hard to do with any football song – let alone this one – when half the away end is lagging – especially if the match is a half-five kick-off!

## CAREFREE! CHELSEA CHANTS AND TERRACE CULTURE

*Batman TV show theme*

**Mark:** Nigel Spackman's a smashing fella. I always like the fact that he only became a Blues player because Wigan Athletic owed Ken Bates a few quid from his time as vice-Chairman at Springfield Park – now that was a proper old-school football ground!

When he bought Chelsea in 1982, Bates was offered players by Wigan in lieu of the debt so he took manager Johnny Neal to a game to see if he thought any of them had potential. Spackers didn't play for The Latics, he was playing for Bournemouth who were Wigan's opponents when Bates and Neal turned up at Dean Court on their scouting mission in May 1983. The following month Spackman signed for Chelsea in a £35,000 deal. A bargain all things considered.

At the time it was common practice for pretty much every player to have their name chanted as they were warming up for games and as 'Nigel Spackman' didn't really lend itself to any melody in particular it was time to get creative. Very creative! The title song of the 1966 *Batman* TV series composed by Neal Hefti was borrowed to very good effect:

*Ne ne, ne ne, ne ne, ne ne, ne, ne, ne ne, ne ne, ne ne, Spackman!*

It's genius to be honest, absolutely brilliant. I sing it every time I walk past the Spackman entrance at Stamford Bridge. I smile at the chant and at the fact Spackers actually managed to get an entrance named after him... something which puzzles me to this day. A very decent workhorse of a midfield player across two stints for Chelsea was Nigel, but the entrance thing well I'm sure even he must chuckle a little at that.

*Skip to My Lou*

**Mark:** Enlisting with Johnny Neal's Blue and White Army the same summer as Spackers was Scotland Under-21 international Joe McLaughlin who signed from Greenock Morton for £95,000. 'Big Joe' was a proper centre-half and served Chelsea well for six years.

As football chants go, the use of American children's song *Skip to My Lou* is common or garden. *Skip, skip, skip to my Lou, Skip, skip, skip to my Lou, Skip, skip, skip to my Lou, Skip to my Lou, my darlin'* has been widely used in a modified form by supporters of all clubs for decades.

In my time of watching Chelsea, *Joe, Joe, Super Joe McLaughlin* was hugely popular as was *Dan, Dan Super Dan Petrescu*. The ultimate Blues version I guess is the one sung in honour of record goal scorer *Super, super Frank, super, super Frank, super, super Frank, super Frankie Lampard*.

*Skip to my Lou* was also used amusingly during the early-mid 1980s when news broke of a daring (unbelievable) feat of terrace warfare bravado. Example: *Tottenham, Tottenham run from Watford*. In pre-internet days it was hilarious how these rumours started, a bit like Chinese whispers going from pub to pub. It would start off in one drinker as such and such a firm got properly served up at Victoria, and by the time you were on the terraces and it came to you via fifteen other boozers and a thousand people, the firm that got a pasting were now the feared top boys who ran London! Watford!

## We Don't Need Another Hero

**Mark:** There was a shabby phase in the late '80s and early '90s at Stamford Bridge when the matchday DJ dispensed with tradition and played a weird assortment of tracks as the teams came out on the pitch. Van Halen's *Jump*, being one... Europe's *The Final Countdown*, being another and then of course there was the Tina Turner version of *The Best*, which stormed the pop charts in 1989 and made it onto TTs *Simply The Best* greatest hits compilation which was released in October 1991.

Among the tracks, which included classics such as *Nutbush City Limits, What's Love Got To Do With It and Private Dancer*, was *We Don't Need Another Hero (Thunderdome)*, a single release from 1985 that featured in the film *Mad Max Beyond Thunderdome*.

A month into the new year (1 February 1992), Chelsea manager at the time, Ian Porterfield, traded defender Tom Boyd with Celtic for striker Tony Cascarino a former ladies' hairdresser who had scored goals aplenty for Gillingham and Millwall before moving to the midlands and Aston Villa and then up to Scotland.

In a day and age before squad numbers, a week later, Cascarino pulled on the No. 9 shirt worn for many seasons with distinction by the then injured Kerry Dixon, and promptly scored on his debut (8 February) netting an 87th minute equaliser in a 1-1 home draw with Crystal Palace.

The late goal and a sparse crowd of 17,810 meant that The Shed had already thinned out by the time 'Cas' scored. Those who remained burst into Tina Turner-inspired song in appreciation of the new Chelsea centre forward.

# CAREFREE! CHELSEA CHANTS AND TERRACE CULTURE

*We don't need another hero.*
*We've got Tony Cascarino.*

Unfortunately, Porterfield decided to find other potential heroes at the end of the season, namely John Spencer, Mick Harford and Robert Fleck!

Cascarino's Chelsea career would subsequently be dogged by injury, poor form, and the signing of diminutive striker Mark Stein by Glenn Hoddle who succeeded Porterfield (sacked 15 February 1993 and replaced by caretaker boss David Webb) as permanent Chelsea manager in June 1993.

Cascarino's last appearance for Chelsea came as a substitute in the 1994 FA Cup Final (14 May) against Manchester United at Wembley. Chelsea were already 3-0 down when Cas replaced Stein in the 78th minute. There were to be no heroics though as the Blues went on to lose 4-0 on a miserable rain-swept day at the home of English football and Cascarino moved to French side Marseille on a free transfer at the end of the season.

## Hava Nagila

**Walter:** Dmitri Kharine joined Chelsea from Dynamo Moscow in December 1992. Renowned for his long curly hair and wearing tracksuit bottoms our Russian goalkeeper was regularly serenaded with the popular chant *Kharine, Dmitri Kharine, Dmitri Kharine, Dmitri Kharine, hey!*

I listened to several traditional Russian songs on *YouTube* to find the tune. I ruled out *Zorba, Kalinka, Loy Loy Cosak, Troika, Occhi Chorni* and a new-found favourite *Gari Gari* before asking *Twitter* for help. Within minutes, @phantomantle tweeted me back with the answer. Surprisingly, Kharine's song isn't to a Russian number at all, but an Israeli folk song that was composed in 1915! *Hava Nagila* (Hebrew: הבה נגילה, Havah Nagilah, *(Let us Rejoice)* is traditionally sung at Jewish celebrations!

**Mark:** Long before England failed to qualify for the 1994 World Cup Finals held in the United States, myself, Ugly John, Tall Phil and No Nickname Rich had decided we were going to attend and do a fly-drive type holiday.

When Graham Taylor, bless his dear soul, flunked his managerial duties we decided we'd still attend and logically decided we'd follow the fortunes of the country with the most Chelsea players in it. Looking at the Blues current first team which is wedged with internationals, if we were pulling the same stunt for next summer's finals in Russia we'd probably end up squabbling about cheering on Spain, Belgium or Brazil.

Back in 1994 it was a toss-up between Norway (Erland Johnsen) and Russia (Dmitri Kharine). They were Chelsea's only representatives and we opted for Kharine because he was more assured of starts and also because Russia's opening game against Brazil was being played in Palo Alto which oddly enough fitted with our fly-drive plans as it was relatively close to San Francisco our destination airport from London.

Long story short, the four of us found ourselves in among a sizeable crowd of 81,061 at the Stanford Stadium getting the *Kharine, Dmitri Kharine* chant going. We even got a wave from Kharine who despite the game being played in the early afternoon in baking sunshine with the temperature approaching 100 degrees Fahrenheit was still wearing his trademark trackie bottoms!

For the record Russia lost 2-0 and a few days later we ended up in Las Vegas and that was the end of the football… but that's another story!

*Matthew Harding's Blue and White Army*

There are plenty of Chelsea manager's who've had a *Blue and White Army* chant down the years. Typically, it was dependent on whether or not the gaffer's name fitted properly. Eddie McCreadie, Johnny Neal, Bobby Campbell were easy enough to work into the simple chant, but things got a little complicated when Ken Bates went continental with Ruud Gullit, in fact thereafter, with the notable exception of Avram Grant and Claudio Ranieri to a lesser extent as just his surname was used, the *Blue and White Army* chant became associated principally with iconic Chelsea hero Matthew Harding who was tragically killed in a helicopter crash away at Bolton Wanderers, (22 October 1996, Bolton 2 Chelsea 1, Scott Minto), when returning home from watching the Blues play a Third Round League Cup tie.

**Mark:** Matthew Harding's formal involvement with Chelsea came during the 1993-94 season. Ken Bates later recalled the telephone conversation that launched their unlikely and some might say unholy alliance. "Ken Bates here," he said. "I understand you're richer than I am, so we'd better get together." Harding, immediately weighed Chelsea in with £5 million to fund the construction of a new North Stand, and also lent the club more than twice that amount to purchase players. But there was no question of the younger man adopting the traditional boardroom values so beloved of Mr Bates. To the best of my knowledge I never saw Ken Bates wearing a Chelsea replica kit, or drinking with supporters in The Imperial public house on the Kings Road before a game. Who can forget Matthew turning up at the unveiling of Gianluca Vialli as a Blues player clutching a brand new home shirt already emblazoned with his name and number? "I'm just a fan who's done rather well," he once said, and the Chelsea massive took him to their hearts.

Bates' priority was to build a futuristic stadium, Harding wanted a swashbuckling team to match the heroes of his youth. The two men were on a collision course which eventually resulted in Bates banning Harding from the directors' box, citing "behaviour related to your heavy drinking both home and away". The letter sent to Harding contained a P.S. which read: "Please ensure that your 'Bates Out' banner in the Main Stand does not obscure the valuable advertisement panels". "Never mind," replied Matthew, "I'll go and sit in the North Stand. I presume that's alright with you. After all, I did pay for it." The bitter public feud rumbled on with Harding pledging that Chelsea fans would be given a vote in the future of the club if he won his power battle with Bates. "If I become chairman I intend to break some moulds, and one plan I have is to give club members the right to re-elect me as chairman. Chelsea have more than 25,000 members and they are the emotional shareholders of the club. I would go to them every summer and I'll promise you this now. If there was a majority voting against me I would stand down instantly."

Harding's words stirred the True Blue soul … *Matthew Harding's Blue and White Army, Matthew Harding's Blue and White Army* … the chant would echo (as it still does to this very day) around the Bridge on each and every matchday a testament to the faith supporters had in him. In December 1995, the club announced after a board meeting that the pair would lunch and sit together at the home Premiership match against Newcastle. That implied Bates had agreed to lift the ban on Harding taking his seat in the directors' box and using the boardroom facilities, though at the time both men refused to comment. By October 1996, Matthew Harding had committed £26.5 million to Chelsea Football Club and the irony was that both he and Bates were on the way to realising their own idealistic dreams. Had he lived, Matthew would have seen the Blues win the FA Cup at the end of the season and his journey to glory would have been complete.

Chelsea's next home game on 26 October 1996 was against arch rivals Spurs. The game itself was destined to be a sideshow from the minute Ken Bates took the decision was taken not to postpone it and, as wakes go, it turned into quite a knees-up-mother-Brown party. Wreaths from both clubs were laid in the centre circle before the match, with a pint of Guinness for Harding standing on the centre spot; Dennis Wise and Steve Clarke, team captain and club captain respectively, carried out a floral message reading "Matthew RIP" and presented it in front of the newly named Matthew Harding Stand.

**Walter:** I'd bought a programme every game that season, but completely forgot to for this match. I'd never seen people cry at the football before – I lost count of the number of men and women in tears. For all the rivalry, it should never be forgotten how respectful Tottenham fans were that day.

**Mark:** As the Chelsea players linked hands and stood, like the rest of us in the ground, waiting for referee Roger Dilkes to blow his whistle to signal the start of a minute's silence I wondered if this moment of reflection would be tarnished by ignorant morons as they usually were. Chelsea v Tottenham? It's never been a marriage made in heaven now has it? From the first second to the last, you could have heard a pin drop. The hairs on the back of my neck stood on end. That Chelsea fans stood silent was not unexpected, that Spurs fans followed suite only added to Matthew Harding's legend. Every supporter inside Stamford Bridge no matter what their allegiance recognised a part of themselves in Matthew… a supporter first and foremost… one of us.

Matthew Harding's favourite expression was "Enjoy the game!" and boy would he have enjoyed this one. Chelsea took Spurs apart with a 3-1 victory, the goals coming from Ruud Gullit, David Lee and Roberto Di Matteo. "Everyone in the stadium today participated in a special way," Gullit said in his post-match interview, "including the Tottenham supporters, and on behalf of the team and the staff I want to thank them. Everybody's just happy about the way they played, and it was a perfect tribute to Matthew."

Matthew Harding was only involved in the running of Chelsea Football Club for three years or so which makes it all the more remarkable that he could have made such an impression on Blues fans in such a short space of time. That he did is a testimony to the man and his principals. Chelsea supporter first and foremost, businessman second… a true man of the people, born on The Shed.

Matthew Charles Harding
26 December 1953 - 22 October 1996
RIP

# CAREFREE! CHELSEA CHANTS AND TERRACE CULTURE

*Lola*

**Walter:** *Lola* by The Kinks was released in 1970 and reached number two in the UK charts. Gianfranco Zola signed for Chelsea in November 1996 and went on to become a bona fide Blues legend. *Lola* / Zola it wasn't going to take too long to work that one out. *Zola! La, la, la, la, Zola!*

The chant soon gained momentum as new verses were added.

21 December 1996 was special! Chelsea 3 West Ham 1, Mark Hughes x2, Gianfranco Zola. After six minutes, Zola's lovely flick set up Hughes for Chelsea's first goal. After ten minutes, Zola tore the Hammers left back Julian Dicks a new one, twisting him inside and out before scoring a peach of a goal.

*If you wanna know the meaning of taking the piss,*
*Go down to West Ham and ask Julian Dicks about Zola!*
*La, la, la, la, Zola!*

The billion-pound game (or so we were led to believe) took place on 11 May 2003 and saw a monumental win for Chelsea; Chelsea 2 Liverpool 1, Marcel Desailly, Jesper Grønkjær. In his last game for Chelsea, a sublime piece of Zola footwork left Liverpool's Jamie Carragher on his backside by the corner flag and another verse was born.

*Give him an inch and a blade of grass,*
*Watch him leave Carragher on his arse.*
*That's Zola! La, la, la, la Zola!*

*DAY-O (The Banana Boat Song)*

*Day-O (The Banana Boat song)* is a traditional Jamaican folk song the best-known version of which was recorded by Harry Belafonte in 1956. Twenty-one years later Chelsea supporters came up with a new version after Chelsea came from behind to knock Liverpool out of the FA Cup at the Fourth Round stage: 26 January 1997 Chelsea 4 Liverpool 2, Mark Hughes, Gianfranco Zola, Gianluca Vialli x2.

**Walter:** Manager Ruud Gullit started with Vialli and Zola up front. Less than half an hour was gone and Chelsea were 2-0 down, and it should've been three. Gullit brought Hughes on for Scott Minto at half time and the Welshman scored five minutes later. Liverpool couldn't handle him. Hughes' play opened space for Vialli (who scored twice) and Zola (who scored once) had a free role all over the final third of the pitch.

The thing about Zola's goal is, (if I close my eyes I can still see it arcing in) is this incredible split-second of silence. I can remember it at the time, and when you see the footage of the goal it comes across perfectly. Before Zola shoots, the crowd at the Bridge, (which was on fire, it should be said), give it that, *"Go ooon"*, of excitement as he receives the ball. Then Zola hits it…

Then comes this almost inconceivable moment of absolute silence. 27,950 people, (The Shed End was being renovated), held their breaths as the ball arrowed towards David James – and rocketed into the top corner. Mayhem ensued. The *Day-O*-themed chant that evolved after this game was:

*Day-O! Di Matteo! Vialli scores and the Scousers go home.*
*Not one, not two, not three, but four!*
*Vialli scores and the Scousers go home.*

## *Flipper*

29 March 1998 League Cup Final Chelsea 2 Middlesbrough 0
Frank Sinclair, Roberto Di Matteo

**Walter:** The night before the final at Wembley I'd been out at a fancy-dress party dressed as a cowboy. I hate parties, and this one was particularly shocking. A mate worked at the local Tesco's, and it was a staff party. Lionel Blair (a patron!) was there dancing and singing. Bizarre! At the end of the night, my feet were killing me. Back at my pal's, there was a bloke in the recovery position off his nut. The next morning, I was hanging in a bad way. I couldn't drink a pint! Fortunately, by the time I got to Wembley, I perked up on the concourse with a couple of beers. Celery was everywhere. It was war. I don't think I'll ever witness celery wars like it again.

Paul Gascoigne was in the Boro team and had been accused of domestic violence towards his wife. I had my back against the wall, and there was a bloke singing a song about Gazza that caught on. The whole concourse was singing it for about twenty minutes, once again though it never made it into the ground. It was to the theme tune of *Flipper*, an American TV drama that ran from 1964 to 1967 about a dolphin. For you younger lot out there, yes, you did read that right. It was a TV show about a dolphin.

*They call him Gazza, Gazza, what a fat b\*stard!*
*Everyone knows, he broke his wife's nose.*

# CAREFREE! CHELSEA CHANTS AND TERRACE CULTURE

*Son Of My Father*

**Mark:** Sometimes football chants which start out as taunts come back to haunt the originators spectacularly. In June 1997 former Millwall, Nottingham Forest and Tottenham Hotspur striker Teddy Sheringham signed for Manchester United. At 31-years of age the prolific centre-forward who'd occasionally been linked with a move to Chelsea had yet to win any honours.

Sheringham's first season at Old Trafford was disappointing, and when Man U rocked up at Stamford Bridge just after Christmas the following year (29 December 1998, Chelsea 0 Manchester United 0) the striker found himself on the bench. Joining the action on the hour mark as a sub for Paul Scholes, Sheringham was taunted by Blues supporters with the chant, *Oh Teddy, Teddy. You went to Man United and you've won f\*ck all.*

The melody was borrowed from Chicory Tip's chart-topper from 1972, *Son Of My Father,* a cracking tune co-written by disco-synth innovator Giorgio Moroder. Ironically, later that season, Sheringham would come off the bench to score in the FA Cup Final against Newcastle and once again in the Champions League Final against Bayern Munich. United won both trophies and the Premier League to complete an impressive treble. That version of *Oh Teddy, Teddy* was never sung again.

**Walter:** The next time we played Man United after their treble was on 03 October 1999 and our famous 5-0 rout of the Mancunians. Nicky Butt was sent off for kicking Dennis Wise, who had pinched him as he lay clattered on the turf. Sheringham was a substitute and was serenaded with; *Oh Teddy, Teddy. He went to Man United and he's still a c\*nt.*

In May 2000, Jimmy Floyd Hasselbaink signed for Chelsea from Atlético Madrid for a then club record fee of £15 million, and the next month Eidur Gudjohnsen arrived from Bolton Wanderers for a more modest £4.5 million. Jimmy won the Golden Boot at the end of his first full season at the Bridge.

His popular *Son of My Father*-flavoured *Oh Jimmy, Jimmy! Jimmy Jimmy Jimmy Floyd Hasselbaink!* still gets sung these days if the boozer or the train is feeling nostalgic. *Eidur Gudjohnsen (clap clap clap clap clap)* was the perfect partner for Jimmy. The following season they hit 52 goals between them in all competitions!

## The Adventures of Rupert Bear

**Mark:** Albert Ferrer was a Chelsea cult hero pretty much from the moment he signed from Barcelona in 1998. "Nobody knows who I am in England, and that's the way I like it," announced the diminutive, tough-tackling right-back shortly after arriving in London. Ferrer was an instantly recognised superstar in his native Spain having won it all with Barca.

That statement coupled with always-enthusiastic performances deserved a decent chant, and whoever came up with the idea of linking Ferrer with the theme tune from kids television show *The Adventures of Rupert Bear*, sung by Jackie Lee, which aired from 1970 to 1977 can consider themselves a genius.

*Albert, Albert Ferrer… Everyone knows his name.*

Abiding memory? Singing *Albert, Albert Ferrer* outside a bar in Milan's Piazza del Duomo prior to the epic Dennis Wise goal game with AC Milan. 'Who is this Albert Ferrer? I don't know his name?' our waitress kept asking, a cue to sing his song even louder.

**Walter:** It started out as *Albert, Albert Ferrer! Everyone sing his name* which is the right adaptation of the song's original lyrics, although, for some reason, most people sang *Everyone knows his name* instead.

## Yes Sir, I Can Boogie

**Walter:** Denmark international defender Jes Høgh arrived in 1999 as back-up to Marcel Desailly and Frank Lebouef. He only made 17 league appearances for Chelsea, but he had a brilliant song. In 1977, María Mendiola and Mayte Mateos aka Spanish vocal duo Baccara had a No. 1 hit with *Yes Sir, I Can Boogie*. Maybe if the Dane had more luck with his fitness, his song based on the track would've taken right off:

*Jes Høgh, I can boogie.*
*But I need a certain song.*
*I can boogie, boogie boogie.*
*All night long!*

## CAREFREE! CHELSEA CHANTS AND TERRACE CULTURE

*Car Wash*

**Walter:** Let's not beat around the bush, Gustavo Poyet was an absolute superstar for Chelsea Football Club. Slice out the fact (for now) he left for Tottenham and kissed the cockerel on his chest, what he did for this Club goes down in history.

When he was manager of Brighton, Chelsea had been away at West Brom and the Seagulls had won away at Walsall to secure promotion. (16 April 2011, Walsall 1 Brighton 3: West Brom 1 Chelsea 3, Didier Drogba, Salomon Kalou, Frank Lampard.) Taxi Alan, Big Chris, Smiffy and I were utterly demolishing a service station KFC when the Brighton team bus pulled into the services. Smiffy and Big Chris bolted out the door faster than I've seen them move since they were single and two treacles on Putney High Street were strolling on the other side of the road. In the service station car park, the lads ended up chatting to Gus and once they said they were Chelsea, Gus told them he regretted his Spurs-related actions, and warmly embraced them.

Anyway, during his time Poyet as a Blue (1997-2001), the intro to the 1976 disco classic *Car Wash* by Rose Royce was mirrored to applaud our Uruguayan – *(clap, clap, clap-clap-clap, clap, clap)* GUS!

It sounded great when the whole end was doing in it unison. My most significant memory of this was all the Chelsea at Wembley in the FA Cup semi against Newcastle (9 April 2000, Chelsea 2 Newcastle United 1) when Poyet scored both goals to take us to the final against Aston Villa. He converted a cross by Jon Harley – a player the Blues crowd always seemed quite fond of – *Jon Harley! Jon Harley! Jon Harley!* was the cry.

**Mark:** The Harley love was due to the fact the talented young left-back was a product of Chelsea's youth set up... and guess what, first team chances were hard to come by! The presence of Graeme Le Saux and Celestine Babayaro restricted his opportunities and he eventually left for Fulham. At the time of writing Jon is currently Under 16 Lead Coach at Stamford Bridge.

*Black Night*

**Mark:** Scoring a goal on your Chelsea debut is a fantastic way to make an immediate impact on Blues supporters, and Mario Stanić took this to another level when leathering a 35-yard piledriver past West Ham keeper Shaka Hislop in a classic London derby at Stamford Bridge (19 August

2000, Chelsea 4 West Ham 2, Jimmy Floyd Hasselbaink, Gianfranco Zola, Mario Stanić x2.) The Croatia international scored a brace against the Hammers and his stunning strike deservedly won *Match of the Day*'s Goal of the Month competition.

Stanić almost immediately became a cult hero at the Bridge, and as befitting such status he needed a song. These things are never obvious, but sometimes they just work. At the time, we used a matchday King's Road drinker called the One Bar (historically the Nell Gwynne, currently the Jam Tree), it was a lively place and would get packed out with people regularly standing on tables and getting the singing going. I heard a lot of new chants from this period aired for the first time here and as Walter has mentioned there were plenty that never made it out of the door. One that did borrowed the opening guitar riff from hard rock band Deep Purple's classic 1970 hit *Black Night* and simply added Stanić to the end of it.

*Der, der, der, der, der, der, der, der, der, der, der. Stanić, Stanić!*

It's bonkers and beautiful and probably one of my favourite Chelsea chants of all time simply because it just shows how inventive football songsmiths can be when going in search of a melody to fit with a footballer's name.

**Walter:** With Netherland's international Mario Melchiot having signed the previous summer, the arrival of Mario Stanić meant that Chelsea now had two players called Mario… which merited a unique song of its own courtesy *La Donna e Mobile* (again).

*We've got two Mario's! We've got two Mario's!*

## Macarena

**Walter:** Nigeria international left-back Celestine Babayaro had a couple of songs. Firstly, to Los del Rio's 1995 chart hit *Macarena*.

*Baba one, Baba two, Baba three Babayaro.*
*Baba four, Baba five, Baba six Babayaro.*
*Baba seven, Baba eight, Baba nine, Babayaro. Ohhhhh Babayaro!*

You'll be pleased to know that it never really took off – mainly because we're not Arsenal (Google Per Mertesacker *Macarena*). However, seeing Big Chris doing the actions after a skin-full is a sight I'll take to my grave.

## CAREFREE! CHELSEA CHANTS AND TERRACE CULTURE

*Barbara Ann*

**Walter:** Originally recorded by The Regents in 1961, The Beach Boys had a global smash hit with *Barbara Ann* in 1965 and the melody provided a second chant for young Celestine. This never took off either, despite Big Chris doing all the harmonies.

*Ba-ba-ba-ba-Babayaro, ba-ba-ba-ba-Babayaro!*
*Oh Babayaro, take my hand, oh Babayaro.*
*You got me rocking and a rolling, rocking and a reeling, Babayaro.*
*Ba-ba-ba-ba-Babayaro!*
*Went to the dance, looking for romance, saw Babayaro so I thought I'd take a chance.*

Yep – you had to be there.

*Only Fools and Horses TV show theme*

*He stuck a Veron in his pocket, he nicked Glen Johnson from West Ham.*
*'Cos if you want the best ones, and you don't ask questions, then Roman he's your man.*
*'Cos where the money comes from is a mystery, is it from the drugs or the oil industry?*
*So come on Chelsea chuck your celery 'cos we are the famous CFC ...*
*la la la la la, la la la la la.*

**Walter:** There is early footage of this chant being sung in the One Bar. In truth, the chant transferred from the pubs to the Matthew Harding Lower with a varying degree of success, but often lyrics kept changing. Veron got changed to Drogba or Tiago – or the first line became, *He's got a billion in his pocket!*

It's an absolute classic that deserves its place here.

These were great times at Stamford Bridge. We'd qualified for the Champions League, our debt had been wiped out by Roman Abramovich and the Club signed a wealth of talent during the summer transfer window including Geremi, Glen Johnson, Joe Cole, Damien Duff, Hernan Crespo (*Hello, Hello...* what a player), Juan Sebastian Veron, Claude Makélélé and Adrian Mutu.

We'd got off to a decent start beating Liverpool at Anfield (17 August 2003, Liverpool 1 Chelsea 2, Juan Sebastian Veron, Jimmy Floyd Hasselbaink) – our away kit looked like a packet of Embassy Mild cigarettes and our away support waved banknotes at the Scousers and taunted them with chants of, *load's and loads of money!*

In our first eight league games, we won six and drew two and qualified for the group stages of the Champions League. It was breath-taking. These months were one of the best buzzes I can remember following the team.

## The Adventures of Robin Hood TV show theme

**Walter:** Another gem that could be heard in the One Bar around this time was a quality tribute to Chelsea winger Arjen Robben who was absolute dynamite, and a privilege to watch at times.

His song which borrowed the theme tune from the television show *The Adventures of Robin Hood* (original series first aired in 1955!!) never really got going – maybe because it was lifted for Man Utd's song about Ryan Giggs.

*Robben's good, Robben's good, running down the wing.*
*Robben's good, Robben's good, hear the Chelsea sing.*
*He ain't got no hair, we don't f\*ckin' care!*
*(Or: Loved by the Blues, feared by the Reds!)*
*Robben's good, Robben's good, Robben's good.*

**Mark:** The Willian song and it drawing on *Tom Hark* has had a chapter devoted to it and rightly so, the tune also formed the basis of another classic One Bar tribute to Arjen Robben which went like this:

*I told my mate the other day that I have found the white Pele.*
*My mate said who, who is it then? I told him that it was Arjen Robben.*
*Arjen Robben! Arjen Robben! Arjen Robben! Arjen Robben!*

## Mambo No.5 (a little bit of)

**Mark:** It helped immensely that Harriet (Tara) Trayner, the manager of the One Bar at the time was Proper Chels and had no problem with people standing on tables and getting the singing going. There were so many clever songs conceived in that drinker during the early days of the Roman Abramovich era that it was to football chants like the 100 Club was to Punk Rock.

First heard in the One, was this little ditty based on *Mambo No.5* a jive song composed in 1949 by Cuban Dámaso Pérez Prado and sampled by German singer-songwriter Lou Bega who had a smash hit with it exactly 50 years later.

*A little bit of Sheva in our lives.*
*A little bit of Ballack down the sides.*
*A little bit of Terry is what we need.*
*A little bit of Shauny with his speed.*
*A little bit of Ashley in defence.*
*A little bit of Drogba he's immense.*
*A little bit of singin' from the fans.*
*A little bit of José he's our man.*

## My Bonnie Lies Over the Ocean

**Walter:** Here we have a traditional Scottish folk song written about Bonnie Prince Charlie (Charles Edward Stuart not Charlie Cooke) that dates back to the 18th Century and whose melody was borrowed for a chant composed in honour of Frank Lampard.

*Our leader it used to be Dennis, and now it is John Terry...*
*And in the middle is Frankie, he plays for the mighty Chelsea.*
*Lampard, Lampard, he plays for the mighty Chelsea, Chelsea.*
*Lampard, Lampard he plays for the mighty Chelsea.*

Originating on a Midlands Metro tram journey back to Birmingham New Street Station after an away game with WBA, (04 March 2006, WBA 1-2 Chelsea, Drogba, Joe Cole), the song *Lampard, Lampard he plays for the mighty Chelsea* never made it back to London let alone Stamford Bridge. The match sticks in the memory because it took place only three days after Peter Osgood passed away.

## Rio

**Mark:** Rio Ferdinand was never the most popular of players with the Chelsea crowd. A regular rival for the England captaincy with Blues legend John Terry, Ferdinand, who started his professional career with West Ham before moving to Leeds, Manchester United and finally QPR, was the subject of numerous versions of Duran Duran's 1982 hit *Rio*.

In September 2003, Ferdinand missed a drugs test at Old Trafford and was banned from competition for eight months from the following January until September 2004. Preceding the ban, Ferdinand had been ahead of Terry in the England central-defensive selection stakes, but manager at the time Sven Goran Eriksson drafted in the Chelsea man who did an exemplary job.

Be it at Old Trafford or Wembley, for the duration of the ban, Ferdinand was restricted to the role of spectator. Chelsea's penultimate game of the 2003/2004 season was away at United, (8 May 2004, 1-1, Jesper Grønkjær), and although credit for the chant lies elsewhere, with plenty no doubt trying to claim the glory, travelling Blues fans kept themselves entertained throughout the afternoon singing; *His name is Rio and he watches from the stands.*

## Nel Blu Dipinto di Blu

Better known as *Volare*. Recorded in 1958 by Italian singer-songwriter Domenico Mudugno and made globally popular by Dean Martin, the melody for this song has formed the basis of many a football chant.

**Walter:** At Chelsea this came in the form of a tribute to Tiago Cardos Mendes who had one stellar season for the Blues, ending the 2004-2005 campaign with a Premier League winners medal.

*Tiago wohoah, Tiago wohoah.*
*He comes from Portugal, he hates the Arsenal.*

## Rock the Casbah

*London Calling* by the Clash is regularly played over the Tannoy at Stamford Bridge, and, like the Madness track *One Step Beyond* it's a song and indeed a band that Chelsea supporters readily identify with.

*Rock the Casbah* is a classic Clash song and it spawned a couple of chants that entertained briefly and were related to José Mourinho's regular spats with UEFA whom he regularly suggested were conspiring against him... and Arsenal... pick any season... you could write a standalone book on his issues with the Gunners.

**Walter:** *Mourinho don't like 'em – f*ck UEFA! F*ck UEFA!*

**Mark:** *Mourinho don't like 'em – f*ck the Arsenal! F*ck the Arsenal!*

## Singin' In the Rain

**Walter:** *Singin' in the Rain* was first published in 1929 and covered by a number of artists including Judy Garland. Gene Kelly's version is probably the most renowned from the 1952 musical of the same name.

It's 15 November 2008, and Chelsea are away at West Bromwich Albion (West Brom 0 Chelsea 3, José Bosingwa, Nicolas Anelka x2), it's pouring down and we're singin' in the rain.

José *'The Unibrow'* Bosingwa opened the scoring with a scorcher past Scott Carson and some bright spark started singing, *Bosingwa in the rain, Bosingwa in the rain. What a glorious feeling, I'm happy again!*

I don't remember it being sung much in between times, but then away to Portsmouth on a Tuesday night in March (3 March 2009) the scene was set. There was an absolute monsoon on the South Coast. I can't remember watching a game in such heavy rain. Bosingwa was playing. I started the chant, a few joined in, and then it fell on its arse and that was that. Win some, lose some. For the record, Chelsea won 1-0 with a goal from Didier Drogba in the 79th minute and Petr Cech was named Man of the Match.

### *Paokora Exo Trela*

**Walter:** Defender Alex Rodrigo Dias da Costa, better known as Alex scored some blinders during his time at Chelsea (2007-12). As cheerful as always, my pal Simon Lorch grinned widely as he told me: "Probably my favourite one to never fully take off, always sung in bars at Euro aways for Alex...

*Oooh Alex Rodrigo, Dias da Costa, he's from Brazil!*
*He plays alongside Terry and he's just as f\*cking hard,*
*He gets the ball outside the box and scores from thirty yards!*

The tune is stolen from PAOK FC from Thessaloniki in Greece. They sing *OOO Paokara exo trela...* (*Oh PAOK, I have madness in my mind*)... Liverpool also started singing it around this time, but we were first!"

### *La Bamba*

**Mark:** I'm probably in a minority here, but I think the significance of what Carlo Ancelotti achieved in winning the Double has been largely over looked by Chelsea Football Club who hardly covered themselves in glory by despicably sacking him less than a year after achieving such a notable feat.

A great manager who had the respect of his players because he'd done it all himself on the pitch, Carlo was both media-friendly and clearly a decent bloke who liked a crafty fag and probably a glass or two of vino. Such traits deserved a decent song and so it came to pass in the form of a ditty that borrowed the melody from *La Bamba* a Mexican folk song that was made globally popular first by Richie Valens and later by Los Lobos.

*Ancelotti, Ancelotti! His name is Ancelotti.*
*His name is Ancelotti, and Didier Drogba and Super Frank Lampard!*
*Ancelotti, Ancelotti! His name is Ancelotti.*

It sounded great when everyone got behind it and incorporated whistling and clapping into the refrain.

## *Kumbaya*

**Mark:** A campfire song beloved of the Scouting movement, *Kumbaya* (Come By Here) is a simple appeal to God to come and help those in need.

*Kumbaya my Lord, Kumbaya. Oh Lord, Kumbaya*

Two Chelsea versions found popularity in recent years.

*Lampard scores My Lord, Lampard scores* for which there is a video on the Gate 17 Chelsea *YouTube* channel and *Juan Mata My Lord, Juan Mata* in praise of the much-loved, much-missed Spanish magician whose talent was squandered by a spiteful José Mourinho. (Bizarre how things worked out in the end with Mata and Mourinho reunited, literally, at Old Trafford.)

The Lampard version never made it big unlike Mata's which proved to be his main tribute chant during his all-too-brief stay at the Bridge.

## *Give It Up*

**Mark:** KC and the Sunshine Band's disco stomper which went to No. 1 in the UK charts in 1984 has seen plenty of use by football supporters, notably by Man United fans who used the tune to tribute Nicky Butt. Fair play to them, that could have been tricky. Chelsea's version was sung in homage to Ghana midfield star Michael Essien… I loved him.

*Essien, Essien, Michael Essien!*
*Na-na-na-na-na-na-na-na-na-na-now!*
*Essien! Essien! Michael Essien!*

## CAREFREE! CHELSEA CHANTS AND TERRACE CULTURE

*King Billy's On The Wall*

**Walter:** Personally, I loathed the *Juan Mata My Lord* song. He deserved so much more than that and Serious Face Gary, a season ticket holder in the Matthew Harding Upper, penned a tribute chant that ticked all the boxes.

Harnessing the melody of Glasgow Rangers fans' favourite, *King Billy's on The Wall*, a famous Loyalist song about King William of Orange's triumph at the Battle of the Boyne, Serious Face Gary came up with:

*Juan Mata's on the ball, Juan Mata's on the ball.*
*He drifts out wide, he cuts inside, he can beat them all.*
*Thousands come to see him, they stand and gaze in awe, from minute one to ninety,*
*Juan Mata's on the ball.*

Gary's pal Tape Mix Tim took it into the Gate 15 concourse of the Matthew Harding Lower. It was sung every home game by the regulars in Gate 15, but it sadly never kicked on further, which is what it truly deserved:

I haven't met a supporter who wanted Mata sold. Looking at it objectively, of course, it's true that if José felt he was a square peg in a round hole, then that was that and we had to trust José's decision to sell him. Sure enough, the league was won the following season and Fàbregas broke assist records.

I know all that, you know all that – but... it's Juan Mata though! What a man!

Mata was voted player of the season in both 2012 and 2013... only the fourth player to win back to back awards. The others are Sir Frank in 2004 and 2005, Ray *'I Couldn't Agree with You More, Splendid'* Wilkins in 1976 and 1977, and John Hollins in 1970, 1971.

When José subbed Juan Mata at Southampton on New Years Day 2014, (Southampton 0 Chelsea 3, Fernando Torres, Willian, Oscar), we all feared the worst. The writing was on the wall. Visibly upset, Mata took his place on the bench and was consoled by his teammates. On 24 January, he signed for Man United. I don't think I've ever recovered!

*Crazy Horses*

**Mark:** The first of two eccentric nods to Premier League title-winning wing-back hero Victor Moses come in the form of a simple but effective rework of The Osmonds 1972 chart hit *Crazy Horses*.

On 25 September 2012, the Blues ran Wolves ragged. Chelsea 6 Wolverhampton Wanderers 0, (Gary Cahill, Ryan Bertrand, Juan Mata, Oriol Romeu, Fernando Torres, Victor Moses), and manager Robbie Di Matteo handed Moses a first start for Chelsea and the Nigeria international duly obliged with a goal and his trademark backflip celebration.

Two days later, a video of the goal appeared on the Gate 17 Chelsea *YouTube* channel accompanied by the chant *Victor Moses* which replaced the *Crazy Horses* words and was complete with that mad screeching wah-wah guitar effect.

*From Paris To Berlin*

Next up, a Moses chant that harnesses the melody of *From Paris To Berlin* Danish pop act Infernal's chart hit from 2005… and why not?

**Walter:** In 2014, Young Simon Lorch and his pals travelled from London to watch Chelsea play Champions League group stage games in Lisbon (30 September, Sporting Lisbon 0 Chelsea 1, Nemanja Matić), Maribor (Maribor 1 Chelsea 1, Nemanja Matić) and Schalke (Schalke 04 0 Chelsea 5, John Terry, Willian, Jan Kirchhoff own goal, Didier Drogba, Ramires). The final was to be held in Berlin at the end of the season, so with a belly full of Caipirinha's they gleefully sang:

*From London to Berlin and every cross that he puts in,*
*His name is Victor Moses! Victor Moses!*
*And when he's parting the Red Sea and burning bushes for me,*
*His name is Victor Moses! Victor Moses!*

However, Paris Saint-Germain cruelly knocked Chelsea out by virtue of the away goal rule in the first knockout round (17 February 2015, PSG 1 Chelsea 1, Branislav Ivanović. Chelsea 2 PSG 2, Gary Cahill, Eden Hazard) and that was the end of that.

As is often the way of things at Stamford Bridge, Victor Moses was on loan at Stoke City during this campaign so he wouldn't have made it to Berlin anyway. Even so it's a great song and with Moses currently part of the Blues first team set up there's still time for it to make a breakthrough, you never know!

### Papa's Got A Brand New Pigbag

**Walter:** Another ditty for Moses was derived from the 1981 instrumental *Papa's Got A Brand New Pigbag* performed by the British dance-punk band Pigbag.

*Do, do, do, do. Victor Moses!*

The tune was also used for; *Do, do, do, do. André Schürrle!*

*Sloop John B* features plenty of times in the book, and again now while we're on the subject of Victor Moses. Moses' role as right wing-back would be pivotal in the 2016/2017 title-winning campaign and when Chelsea's opposition played in red it was always worth having a pound on him to score anytime and then belt out; *He parts the Red Sea, he parts the Red Sea! Victor Moses, he parts the Red Sea!*

**Mark:** May as well add in a few more *Sloop John B* gems in here. The ironic but good-natured *He scores when he wants, he score when he wants* chant proved popular for both Fernando Torres and John Obi Mikel as did *He cuts his own hair, he cuts his own hair* for Travis Bickle lookalike and fellow Champions League hero Raul Meireles… then there was the tweaked *He does what he wants* version for one of the great hopes from Chelsea's fabled academy Josh McEachran.

McEachran's first team star flickered briefly and brightly over Stamford Bridge and then predictably vanished over the horizon via Swansea, Middlesbrough, Watford, Wigan and Arnhem before reappearing in all its twinkling glory at Griffin Park, Brentford.

**Walter:** I remember McEachran's *Twitter* feed mainly consisted of him reporting on going for a Nando's, having a nap, and seeing some sort off of *Coronation Street*. His chant led you to believe otherwise:

*Josh McEachran's having a party! Bring your vodka and your charlie!*

### Our House

**Mark:** McEachran's chances of featuring in Chelsea's midfield weren't help by the constantly revolving managerial door. Carlo Ancelotti, Andre

Villas-Boas, Roberto Di Matteo, Rafa Benitez and José Mourinho – pity the kid and all the youth players for that matter having to cope with such a lack of continuity. Not much has changed in that respect!

**Walter:** Another young midfielder, Nemanja Matić, had hardly featured in his first stint at Stamford Bridge and was used as a makeweight in the deal with Benfica that brought David Luiz to Chelsea first time around in January 2011, four months before Ancelotti was sacked. When Mourinho was rehired in 2013, he asked for Matić. The Serbia international's return to the Bridge in January 2014 saw a Madness *Our House*-based anthem spring forth:

*Matić, in the middle of our pitch!*
*Matić, in the middle of our pitch!*

Southampton had sung similar for their player Claus Lundekvam, 1996-2008. When my good pal Blanco the Saint has been on the sauce, he sends me clips of him singing; *Our Claus! In the middle of our pitch!* while simultaneously banging on the toilet door he's frequenting.

### This Is How It Feels

**Mark:** 27 January 2013, and 12,146 fans crammed into Brentford's cosy home at Griffin Park for the Bees 4th Round FA Cup tie with Chelsea. The most enticing aspect of the tie for Blues supporters wasn't the high-octane thrill of a west London derby, chuckle… it was the prospect of standing on terraces under a lowish roof and giving it the retrospective large one. Personally, I was looking forward to doing impressions of a seagull squawking and going *ugh ugh ugh ugh… you're shit… argharggggggggh* every time Brentford's goalie Simon Moore took a goal-kick in front of our end. Faded Shed memories for me.

Chelsea fans were packed together like a tin of Blue and White sardines in the Brook Road Stand, whimsically referred to as the Wendy House by the home crowd. 1,285 supporters stood on the terrace behind the goal, 600 in the seats above. Despite the midday kick-off restricting pre-match drinking time, the atmosphere sizzled. This was nothing to do with the opposition, it was more to do with the environment, oh and the latest drama to have enveloped the Blues which this time had come in roly-poly frame of goatee-bearded former Liverpool manager Rafael Benitez.

*Fat Spanish Waiter* was recited repeatedly early on though as League One outfit Brentford took the game by the scruff of the neck and threatened an upset, leading the game 2-1 (Oscar) with less than 10 minutes left, the more appropriate chant *You don't know what you're doing* was directed at Rafa.

The unpopular interim Blues boss might have thought Fernando Torres 82nd minute equaliser which took the tie to a replay would have spared him from further torment, but he was wrong.

Shortly after Benitez arrived at Stamford Bridge, a protest chant with words set to the wonderful indie melody of *This is how it feels* by the Inspiral Carpets gained popularity.

*We don't are about Rafa.*
*He don't care about us.*
*All we care about is Chelsea FC.*

At Griffin Park, Benitez was left in no doubt about the magnitude of ill will towards him as he had no option other than to walk past irate Blues fans congregated in The Wendy House to reach and leave the dug-out.

Rafa being Rafa, in his post-match interview the Spaniard had the temerity to argue against the suggestion that he didn't know what he was doing by defiantly stating that he did. "I guarantee that sending on Juan Mata and changing the game showed we do know what we are doing." His words only served to fan the flames of supporter angst.

**Walter:** The Porky Interim got absolute hell. *You're not wanted here! You're not wanted here! F*ck off Benitez, you're not wanted here* (*Sloop John B*) was also sung at most games and *We don't care about Rafa* evolved into *We don't care about Rafa (fat c*nt), he don't care about us (chorizo) All we care about is Chelsea FC!* Big Chris takes the credit for inserting *'chorizo'* into the song. He does an action to it too, pretending to munch on a big Spanish sausage. Another ditty often resounded in the Wee Imp pub both pre-and post-match.

*When Rafa leaves Chelsea! When Rafa leaves Chelsea!*
*We're gonna have a party,*
*We're gonna have a party,*
*We're gonna have a party,*
*When Rafa leaves Chelsea.*

## I Am The Music Man

**Mark:** If Rafa Benitez was the scourge of Chelsea fans, a player who arrived in the January transfer window during his tenure as interim boss was anything but. Senegalese striker Demba Ba had made a name for himself on Tyneside scoring goals for Newcastle United and with £50 million record signing Fernando Torres regularly struggling for form, the 27-year old was hired to do the same for Chelsea and proved an instant hit.

Scoring two goals on his Blues debut in a 5-1 thrashing of Southampton at St Mary's in the 3rd round of the FA Cup (5 January 2013, Demba Ba x2, Victor Moses, Branislav Ivanović, Frank Lampard) and following it up with a goal on his home debut against the same club (16 January 2013, 2-2, Demba Ba, Eden Hazard) was enough for Ba to achieve instant hero status and better still be fêted in song.

Ingeniously, the lyrics of the traditional children's folk song I Am the Music Man, which in 1990 had been taken to the giddy heights of No. 52 in the UK Singles Charts by novelty party records specialists Black Lace, was given a Chelsea makeover by Blues supporter Dan Shiel.

*I am the music man, I come from far away and I can play, (What can you play?) I play the piano.*
*Pia pia piano, piano, piano, piano…*

became:

*I am an African, I come from far away, And I can play, (What can you play?)*
*I play football.*
*Demba, Demba Demba Ba, Demba Ba, Demba Ba.*
*Demba, Demba Demba Ba, Demba Demba Ba!*

**Walter:** I asked Dan (@DMANUTC) how the song came about.

**Dan:** "I remember singing the song to a load of the boys in the boozer before the Brentford cup game and getting told: "There are too many words to get that started in our end!" Loads of us were shouting, *I am an African!* for the whole first half, and no one was having it. After venting some anger out on Rafa at half-time, I think everyone fancied it and the whole end was singing it. Credit to The Chelsea Smiths Firm for sticking with it through the first half."

**Mark:** Ba, a late substitute for Ryan Bertrand against Brentford, was treated to his special chant for the rest of his brief Chelsea career which concluded at the end of the following season.

There is no doubting the catchiness of the *Demba, Demba, Demba Ba* chant but at the time its singing was restricted to Chelsea fans. Nobody, however, could have predicted then that 49 games into his 51-match stint with the Blues, Ba would score a goal that would immortalise him in football folklore and spawn a chant that would be heard at every stadium in the Premier League.

*Que Sera, Sera (Whatever Will Be Will Be)*

**Mark:** 27 April 2014, and table-topping Liverpool, on the back of an eleven-game winning streak, looked destined to win their first ever Premier League title. Visitors Chelsea, with one eye on a midweek Champions League semi-final second leg tie with Atlético Madrid, Petr Cech and John Terry injured, Oscar in the stands, and Gary Cahill and Willian on the bench were the bookies favourites to take a beating.

As Reds manager Brendan Rodgers and his players arrived at Anfield, the team coach was surrounded by fans singing *We're gonna win the League*. The sense of self-entitlement was palpable with stalls outside the ground already selling merchandise proclaiming Liverpool champions.

Following a recent victory over title rivals Manchester City at Anfield, Reds skipper Steven Gerrard, sensing that the opportunity had finally arrived to silence opposition fans who had taunted him with the chant *Have you ever seen Gerrard win the League?* throughout the latter stages of his career, had delivered an expletive-laden team talk that was beamed around the world. "This does not f*cking slip now," he'd said, not once, but twice, just in case anyone wasn't listening or didn't understand.

Little did Gerrard know then, or indeed when he led Liverpool out onto the pitch to face Chelsea, that his words would come back to haunt him in a way he could never have imagined even in his worst nightmares.

As the game kicked off, Blues boss José Mourinho's game-plan to hand 20-year old centre-back Tomáš Kalas a Premier League debut and ask him to mark hotshot Reds striker Luis Suárez out of the game looked fundamentally flawed... but that's just what the steadfast young Czech did.

As first-half injury time drew to a close, it was clear that Mourinho's containment tactics were working. Rodgers knew he had the lemon-break coming to figure out a way to breach Chelsea's defence, Liverpool had the lion's share of possession... score one and they'd score more.

And then it happened.

Reds defender Mamadou Sakho squared an innocuous-looking ball to Gerrard who inexplicably miscontrolled it then slipped and fell while trying to recover. The ball ran loose to advancing Blues striker Demba Ba who scuttled away from Gerrard and scored at The Kop End. Ba dropped to his knees in celebration and kissed the pitch leaving Gerrard to pick the ball out of his own net.

Chelsea went on to win the game 2-0 thanks to a stoppage time Willian goal, but it was Gerrard's slip that dominated the news while social media came alive as replays of the incident were cruelly customised to poke fun at the Liverpool captain.

Rodgers, Gerrard, and co. failed to recover their composure. In their next game away to Crystal Palace, Liverpool blew a three-goal lead to end up drawing a game they should have won and with that their dreams of the title were over.

At the same time, a new chant was born.

Annexing the melody from *Que Sera, Sera (whatever will be, will be)* a song was born that would ensure the football world would never forget the real reason why Liverpool failed in their quest to win the league.

*Steve Gerrard, Gerrard, he slipped on his f\*cking arse, he gave it to Demba Ba, Steve Gerrard, Gerrard.*

Quirkily, the chant caught on with supporters of other teams in opposition to Liverpool and despite both Ba and Gerrard having long since departed the Premier League it can still be widely heard today.

On 10 May 2015, sportingly, Gerrard was given a standing ovation by Blues fans the last time he faced Chelsea in a Liverpool shirt at Stamford Bridge. Despite this noble gesture however, Gerrard, who had suffered further ignominy when a racehorse named Gerrard's Slip found its way into the winners' enclosure at Southwell earlier that year, had little in the way of praise for Chelsea followers. "The Chelsea fans showed respect for a couple of seconds, but slaughtered me all game," he said in a TV interview after the match. "It's nice of them to turn up for once today," he concluded somewhat spitefully.

While there is no doubt that the Gerrard chant retains popularity, there are plenty among Chelsea's hard-core match-going support who frown on it and refuse to sing it. I asked *cfcuk* editor David Johnstone to outline the reasons why.

**David:** "The *Ba/Gerrard* song was, on that day at Anfield, sharp, to the point and funny. However, when Chelsea supporters started singing it every time Liverpool were subsequently the opponents, to my mind at least, it became boring, unnecessary and unfortunately highlighted the lack of 'invention' and originality in the repertoire.

When it started getting sung (for instance) versus Bolton Wanderers at Stamford Bridge in the League Cup 3rd Round (24 September 2014, Chelsea 2 Bolton 1, Kurt Zouma, Oscar) or at Southampton away in the league the same season (28 December, Southampton 1 Chelsea 1, Eden Hazard) and simply for the sake of singing a song, it became totally embarrassing.

Whilst I appreciate the rivalry between Chelsea and Liverpool that has developed since 2004/5, I feel that Blues supporters should show more 'class'. It's on a par with the Liverpool fans singing their *You ain't got no history* version of *Carefree* – and we all know how boring, stale and monotonous that one is!"

*Superstar (Jesus Christ Superstar Song)*

**Walter:** The Senegal international striker also was the subject of another chant which borrowed the title track from Andrew Lloyd Webber and Tim Rice's *Jesus Christ Superstar* rock opera concept album which did the rounds of the pubs. *Demba Ba! Superstar! Hates Tottenham and he loves Allah!*

**Mark:** That's quality! Weird how a player who had such a short Chelsea career ended up with some landmark chants while others can spend years with the club with nothing of any note sung about them. My first recollection of *Superstar* being the basis for a song goes back to my schooldays. *Georgie Best! Superstar! Walks like a woman and he wears a bra!*

*Englishman In New York*

**Walter:** There had been some growing chatter on social media that the Willian song, the Gerrard chant and others were too prevalent and over used. Frankly, many regular supporters were sick of the sound of them.

Mata (loved and adored by everyone) had gone to Manchester United without a chant to his name that properly caught on, and this caused many supporters to clamour for a song for Oscar. The skinny lad from São Paulo put himself about, never stopped hassling when not in possession, his sleight frame bizarrely not often an issue as he seemed to bounce off opposition defenders and midfielders at times.

A tweet was going the rounds to the tune of *Englishmen in New York* by Sting with the first two lines in place, but nothing else: *Oscar! He's a Brazilian, he is f*cking brilliant....* So, I Googled our young star looking for inspiration to find that his full name seemed to fit quite well: *Oscar! He's a Brazilian, he is f*cking brilliant, dos Santos Emboaba Júnior!*

Up in a boozer in Geordieland before a 1245 kick off, (6 December 2014 Newcastle United 2 Chelsea 1, Didier Drogba), my travelling companions Spanish Stan, The Baron, Bacon Roll Campo and Criminologist Scott shuddered as Big Chris sank a fifth pint and tried for the fiftieth time to get the song going.

On each occasion, Spanish Stan corrected Chris's pronunciation of 'Emboaba'... Chris tried again, it sounded even worse. Everyone laughed in their pints and it went down in history as a, 'you had to be there' moment amongst the 'privileged' few.

*Englishman in New York* was released by Sting in 1988. Surprisingly it only reached No. 51 in the UK charts thereby flopping almost as badly as the Oscar version.

At the time of writing, it is not known if supporters of Shanghai SIPG have come up with a chant for Oscar who left Chelsea for the Chinese Super League club in December 2016. Given the fact he cost an eye-watering £60 million, you'd think they'd make an effort.

## My Old Man's A Dustman

**Walter:** The duo that helped drive us to winning the Premier League title in 2015 were Diego da Silva Costa and Francesc Fàbregas Soler.

Diego got the *Diego! Diego! Diego!* Treatment... that fitted his character perfectly, but it took a while for Fàbregas to win over the support, including me. I just couldn't take to him. His clashes with our players... especially Super Frank while at Arsenal, and particularly with snidey Barcelona... all these were in my mind. Every time I tried to take to him, I saw him in an Arsenal shirt holding up celery with disgust on his face.

It took me a while, but I finally came around to him. The *Magic Hat* song, (*My Old Man's A Dustman* by Lonnie Donegan released in 1960), has been around at the football for a while. Oldham Athletic fans were singing it to Andy Ritchie in 1987, Man United to Roy Keane six years later. Ben Sewell sent me this brilliant email that explains the origin of Chelsea's version.

**Ben:** "I was born in 1993, and I've been a season ticket holder since 2009. I was a 'Young Blues Badge Holder' for most my early life! My Family are massive Chelsea fans. My mum was born in Chelsea, my dad in Staines – they met in The Shed at a friendly against Atlético Madrid in 1979! (11 December, a waterlogged pitch saw the game called off!)

My Granddad was a steward in the East Stand Directors Box – so I was always going to be Chelsea! My first game was when I was eight-years old, we beat Bolton 5-1, (23 December 2001, Eidur Gudjohnsen, Jimmy Floyd Hasselbaink, Boudewijn Zenden, Colin Hendry own goal, Frank Lampard), and all I can remember was Jimmy's screamer and Hendry scoring an own goal.

On the way home, we were driving near Richmond, Gianfranco Zola pulled up next to us at the lights and I was star-struck! I showed him the Chelsea badge on my shirt and he put his thumb up! I'll never forget that moment. On the morning of Arsenal away (26 April 2015, Arsenal 0 Chelsea 0) we were on our way to winning the league under Mourinho again. I was drinking in The Shakespeare's Head in Holborn in the corner with a few of my mates, my Dad and my brother. We were talking about how we needed to come up with a song for Fàbregas.

A few years back in Barcelona, I tried to start *Gary Cahill's magic*, but it didn't work or take off at all. Then, in the corner, it came into my head and I tried to fit Fàbregas into it and it just clicked. We started singing it:

> *Oh Fàbregas is magic, he wears a magic hat,*
> *He could've signed for Arsenal but he said no f\*ck that!*
> *He passes with his left foot, he passes with his right!*
> *And when we win the league again we'll sing this song all night!*

The rest of the pub joined in as it got louder and louder, next minute the whole pub was on their feet singing it for a good half an hour! Videos of the song, went flying around social media, and every Chelsea fan in north London was singing it. I remember in the tube station on the way to the ground everybody was shouting it on the escalator. I didn't expect it to kick off like it did. I thought it would've just been sung because we were playing

Arsenal and it's always good to wind that lot up! But I was wrong, it's still sung to this day. I messaged Fàbregas after Stoke away (18 March 2017, Stoke City 1 Chelsea 2, Willian, Gary Cahill) telling him I came up with his song and he replied 'Amazing, thank you so much', I mean it's just been brilliant."

### Lost In The Supermarket

**Walter:** A decent song for defender Papy Djilobodji circulated on *Twitter* via @CFCCallum and harnessed *Lost In The Supermarket* one of the finest tracks ever recorded by The Clash.

*All lost in transfer market can no longer shop happily came in here for that special offer Papy Djilobodji!*

Papy never made the grade at the Bridge so the song led a brief life on social media and no doubt in the odd pub or train carriage before flickering and dying like a moth to the flame.

**Mark:** This is probably my favourite hit-the-post creation. The funny thing about Papy was that Chelsea's board, having paid Nantes £3.18 million for him in on summer transfer window deadline day 2015, and got slaughtered for doing so, sold the Senegal international to Sunderland less than a year later for £8.55 million. Papy's Blues career had amounted to a one minute cameo appearance in injury time as a substitute for flop loan striker Radamel Falcao in a Third Round League Cup victory away at Walsall (Walsall 1 Chelsea 4, Ramires, Loic Remy, Kenedy, Pedro).

Incredibly, an official statement (I think they have a template for this) on the Chelsea website rattled on about thanking Papy for his service to the club. I'm not sure if they bothered with anything when they ended Falcao's loan deal from Monaco early.

The Colombian's greatest Chelsea-related moment came not when he scored his only goal for the Blues (29 August 2015, Chelsea 1 Crystal Palace 2) but when he returned to the Ligue 1 side and faced Tottenham Hotspur at Wembley in a Champions League Group E match in September 2016. Spurs fans taunted Falcao with the chant *Chelsea reject* as he left the pitch and the striker responded by raising his left hand and flicking out the final score with his fingers. 2-1 to Monaco.

# CAREFREE! CHELSEA CHANTS AND TERRACE CULTURE

*Too Shy*

In July 2016 Michy Batshuayi signed for Chelsea from Marseille in a deal worth £33 million to the Ligue 1 side. At the time the Belgium international became the Blues second most expensive signing after Fernando Torres. Big things were expected of the then 22-year old, and a couple of tribute songs bubbled up from Chelsea supporters as he showed great promise in the early games of the 2016/17 season.

**Walter:** The chorus of Kajagoogoo's 1983 No.1 hit *Too Shy* was changed to *Too shy shy, hush hush Batshuayi*.

*That's The Way (I Like It)*

Better still, KC and the Sunshine Band's 1975 hit *That's the Way (I like it)* became *Batshuayi, I like it uh-huh, uh-huh*.

Unfortunately for Michy, Antonio Conte's switch to a 3-4-3 set up coupled with the goal-scoring form of Diego Costa meant that first-team opportunities would be hard to come by... though the likeable young striker would have a big shout in the order of things come the end of the campaign, more on this soon.

*Heartbeat*

**Walter:** At the time of writing, Marcos Alonso is my current favourite Blues player. I was privileged enough to receive a cheque on the pitch on behalf of the *Chelsea Supporters Group* for SW15 based charity *REGENERATE* before Chelsea's home game with Swansea City (25 February 2017, Chelsea 3 Swansea 1, Cesc Fàbregas, Pedro, Diego Costa).

As I left the tunnel and went up the steps to the edge of the pitch, I noticed players were still warming up. I had to pinch myself I was so close so them, and I scolded myself for downing that last large glass of vino. Fàbregas, Costa, Hazard and Matić all jogged past me to go back down the tunnel. I patted each of them on the back. Alonso returned the gesture, patted me on the back and said, "Hi, how are you?" All I could do was chew my tongue in response, and then off he went.

*Oh Marcos Alonso! Oh Marcos Alonso!* (*Seven Nation Army*) was the first chant for Alonso, and then at the end of the 2016/17 season a new one sprung up to the chorus of *Heartbeat* by Buddy Holly, released in 1958:

*Oh Marcos, Marcos Alonso runs down the wing for me!*
*Der-der-der-der-der, der-der-der-der-der, der-der-der-der, der-der-der-der-der!*
*Oh Marcos, Marcos Alonso runs down the wing for me!*

I had a feeling this might take off… and then up at Leicester (09 September 2017 Leicester City 1-2 Chelsea Morata, Kanté) most the away end was blasting it out.

**Mark:** After Alonso's heroic two-goal salvo against Spurs at Wembley in the Premier League (20 August 2017, Tottenham 1 Chelsea 2) there's no reason why this shouldn't take off. It seems boring to me that three Spaniard's, Alonso, Alvaro Morata and Pedro who featured against Spurs in this game all have the same *Seven Nation Army* chant. So, keep *Oh Marcos… Marcos Alonso runs down the wing for me!* going and going and going and fingers crossed Chelsea don't sign Alex Sandro from Juventus or his days at left-wing-back could be numbered.

**Walter:** Credit goes to Shaun Long (@ShaunyLong) and his pals in The Shed Jug and Tug for persevering with the song since the 2017 FA Cup Final. I've since heard that Liverpool sang the same tune for Maxi Rodríguez (2010-2012) so I've added some fresh verses. It might be time to wear an Alonso mask and make another Gate 17 video.

*Oh Marcos… Marcos Alonso runs down the wing for me!*
*He scored… Two goals past Hugo Lloris at Wembley!*
*He looks… Just like George Michael in 1983!*
*So, Marcos… Marcos Alonso will you marry me?*

**Mark:** To be honest, I think this is genius on a par with the Willian song. I can imagine people reading this book pausing to sing it right now and smiling. Be great to hear it reverberating around the Bridge.

## *Club Tropicana*

**Walter:** It was the lovely Alexandra Churchill @CFCgwlb who first noticed that Alonso's hair (after he grew it over the summer) was now resembling an early 80s George Michael. This prompted *Twitter* links to the song *Club Tropicana*, released by WHAM! in July 1983, which then resulted in Callum West @CFCCallum to tweet the quite brilliant:

*Marcos Alonso number three!*
*Fun and sunshine, there's enough for everyone!*
And before you ask, yes, I did try getting this going in the boozer (9

September 2017) up at Leicester (Leicester City 1 Chelsea 2, Alvaro Morata, N'Golo Kanté). It nose-dived, but I'm determined! There's always the next game.

*September*

**Walter:** Since 1994/95, Chelsea had qualified for Europe every season until the disastrous 2015/16 campaign. The season out of Europe simply fanned the flames of desire to return – especially away. This long-awaited Euro away match fell on 27th September (Atlético Madrid 1 Chelsea 2, Alvaro Morata, Michy Batshuayi) and 2,500 buzzing Blues fans made the trip.

It was hot, there was alcohol aplenty consumed, there were videos of a new emerging song – footage from bars, streets, then later on the metro-line and finally on the pre-match concourse with lyrics uploaded. Earlier in the day, Ryan Arif (@ryan190512), sat in the sun, drummed his fingers on a white table with bottles of Spanish lager and jugs of Sangria aplenty outside a bar a few miles from the stadium, and continued singing his new chant for midfield powerhouse Tiémoué Bakayoko.

Ryan told me: "A few of us managed to get it going on Terrace bar in Stoke a few days before our trip to Madrid. (23rd September 2017, Stoke City 0 Chelsea 4, Pedro, Alvaro Morata x3.) There was a handful of us singing it there. Seemed like everyone knew it by the time we got to Madrid."

Seeing as it was the month of September, it was rather apt that the chosen song that emerged was to the 1978 smash hit *September* by Earth, Wind and Fire. Those that were too intoxicated to pronounce *Tiémoué* sang *Timmy* instead! At the end of the game in Atlético's spanking new stadium during the lock-in, the song had caught on so rapidly, the whole away end bounced to it, celebrating a famous victory:

*Ba de ya – Tiémoué Bakayoko*
*Ba de ya – together with N'Golo*
*Ba de ya – he never gives the ball away*

*Pop Goes The World*

**Mark:** Taking another club's chant, reworking the words and reflecting it back at the originators is a fine art which depending on who you support infuriates or entertains.

On 18 October 2014, Chelsea supporters packed into the Arthur Wait Stand at Selhurst Park for a London derby with Crystal Palace were in a buoyant mood. Comfortably top of the table, the Blues were on the march to the title and Palace weren't going to poop the party.

Despite its ricketiness and restricted views, Selhurst Park, offers away supporters a chance to experience and maybe relive the type of old-school atmosphere that is sadly missing from the majority of Premier League stadiums. 24,451 fans had paid good money to see the Eagles play the Blues, a lowish gate by top-flight standards, but Selhurst was bulging at the seams.

After an eight-year absence, this was Palace's second season back in the top tier of English football and something curious had happened to a section of their support along the way that in all fairness deserves applause rather than ridicule it tends to get.

The Holmesdale Fanatics Ultras were conceived during the south London's club sojourn in the Championship in a bid to generate the type of atmosphere seen at stadiums on the continent.

Gathered in the Holmesdale Road Stand, the ultras, dressed in black, made a drum-thumping, crowd-surfing, flare-igniting, banner-scrawling statement... and their chants were never-ending irrespective of what was happening on the pitch and that included Oscar giving Chelsea the lead in the 6th minute with a wonderful free-kick.

*CPFC, CPFC, CPFC, CPFC, CPFC* sang the Holmesdale 'Fanatics' to the remarkably obscure 1987 melody of *Pop Goes The World* by Canadian band Men Without Hats. *Pop Goes The World* failed to make a dent in the UK charts though it did reach No. 1 in Austria and No. 2 in Sweden which doesn't explain why fans of crack Argentine football side River Plate borrowed the melody and came up with the chant *Ooh, vamos, River Plate! River Plate! River Plate! vamos River Plate!* (definitely worth looking up on *YouTube* if you have a spare minute).

It's the best part of 7,000 miles from River Plate's fantastically-named 61,688 capacity Estadio Antonio Vespucio Liberti where the 1978 World Cup Final was played between victorious host nation Argentina and the Netherlands to the altogether more humble confines of Selhurst Park which houses 26,255... but the mysterious reworkings of *Pop Goes The World* sound good in both venues.

Shortly after Oscar's goal, Chelsea supporters picked up the melody and *CPFC, CPFC, CPFC, CPFC, CPFC* became *Sh\*t football team, sh\*t football team, sh\*t football team, sh\*t football team, sh\*t football team.*

Cesc Fàbregas, doubling the Blues lead early in the second half with his first goal for the club, a sublime effort involving Oscar and Eden Hazard in the build-up, was the cue for another variation of the chant which gained momentum for the remainder of the game. *We're top of the League, we're top of the League, we're top of the League, we're top of the League, we're top of the League.*

Frazier Campbell scored a last minute goal for Palace, but Chelsea's 2-1 win strengthened their position at the top of the table where they would remain for the remainder of the campaign. As a consequence of this; *We're top of the League* would be sung by Blues fans at every game for the remainder of the season.

**Walter:** The catchy tune is also lent to Chelsea singing; *You're f\*cking sh\*t!* to the opposition, and then reminding them; *We've won it all! We've won it all! We've won it all!*

**Mark:** The melody to *Pop Goes The World* would go on to lend itself perfectly to a chant in honour of current (at the time of writing) Chelsea manager Antonio Conte.

*Antonio, Antonio. Antonio, Antonio, Antonio.*

As Conte revitalised the Blues following the demise of José Mourinho and won the Premier League title at the first attempt, the *Antonio* chant unified Stamford Bridge in the same way Mourinho's *La Donna e Mobile*-inspired tribute once had. Beautiful and uplifting to hear, there's nothing quite like a crowd singing from the same hymn sheet.

## *Ain't Nobody*

**Walter:** *Antonio Antonio* was an emotional improvement on the initial chant Chelsea supporters had concocted for Conte. First heard away at Watford (20 August 2017, Watford 1 Chelsea 2, Michy Batshuayi, Diego Costa) to the melody of *Ain't Nobody* the 1983 hit by Rufus featuring Chaka Khan came: *Antonio Conte does it better, makes me happy, makes me feel this way!*

I say, 'emotional improvement', because it really is something hearing the whole Bridge chanting *Antonio Antonio.* In the reverse league fixture against Watford at home (15 May 2017, Chelsea 4 Watford 3, John Terry,

César Azpilicueta, Cesc Fàbregas, Michy Batshuayi), the singing of our manager's name was so powerful, his wife Elisabetta was reduced to tears. What great supporters we are. What a job Conte had done.

*We Shall Not Be Moved / For He's A Jolly Good Fellow*

**Walter:** Rewind three days to 12 May 2017, the date that Chelsea won the Premier League title at The Hawthorns (West Bromwich Albion 0 Chelsea 1) with a goal by Michy Batshuayi. There have been a few occasions in the run-up to our title winning seasons in 2004/05, 2005/06, 2009/10, 2014/15 and 2016/17 where I have been lucky enough to be in away ends with goose-bumps when two songs are sung: *We Shall Not, We Shall Not Be Moved! We Shall Not, We Shall Not Be Moved! Just like a team that's gonna win the Football League – We Shall Not Be Moved!* Followed by: *We're gonna win the League! We're gonna win the League! And now you're gonna believe us, and now you're gonna believe us, and now you're gonna belieeeeeve us! We're gonna win the League!* I only sing them when it's practically in the bag.

**Mark:** A couple of terrace bangers there from Walter that get put to good use (sometimes too early… cough… Liverpool, Tottenham Hotspur) by supporters of clubs with hopes of winning a league title. *We Shall Not Be Moved*, which started out life as African American spiritual *I Shall Not Be Moved*, was brought to wider attention by Australian band The Seekers who released it as the B-side of their 1965 No.1 chart hit *The Carnival Is Over* while *We're Gonna Win The League* borrows the melody of the traditional song *For He's A Jolly Good Fellow*, the same tune as used in the popular children's ditty *The Bear Went Over The Mountain*.

*Psalm 23*

**Walter:** I wasn't at WBA, and much has been already been written and said, so I will only add my short version of events. My plan was to leave work at 4.30pm, get a train to SW6 and watch the game in a pub near the Bridge – but I did my back in. I had to work the following day, so I weighed up my options. I've had a bad back twice before, I didn't want to make it worse. A train journey, the pub, potential celebrations and another train home wasn't really the best choice to make. So, I went to bed with an ice-pack (alternating it with a hot wheat bag) and put the game on the radio.

Can you believe it? The radio!
But you know what? It was alright. The best thing was that after the game, the commentators kept talking and talking and all you could hear were the Chelsea supporters singing. There were no ad breaks, no cuts to

the studio, just quality airtime. It was a proper throwback listening to our fans – they went through every player on the pitch and who'd been on the bench, singing their praises over and over and over again.

During the game, a few pals of mine who were there (who know I'm in The God Squad) tweeted me the same picture – some verses from *Psalm 23* that are printed along the back of a tier in West Brom's home end. I believe it's relevant to mention – in this modern age where the love of money and greed has changed English football forever, West Bromwich Albion FC honour how most football clubs were founded – the church and community coming together to form a club to bring unity, hope, identity, sport, support and play beautiful, wonderful, football.

*The Lord's my Shepherd, I'll not want.*
*He makes me down to lie,*
*In pastures green; He leadeth me, The quiet waters by.*

# FINAL WORDS

**Mark:** The idea behind *Carefree!* was to tell a story interwoven with personal experiences and songs that explains the allure of Chelsea from different angles. Great matches, great players, great goals, terrace legends, rivalries and the songs and chants associated with them. History granted, but it doesn't stop here. There's always going to be another great match, great player, great goal and the craic to be had from getting involved.

When finances and real-life permit, going to watch Chelsea isn't just about the 90-minute kick-about on the pitch… it's about connecting with like-minded souls, about interaction, about belonging, about identity. Supporters of any football club will tell you the same thing.

Following Chelsea has given me many life-long friendships that I value dearly. Today sit in Gate 17 at Stamford Bridge with the same group of mates I used to stand on The Shed with almost 40 years ago. Following the Blues has enabled me to broaden my horizons. I've travelled over land and sea (and Leicester) to places I would never have dreamed of visiting.

The shared experience of watching the Chelsea is the glue that binds so many of us together. In an increasingly uncertain world, it's nice to know that some things can remain so constant. Long may this continue!

**Walter:** Thank you to my wife Becky and our kids and to 'Tall' Paul Barnard who took me to my first Chelsea match. *Get off my sister.*

No matter at what stage of life are at… young, middle-aged or old… by the time you've finished this book, new songs will already have been concocted in pubs, clubs, bath tubs, tubes, beaches, swimming pools, concourses, kitchens, living rooms, bedrooms, hills, mountains, planes, trains and automobiles. My advice to you would be to start the next chapter.

If it's in your head to write – if it's in your heart to type – if it is in your very BONES to flip open your phone and press the buttons to form words and sentences because something has captured you, THEN GET WRITING!

If you follow Chelsea, then get on it. Describe your trips, your journeys, your mates, your experiences, the people you meet – and of course THE SONGS! Especially if you're in a privileged position to go all over the

## CAREFREE! CHELSEA CHANTS AND TERRACE CULTURE

country and Europe following your team then I urge you to pick up your pen. It is mighty. Create a pseudonym if need be. Because I for one want to read all about it. Compose the next chapter. Let it flow. You know where to find us to get it printed. Live generously and keep the peace.

# GATE 17
## THE COMPLETE COLLECTION
(November 2017)

### FOOTBALL

Over Land and Sea - Mark Worrall
Chelsea here, Chelsea There - Kelvin Barker, David Johnstone, Mark Worrall
Chelsea Football Fanzine - the best of cfcuk
One Man Went to Mow - Mark Worrall
Chelsea Chronicles (Five Volume Series) - Mark Worrall
Making History Not Reliving It - Kelvin Barker, David Johnstone, Mark Worrall
Celery! Representing Chelsea in the 1980s - Kelvin Barker
Stuck On You: a year in the life of a Chelsea supporter - Walter Otton
Palpable Discord: a year of drama and dissent at Chelsea - Clayton Beerman
Rhyme and Treason - Carol Ann Wood
Eddie Mac Eddie Mac –
Mark Meehan, Mark Worrall, Kelvin Barker, David Johnstone, Neil Smith
The Italian Job: A Chelsea thriller starring Antonio Conte - Mark Worrall
Diamonds, Dynamos and Devils - Tim Rolls

### FICTION

Blue Murder: Chelsea till I die - Mark Worrall
The Wrong Outfit - Al Gregg
The Red Hand Gang - Walter Otton
Coming Clean - Christopher Morgan
This Damnation - Mark Worrall
Poppy - Walter Otton

### NON FICTION

Roe2Ro - Walter Otton
Shorts - Walter Otton

www.gate17.co.uk

Printed in Germany
by Amazon Distribution
GmbH, Leipzig